Wayne Olson
1454 Southview
Prescott, AZ
~~8526~~
86305

Also by Martin Gottfried

A Theater Divided
Opening Nights
Broadway Musicals
Jed Harris: The Curse of Genius
Live and In Person: The Great Entertainers
All His Jazz: The Life and Death of Bob Fosse
More Broadway Musicals
Sondheim
Nobody's Fool: The Lives of Danny Kaye

Simon & Schuster
New York • London • Toronto • Sydney • Tokyo • Singapore

George Burns

and
The Hundred-Year Dash

Martin Gottfried

SIMON & SCHUSTER
Rockefeller Center
1230 Avenue of the Americas
New York, NY 10020

1   3   5   7   9   10   8   6   4   2

Library of Congress Cataloging-in-Publication Data
Gottfried, Martin.
George Burns and the hundred-year dash / Martin Gottfried.
p.   cm.
1. Burns, George, 1896– . 2. Comedians—United States—Biography
3. Entertainers—United States—Biography. I. Title.
PN2287.B87G68   1996
792.7′028′092—dc20
[B]   95-49079   CIP
ISBN 0-684-81483-8

Title page photo: The Kennedy Center

The author gratefully acknowledges permission to use lyrics from the
following songs:

"The Red Rose Rag," by Percy Winrich and Edward Madden, 1911.
Copyright, Warner Music.

"Where Did You Get That Girl?" by Harry Ruby and Bert Kalmar, 1911.
Copyright, Warner Music.

"I'd Love to Call You Honey," words by Ed Rose and William Raskin,
music by Jack Mills. Copyright, Jerry Vogel Music, Inc.

"I Wish I Was 18 Again," by Sunny Throckmorton, 1980.
Copyright, Tree Publishing Co., Inc., BMI.

Acknowledgments

About seven years ago, when George Burns was ninety-three years old and in full command of his faculties, I spent several days interviewing him about his life, his marriage, and his work. As he entered his middle nineties he continued to be sharp and alert, and even at ninety-eight he was lucid and witty.

But nearing one hundred, this amazing mind began to falter. My last meeting with him, at ninety-nine, was brief and depressing. He could still deliver a wisecrack, but alas, his fierce determination could no longer stay the will of nature.

The research for this biography only began with those interviews. Nearly a thousand hours were then spent talking with Burns's family as well as with his friends and professional colleagues. There is not a word of dialogue or any incident in this book that was not directly witnessed by at least one of these sources or another participant whose account appeared in print.

This research provided an incidental benefit—the opportunity to meet people I might otherwise never have known. I am grateful for their good company and appreciate the memories they shared. This work could not have been done without the time generously given to me by Ronnie and Sandra Burns, Louis Weiss, Bernard Kamber, Benay Venuta, Dina Consolini and Ron Simon at The Museum of Radio and Television Broadcasting, Lenny Sallis, Joan Benny, Peter Stone, Lauren Bacall, Herbert Ross, Fred De Cordova, Rod Amateau, Carol Channing, Charles Lowe, Carl Reiner, George Balzer, Milton Berle, Buddy Arnold, Warner Leroy, Jan Murray, Harvey Silbert, Patricia Zeitman Rosenberg, Barry Mirkin, Leah Superstein, Sammy Lewis, Paul and Ruth Henning, Steve Cox, Herbert Browar, Buddy Hackett, Larry Gelbart, Armand Deutsch, Irving Brecher, Lucie Arnaz, Larry Fallon, Melissa Berry, Ray Stark, Tony Martin, Rabbi Richard Chapin, and Leonard Stern.

I was also fortunate to have, yet again, the assistance of all my knowledgeable friends on the staff at the Library of the Performing Arts in Lincoln Center, helping me to draw once more upon the resources of that great institution.

For the first time, my dear Gene Young actually liked my work, which was disconcerting, although pleasantly so. This did not deter her from abusing the manuscript sufficiently, that it might be revised toward some semblance of consistency, coherence, and style. I am sadomasochistically grateful for both the praise and the abuse.

Ann Adelman was the copy editor responsible for cleaning up my grammar, and, for the second time, I was very fortunate indeed to have my friend Chuck Adams as editor at Simon & Schuster.

But above all, I am grateful for the wonderful hours that were spent talking with George Burns, a uniquely sane man whose benevolence and wisdom were rare and genuine. The expression "comfortable in one's own skin" might well have been coined for him. His love of Gracie, of Jack, and of himself bespoke his greatest love, his love of life. This was indeed a man.

New York City, 1995

This is for Melissa Berry,
Joan Benny, and Maggie Fogel.
I could not have done it without them.

1

The picture of George Burns that endures is of him smiling, squinting through his big black round eyeglass frames, and taking three puffs on his cigar. It is the picture of a man who could handle anything. He had the timing.

He was perhaps the most famous and popular old man America had ever known, and surely the funniest. In an age of advice, when Americans were obsessed with magic messages, he offered something that used to be called wisdom.

When he wasn't onstage, he was wise enough to keep his eyes open and his mouth shut. He was secure enough to know that being alone does not have to mean being lonely; that life need not fade so fast, abate with age, or decline with the deaths of friends and family. He loved to do what he did; he saw doing as living, and so he loved living. With that love as his energy, he discovered the secret of renewal. This is the story of that renewal.

The man seemed to get younger as he got older. He had literally *spent* his youth—wastefully and extravagantly, as youth should be spent—as if he knew that there was plenty of time left. When less was left, and it was thus more precious, he would not waste a minute of it.

Perhaps his ninty-ninth year was not his best year. Yet it was only his first tough year, which was not bad for a lifetime. Perhaps an unhappier life might have built up his defenses, but he edited out the bad times. If he had lived through nasty patches, he revised those parts of his story. He would work on his history until he got it right, retelling his past to polish the rhythms and assure the laughs. He preferred the catchy tune to the dirge. When he said, "For me, life is show business," he meant it. He viewed life through show business glasses. It was a prettier sight than reality.

He was never able to fully express his pain over Gracie's death. In private, he might say with a fierce directness, "She made everything possible in my life." But he preferred to do his personal talking in public, where he could turn pain into oblique, self-effacing comedy.

In short, he kept his own counsel, which did not mean bottling things up; it was just smart, and he was a smart guy.

"Daddy doesn't like negative things," Burns's son Ronnie said. "He doesn't like to deal with unhappiness."

The pain of Gracie Allen's death ran so deep that George Burns could not accept its full thrust. He kept her alive by writing about her, talking about her in his act, even talking *to* her when he visited the crypt at Forest Lawn Memorial Park. The story of those visits has become legendary: He would sit in the mausoleum and chat aloud about work, about their friends, about the children, Ronnie and Sandy, and when he left, he would say, "Goodbye, kid—see you next month." He wasn't sure she heard him, he said, but it made him feel better.

The other mean event in his life was Jack Benny's death, and he never stopped talking about his best friend, either.

A friendship like that is as rare as a marriage like that, but it was hardly coincidental that George Burns enjoyed two such relationships. He had a gift for that.

The loss of these two people was severe, but great loss is possible only when there is something great to lose. At ninety-nine, the only thing that was left to lose was his sense of humor. Alas, even that was beginning to slip. He was frail and wizened, shrunk to five feet, his head like a walnut. He seemed small enough to be cradled in your hands, and he deserved to be.

He had once been a fine five feet eight inches tall. He had always been in the supreme condition of a professional dancer. When he stopped dancing, he started to exercise regularly, and even in his nineties had been making gestures in the direction of the Canadian Air Force fitness regimen.

But at ninety-nine, he just sat there, or lay there, and slept. It was not so easy to set this part to a catchy tune. So it was only in a manner of speaking that he was chugging along toward the hundred-year mark. There was not exactly a bounce to his stride; in fact, there was no stride at all. He was confined to a wheelchair and the goal line seemed to be receding.

That goal line was the birthday that was going to make him America's favorite centenarian. There was already a cheering squad waiting along the sidelines. Ahead at the tape, on the birthday itself, January 20, 1996, lay an engagement at Caesar's Palace in Las Vegas. But having got younger as he got older, he was now babelike. The only thing that still had the old push was his heart.

"There's only one reason he's going to make it to a hundred," a family member said, "and that's because he wants to."

Naturally, Burns put it in vaudeville terms: "I can't die—I'm booked."

2

"We knew Dad came from a very poor family. He had eleven brothers and sisters, everyone sleeping on the same mattress in a one-room apartment. But he wouldn't tell it that way. That's not nice. That's not funny."

Instead, Ronnie Burns remembered, his father "would make it funny. As a storyteller he would rather put a vaudeville shine on that reality."

George Burns put a "vaudeville shine" on much of his reality, telling anecdotes about the past, then winking and adding, "I lie a lot." That usually got a laugh for this elderly elf, but he was indeed lying—and not lying. For his stories did not really deny reality, they only improved it, making it colorful and funny, and he was grateful to have gotten into a business that paid him to do that. If he had done it in some other line of work, he might have been locked up.

At the same time, his stories really did alter the truth, and after a lifetime of telling them he did not seem to know the facts from the fiction. Sometimes it even seemed as if the joke was no joke, and that he had come to believe the vaudeville.

"For me," he said, "real life was show business."

As he grew older, it became all but impossible to find the truth or, sometimes, to even understand why it was not to his liking. Perhaps it was the telling of the stories that he liked.

He wrote a small library of memoirs. An anecdote in one often contradicts an anecdote in another; there are similar stories having different punch lines; but they are all inspired by real people and events in his life.

This much is almost definitely certain: He was born Nathan Birnbaum in New York City on January 20, 1896, to Dora (Dassah) Bluth and Louis Philip (Eleazar Shrager) Birnbaum. They were Orthodox Jews who had migrated from Eastern Europe with their son Morris and a nine-month-old daughter, Annie. Like so many immigrants, they gravitated to the Lower East Side of Manhattan. Their tenement was 95 Pitt Street, just off Grand Street, and they did indeed live in that one room—with nine children, anyhow.

The last three would be born in grander quarters. After Nathan's arrival, the family moved a half dozen blocks to an expansive three-room cold-water flat at 259 Rivington Street. This third-floor walk-up was heated by a coal-burning oven in the kitchen. There were only two windows, both in the parlor. The kitchen had a skylight but the bedroom had no natural light at all. Small wonder, then, that Burns became an escape artist, as it were.

As a newborn, he slept in the bedroom with Louie and Dora. The other eight children were in the parlor, from the eldest, Morris, through Annie, Isadore, Esther, Sarah, Sadie, Mamie, and Goldie—who, being Nathan's next-older sister, became his confidante.

Still to be born in that apartment were Sammy, Theresa, and baby Willie, making a grand total of seven girls, five boys, and two adults in three rooms.

They took turns bathing in the kitchen tub, sometimes

using the same warmish water when the hot ran out. The bathroom was an outhouse in the backyard downstairs.

Louis Birnbaum got a job as a helper in the kosher butcher shop that was on the street level of the building. He was also an assistant cantor in the neighborhood synagogue, singing the ceremonial prayers. There, he enjoyed a scrap of importance as a descendant of the *Cohanim*—the tribe of Jews who were the first rabbis. In pre-Christian times, they performed the religious services while the other Jewish tribe, the *Levis*, merely assisted in the services. This distinction between the Cohens and the Levys, as they came to be called, had since lost its meaning, except that a "Ca-en" (as a *Cohanim* was called in Yiddish) was still the first to read from the Torah during synagogue services. Minor as this honor was, there was little else that life seemed to offer Louis Birnbaum in the pride department.

Dora Birnbaum was, by all accounts, a formidable lady. Wearing a *sheitl* (wig), which was the requisite head covering for an Orthodox Jewish woman, she ran her household and fed her children on pennies. It was she who managed to make something of nothing while Louie came home from the *shul* on Saturday mornings, and rested or meditated for the remainder of the Sabbath.

He would sit at the window and read from his prayer books, and it was there at the window, one Saturday afternoon, that he nodded off and died, a forty-seven-year-old victim of the 1904 influenza epidemic.

There weren't enough relatives or friends to make up a *minyan* of ten male mourners, as was required by Jewish custom, to say the Kaddish, the prayer for the dead. And so Dora had to pay people to pray for her husband's soul while she was sitting *shiva*. That was one of George Burns's earliest childhood memories: his mother scrounging for nickels to pay people to mourn for his father.

She was alone at forty-three with no money and twelve children, the youngest of them six months old.

• • •

Even though Burns once told a friend that ever since his mother had to pay for his father's mourners he was against religion, it does not explain why he was never given a bar mitzvah. That was not a matter of money, since the ceremony costs nothing. Many years later, while sitting in a synagogue, he said to a relative, "This is the first bar mitzvah I've ever been to. When does the man come with the knife?"

It was a revealing joke. Of course he knew the difference between a bar mitzvah and a *bris* (circumcision ritual). He never denied his Jewishness, but even before he was thirteen years old, being Jewish was not part of his essential identity. By the time George Burns reached that bar mitzvah age, show business would be his religion.

At six, he entered the first grade at P.S. 22 on Mangin Street. It was only a few blocks from home, but another neighborhood can be another country to a child, especially in a narrowly defined immigrant community. In fact, Mangin Street was Italian territory, but Nathan was already beyond ethnic trivia. A year earlier, he had gotten a taste of performing, improvising a Spanish dance to the music of an itinerant organ grinder. "The people clapped for me," he remembered, "and I got my first feel of an audience."

With his father dead, and nothing for an allowance, he was selling newspapers and shining shoes. At eight, he had a job at Rosenzweig's candy store on the corner of Columbia Street at Stanton. He and two other youngsters, Mortzy and Heshy Weinberger, worked in the cellar, mixing, stirring, and pouring batches of cherry and chocolate syrup. While they funneled the stuff into gallon jugs, they would harmonize, or try to. Such improvised harmony was a tradition in many Jewish homes.

One day, Lewis Farley, the neighborhood postman, stopped into Rosenzweig's for a soda. Overhearing the boys singing in the cellar, he went downstairs to listen.

"Farley," Burns remembered, "wanted the whole world to sing in four-part harmony." All the trio needed for a quartet, he said, was a lead singer, and he suggested a boy named Moishe Friedman who everyone unaccountably called "Toda."

Mr. Rosenzweig let them rehearse regularly in his cellar and the youthful voices started to swell in four-part harmony. Nathan's boyish tenor was far from the sandpaper baritone in his future. Behind the lead singing of Toda, he harmonized with Mortzy (baritone) and Heshy (almost bass). They named themselves the "Peewee Quartet," and Mr. Farley, or "Maestro," as the boys called him, was their manager. He booked the act into such venues as street-corners, schoolyards, even the Staten Island ferry. Like any agent, he also handled the finances, passing a hat through the crowd, collecting whatever was tossed in and then distributing it.

For all intents and purposes, the real life of George Burns had begun.

Eight is not an age for boys to sing. The sense of manliness is too fragile and the voice too thin. But once this crest is surmounted, the sailing is easy, and Nathan began to learn the ditties he would later sing with such relish. A harmony act was a common beginning point and schoolroom routines were popular in vaudeville. The five Marx Brothers were already performing as "The Six Musical Mascots" (including their mother Minnie). Perhaps even the Peewee Quartet had a future.

Lew Farley arranged for them to perform during an amateur night at a neighborhood movie house, the Cannon Street Theatre, and the boys emerged triumphant. They celebrated by spending the five-dollar group prize at Berkowitz's Restaurant on 14th Street, stuffing themselves with steak, potatoes, cole slaw, and dessert. It was dawn by the time Nathan rolled into Rivington Street, and his mother was awake, worried and distraught, which in Yiddish translated as rage.

The wonderful evening was surely worth it, and as if to symbolize its significance, miraculously, he found his bed empty just for him. The three youngest brothers—Sammy, Willie, and himself—usually slept together, but on this warm summer night, Sammy and Willie had decided to cool off on the fire escape. Nathan chose to stay inside and luxuriate in solitary splendor, this night of first stage success.

He quit school after arithmetic threatened to make him a permanent fifth grader. Pulling down the peak of his cap, so to speak, he went looking for work. It was hardly unusual to join the workforce at the age of ten. In fact, that was rather typical on the Lower East Side of 1906. Nathan was thus partly grown up with a burden of responsibility, and partly a child, still roller-skating in the park and venturing uptown to 14th Street for a peek at Huber's Museum, "a sort of combination vaudeville and freak show."

However, there was one difference between little Nathan, who was very little, and most ten-year-olds. They didn't have stage names.

His was acquired after he had quit singing with the Peewee Quartet to become half of a dance act with Abie Kaplan. Abie had taught him the time step, a basic tap-dancing combination, and for practice, they would dance down the street. They would also—as Burns told it—steal coal from the Burns Brothers Coal Yard to help heat their mothers' kitchens. In fact, they so loaded up their baggy knickers with chunks of coal that the kids in the neighborhood began calling them "the Burns Brothers." That, if George Burns is to be believed, became the name of their act. A less entertaining explanation could be that "Burns" came from a shortening of his own name, Birnbaum.

The Burns Brothers, Abie and Nathan, played their first

engagement in 1905 at Seiden's Theatre down the street from Rosenzweig's candy store. This was a "presentation house," so called to distinguish it from vaudeville or movie theatres. Such a place offered a short bill of variety acts between showings of silent movies. Along with Abie and Nathan, the bill included a one-act Yiddish play on the subject of intermarriage. This piece, entitled *Religion Versus Love,* offered a line of dialogue that Burns would treasure, and whenever anyone asked whether he had ever changed his name legally, he would cry, like the young man in the play who was being asked to convert to Christianity, "No! A Jew I was born and a Jew I shall die!"

More often than not, the Burns Brothers were "at liberty," as it was said in the show business. They used the free time to expand their repertoire, hanging out in Hamilton Fish Park on Sheriff Street and teaching themselves the buck-and-wing dance step. Nat also chose a new first name for himself, borrowing George from his favorite brother, Isadore, who called himself George because he hated his own name. "I loved my brother Izzy," Burns said, "and if 'George' was good enough for him, it was good enough for me."

It is easy to believe that you are in show business. All that is required is dressing like an actor, going where actors go, and announcing that you are out of work. As Burns put it, "I was in show business but I wasn't working. I had makeup, I had music, I had pictures but I had no job. But I was in love with what I was doing."

That was his way of telling it cute, but it wasn't always so charming, nor was it easy to allay hunger with a funny story. He found a way to eat for nothing, asking for a cup of hot water and then pouring ketchup into it. He even found that amusing to recall, and like all of his vaudevilizing of hard times, it reflected an easygoing attitude toward life's bumpy ride. Since he liked to eat when he was hungry, and since hot water and ketchup was the only thing there was to eat, he came to like it. Throughout his life he would demand that soup be served boiling hot. The ketchup he added to everything.

It was simple enough for him to mingle with show folk. The teenage hoofer joined the crowd of out-of-work performers who milled under the marquee of Hammerstein's Victoria Theatre at the corner of Seventh Avenue and 42nd Street. Until the Palace was built in 1913, Hammerstein's was the ranking vaudeville theatre in the country and just being near it seemed to provide a sense of connection. Actors would stand out in front all day, gossiping, lying about their bookings and exchanging knowing laughs about the latest in show business, such as Boudini's publicity scheme. That was a story Burns loved to tell.

Boudini was a juggler. His specialty was to hold a fork and pierce objects that were thrown up to him from the audience. As a publicity stunt, his press agent suggested, "Why don't we have somebody drop a watermelon from the roof and you catch it with a fork?"

Boudini gasped. "A watermelon falling from a roof? It'll kill me!"

The press agent was a step ahead of him. "We'll take out the insides. We'll make it very thin."

Reporters and photographers gathered outside the theatre to watch as the juggler's assistant peered over the roof and held out the watermelon.

Boudini stood on the sidewalk with his fork in the air. The assistant dropped the watermelon.

"With nothing in it," Burns chuckled, "it just blew away."

Sharing in such folklore seemed to comfort the unemployed singers and dancers in front of Hammerstein's Victoria. The fourteen-year-old Burns would even (he said) spend hours riding up and down the elevator of the Putnam Building next door, wearing a pair of pince-nez glasses "to look like an actor." The point was that "some agent would see me with the glasses and say, 'What are you doing, kid?' and give me a job.

"But finally, the elevator operator said to me, 'Tell me something, is the elevator the only place you play?'"

True or not, for the next couple of years it might as well have been. By 1912, when he was sixteen, George was just barely in show business. He even took a full-time job with a ladies' blouse manufacturer, Mersky & Company, which at least gave him twelve dollars a week in walking-around money.

Some of it surely went to his mother, but he had suddenly become a ladies' man, and that cost money, too. In fact, his escapades cost him more than money.

As he would tell a lady friend years later, he contracted gonorrhea. He could hardly see the family doctor about it. Idols of all mothers, they were the recognized guardians of health and morals.

The doctor he did find was dainty in referring to Nathan's problem, preferring to call it "Cupid's eczema." The treatment prescribed was a week's worth of self-injections with a stinging purple solution.

Perhaps through some carelessness of Burns's own, an air bubble got into the hypodermic. This not only proved painful but caused his testicles to swell. The infection ultimately was cured, but it was one of the more memorable experiences of his antic youth.

Deflated, so to speak, but unfazed and still the young dandy, he used one of his Mersky paychecks to buy himself an audition outfit: a gray glen plaid suit with a four-button jacket. It was on the sharp side, but he was a dude with show business taste, whether in clothes or for "blondes who called me 'babe' and 'slick.'"

He had the new suit pressed every time he wore it. All actors did the same. An impressive front was important, for nobody wanted to look seedy, therefore unemployed, at an audition. And so like everyone else, Burns would go to the cleaner's and sit behind the curtain in the dressing closet while his suit was pressed. Then he would put it on and head for the audition.

Unfortunately, that meant putting on a flaming hot suit. In order to walk comfortably in it and not brush against the searing material, the actor had to walk stiffly. It made for a unique, if not downright peculiar posture, and when a performer walked down the street that way, stiff-armed and stiff-legged in a "hot suit," he was likely to hear some wise guy cry out, "Going to an audition?"

Auditions taught Burns the importance of promptness. "In vaudeville," he said, "you came in on the first morning and got a check for number one, number two, number three, and so on. Whoever got rehearsal check number one got to sing his first song choice.

"See, there were only three or four great songs, for instance, 'You Made Me Love You.' Everybody wanted to sing that. Everybody sang the same four songs. But if you were there first, you got the number one check—you got to sing it."

It seemed he had more brains and determination than talent. A year later, blaming his unemployment on the glen plaid suit, he borrowed money from a brother-in-law and acquired not only a new suit but a whole new outfit. It came with an elegant, dove gray doublebreasted vest and matching spats. This time, the suit featured five buttons, and it was light blue with a pinstripe. To complete the ensemble, he bought a high-collared white shirt and a polka-dot tie. Finally, as a cover for his already-thinning hair, he popped on "a wide-brimmed straw hat that had a black string attached to my lapel." Thus armed, he was ready, yet again, to brave the booking offices.

But he was already outgrowing certain opportunities. He worked in a schoolroom act, briefly as usual, as one of "The Fourth of July Kids," but at seventeen he was a little old for a schoolroom act. The Marx Brothers had already abandoned theirs and Julius Marx (Groucho) was the same age as George—old enough to be smoking cigars, which in fact both of them already were doing, with sporty George favoring eight-cent Ricoras.

He was looking to form a dancing act, because dancing seemed to be his strongest talent, if he had any talent. He was certainly a good ballroom dancer, good enough to teach the fox-trot, the waltz, and his specialty, the Peabody, which was a fast and intricate glide. His job as a dance teacher was at Bennie Bernstein's Dancing School ("B.B.'s College of Dancing") on Second Street and Avenue B in Manhattan, with a suburban branch on Pitkin Avenue in Brooklyn. Not coincidentally, dance instruction was a good way to meet girls.

From the outset, he was a big laugher. This was his sense of the humor in things. He got more of a laugh from the way people talked than he did when somebody told him a joke.

"Ladies and gentlemen," Bennie Bernstein would announce at the start of an evening. "Please remember that we have dancing in this place Monday night, Tuesday night, Wednesday night, Thursday night, Friday night, Saturday night, and Sunday night, and every night in the week."

Such locutions tickled Burns, yet it did not occur to him that this perception, this taste, was a talent that could be exploited; that he could serve as a catalyst, a comedy go-between. For his sense of humor was a unique one, but at the moment he would not even have known what a catalyst was.

The stories that, years later, he would tell about being perpetually out of work were not quite true. He was in the process of becoming a small-time act, one of a hundred second-rate song and dance men scrambling for bookings and getting them often enough to try for more. There were hundreds of small-time vaudeville theatres to work in, but the work was never steady, and as he approached eighteen, he was only "picking up time," taking anything he could get.

Whether the vaudeville "wheel"—the theatre chain—was a first-class operation like B. F. Keith, or a honky-tonk in the boondocks, all work was called "time." An act could be booked on the Keith time in the East, or on the Orpheum time in the Midwest, or the Pantages time in California. Some of these were the "big" time, requiring only two shows a day in the best theatres with the best pay and the best working conditions. Others were the "medium" time. The small time was a "grind"—four or even six performances a day in theatres so dilapidated that Burns would come to define a theatre as "anything with a toilet."

It was also why the smallest of the small time was sometimes called "the death trail," or "the aching heart."

Most of 1914 he was at liberty and picking up time. He changed his name and his act so frequently that it was remarkable he could remember who he was and what he did. He worked briefly as "Willie Saks and His Little Derby Hat." Under the name "Glide," he was part of "Goldie, Fields and Glide" when they were hired and then fired after one performance. Six months later, he showed up at the same theatre looking for booking under a different name. The manager peered into his face and asked, "Didn't you work here before?"

"No," George said. "And besides, I have a new act."

It was because of this funny life—or at least, this life that he was able to view as funny—that he enjoyed himself instead of being discouraged. He was indomitable, and he was in love with show business. He also had the youth and the freedom from responsibility to indulge that love, and he certainly had a historian's eye. He was a shrewd, devoted, wry, and appreciative observer of what was then called the variety arts.

"If you did seventeen or eighteen minutes," he remembered, "that meant you had a very good spot on the bill. If you only did twelve minutes, you were on number two, which was a bad spot. So when you'd meet an actor on the street, let's say he was playing the Fifth Avenue Theatre, you'd say, 'Hey Jim, how you doin' at the Fifth Avenue?'

"He wouldn't say, 'Great!' He'd say, 'Eighteen minutes.' That meant he had a good spot on the bill."

Just the names of the acts could delight him, especially the names of his own acts. He relished memories of being Jed Jackson of "Jackson and Malone"; Harris of "Harris and Dunlop"; Jose of "Jose and Dolores." He was first Brown and then Williams of "Brown and Williams," an act that opened with a duet, segued into a soft shoe, then an eccentric dance, and closed with tap dancing on skates. The song "The Red Rose Rag" came from this act.

> Down in the garden where the red roses grow,
> Oh, my, I long to go
> Pluck me a flower,
> Cuddle me an hour,
> Lovie, let me learn that red rose rag.

He was going to hold on to this song for the rest of his life. It might have seemed like the latest thing when he first sang it, but in the end it captured for him the innocence, the foolishness, and the joy of the vaudeville days. There were other songs from these times—"Tiger Girl," "In the Heart of the Cherry," "Syncopation Rules the Nation," and "(So I'll Buy a Ring and) Change Your Name to Mine"; however, "The Red Rose Rag" seemed to say it all for him.

But he couldn't even get a job in the U.S. Army in the middle of a war. When he tried to enlist, he was rejected because of poor eyesight.

He insists that he worked as "Willie Delight" only because the name's previous owner quit show business and sold his cards cheap. It was as Willie Delight that Burns sang Kalmar and Ruby's "Where Did You Get That Girl?" He liked its verse better than the chorus, and that made sense for a man who would always bypass the obvious in search of the wrinkle.

Lonesome Johnny Warner, sitting in the corner
Of a swell cafe, eating his heart away
Because he had no girl

At another table, sat a girl named Mabel
With a fellow who Johnny knew
And his brain began to whirl.

He was also Jack Harris of "Harris and Kelly," Phil Baxter of "Baxter and Bates," and Pedro Lopez of "Pedro Lopez and Conchita," a tango team. For that, he grew long sideburns, dyed his hair black, parted it in the center, and plastered it down with Vaseline. The sideburns were shaved off for his next act, a dance trio with the Rosebud Sisters.

"Who cared? I wanted to be in show business."

He was, and there was no business like it. Even when he wasn't booked, he was in show business. He sang and he danced, but while he loved being funny offstage, he never worked as a comedian. Evidently it didn't occur to him that he might be funny, despite one brief stint as "Maurice Valenti and His Wonder Dog," and another as "Flipper and Friend," working with a trained seal—to which he took second billing.

Despite all the names and all the sharp clothes and all the swagger and all the stories and songs, and despite, even, the increasing frequency of work, he was still living at home, and home was still on Rivington Street.

His mother was not well. Dora Birnbaum was taking in sewing and wash, struggling to live on a pitiful budget and focusing on marrying off her daughters. She would even call the Immigrant Aid Society to find out the names of appropriate young Jewish men who were arriving from Europe. She would invite them to dinner, even to sleep over since the apartment was so spacious.

Actually, by 1922 some of the older siblings had moved out and Dora was about to move the rest of her brood to Brooklyn. Ultimately, Sammy would marry an Italian girl and live in New Jersey; George's favorite brother, Isadore, would become a department store executive in Akron, Ohio. Morris would be a professional gambler; and Willie, the youngest, would soon be working with George.

Most of the sisters would raise families in apartments close by Dora, in the Crown Heights section of Brooklyn. It was customary among Jewish families for daughters to live near their mother, although Goldie would ultimately move to San Diego.

Burns's nephew Lenny Sallis remembered, "My grandmother was a brilliant woman," and "It was a well-adjusted family." "Well adjusted" and "brilliant" are defined with typical Jewish pessimism as an absence of negatives. "None of her children got arrested. There weren't any feuds, there were no drug addicts, and nobody went to prison."

As Burns moved into his middle twenties, the Palace Theatre opened in Times Square, succeeding Hammerstein's Victoria as America's premier vaudeville house. The nation's greatest entertainers performed on its giant stage: the fabulous singing women—Eva Tanguay, Nora Bayes, Elsie Janis, Sophie Tucker; the great clowns—Ed Wynn, Bobby Clark, W. C. Fields; legendary teams like Smith and Dale, or Weber and Fields; the new monologists, like Frank Fay, Julius Tannen, Milton Berle, Frank Tinney, and Joe Frisco.

However, the novelty acts seemed to capture best the young and antic spirit of vaudeville. The Lunatic Bakers, for instance, jumped in and out of ovens. The armless Lutz Brothers assembled a car engine with their feet. Marguerite

Webb and Jack Connelly played the piano with fruit in their hands.

There was "Frances White, The World's Smallest Dancer," the Cherry Sisters ("The World's Worst Act"), and "Willard, The Man Who Grows" (a horizon line on the scenery gradually dropped behind him). "McNaughton, The Human Tank" swallowed frogs, while Annie May Abbott, "The Georgia Magnet," defied anyone in the audience to lift her. Even Helen Keller and Annie Sullivan had an act.

But for George Burns, "Swain's Cats and Rats" seemed to sum them all up as the ne plus ultra of fabulously absurd novelty acts. "At the end," he remembered with relish, "the cats would run around a racetrack and the rats were the jockeys. They would sit on the cats."

He seemed to take a sensual pleasure in these details and warmed even to the title of a preposterous act. When he joked about "Madame Burkhart and the Cockatoos," it was the name that made him laugh. He was a writer but he didn't know it, the most literate illiterate in vaudeville.

He was also a man of uncluttered intelligence, tickled by the illogical. Sitting in a restaurant, for example, he overheard a customer ask a passing waiter where the men's room was.

"Please," the waiter said, "I've only got two hands."

A similar sense of the offbeat humor in everyday conversation lay ahead, waiting to make his future, but he seemed to live only in the present. Even if nothing but failure lay ahead, which sometimes seemed to be his fate, he never despaired. What might have looked like reason for frustration to somebody else was adventure and fun for him.

Even so, it was a matter of fact that Burns was a twenty-five-year-old performer without an act of his own, or even a consistent name. His situation looked hopeless—dancing tangos one day, roller-skating the next. "I was a typical small-time, number two act," he said, and number two was the lowest spot on the bill for a talking act (as opposed to a number one or opening act—a dumb act like a juggler or a dog act). It seemed to him as if that was all he ever would be, a small-time, number two act who was unrequitedly in love with show business; who could not be discouraged and was cheerfully, doggedly, and indomitably coping with vaudeville as he was with life; who, smart as he was, did not know what his own act really was.

3

He worked with Sid Gary for a year, which was longer than he had ever been with anyone except Harriet Gibson, and he was living with her. Harriet Gibson was a singer—"a cute little number," by George's description. He was a cute little number, too, he had to admit, in his checkered suits and spats. He was very clothes-conscious. As a matter of fact, he seemed to remember more about his clothes than about his childhood.

According to the same values, an act was more important than a girlfriend. He stayed with Sid Gary rather than going on the road with Harriet Gibson because the act with Gary had the clothes to go with it. He seemed to think that the Burns and Gary costumes alone—matching brown suits, spats, ties, and derbies—were going to move them straight up to a number seven spot, which was the headliner's place on a vaudeville bill.

But the only place he was moving was deeper into his twenties, and that was a ripe age for someone who was not even up and coming. Never a fool, he must have realized that however much he loved to sing, the audience did not seem to enjoy it. This was a decided drawback of his singing acts.

The problem with dancing, which was definitely his greater talent, was that in vaudeville, dancing did not work as a solo. A hoofer had to choose between being in a song and dance act with another man, or doing a ballroom routine with a woman. Burns decided to try a ballroom act again. He found a lovely Jewish girl for a partner, a dancer named Hannah Siegel, and promptly dubbed her "Hermosa Jose" (after Hermosa cigars, he said). He was planning a Latin act because he had leftover Spanish material from his old act, "Pedro Lopez and Conchita." The material consisted of a tango, which was his best dance not counting the Peabody, plus the sheet music for "La Czarina," which was a Russian mazurka that he mistook for Spanish.

At this point, he once again paints his memories in greasepaint. He and Hannah, he drolly claims, were offered a twenty-six-week tour which they could accept only if they got married. That was the stipulation made by her parents, who were devout Jews.

There are a couple of reasons to question this story. In the first place, a twenty-six-week tour was an improbable engagement for this sporadically employed, second-rate song and dance man. Second, if George and Hermosa were a brand-new act, it was not likely that they would get such an offer. They must have been working somewhere to receive it. If so, he says nothing about it.

They got married—at City Hall in Manhattan—just, he insisted, for the booking. "The whole marriage, we never slept together."

If this was possible, it is not plausible. Perhaps he is avoiding an unpleasant subject yet again. He jokes about this twenty-six-week marriage of theatrical convenience, but never describes Hannah or his experiences with her. He does not say how he met her, or why her devout Jewish parents approved of a civil wedding ceremony. He says that they were divorced but not *when* they were divorced—if they were divorced at all (a memorable Jewish ritual), rather than the marriage being annulled on grounds of non-consummation. He does not say what the act was or where it was booked or how it was abandoned or even what its name was. In view of his nostalgia about the names of acts—his loving, lengthy enumeration of the assorted *noms de théâtre* under which he worked—this omission is most peculiar.

The name of the act with Hannah, in fact, was "Jose and Smith."

Was it really no different, and no harder, to break up the act than the marriage? Perhaps not for George. Perhaps he couldn't tell the difference between an act and a marriage. If he had been asked at the time what the difference between them was, the answer would surely have made a funny chapter in his jokebook of changing the subject.

His next partner, Billy Lorraine, was a stammerer but it didn't make a difference since Burns and Lorraine weren't a talking act, and Billy didn't stammer when he sang. Burns himself would stammer in later years, but at the moment he didn't even talk onstage.

Burns and Lorraine were singing impressionists. "We opened with syncopated patter," George remembered. "Then we did our imitations." His specialty was George M. Cohan. Billy did Jolson and Cantor. They called the act "Burns and Lorraine, Broadway Thieves," and George didn't need Flo Ziegfeld to tell him that if it had taken two decades to get this far, he might think about getting into another racket. But he never considered another racket.

During this stretch, Milton Berle worked on a bill with Burns and Lorraine. The comedian was doing a double with Elizabeth Kennedy, which they called "The Twinkling Stars." Berle was only fifteen but he already had higher billing than Burns.

Standing in the wings and waiting to go on, he watched

as the "Broadway Thieves" did their turn. The costumes were the usual song and dance—blazers, straw hats, and canes.

The opening number was typically corny for the small time, "Last Night at the Actors' Ball," which served to cue the impersonations. Then again, Berle thought everything about this act was "second rate. Everything George was doing then was small time."

Burns would come to agree, and be funny about it, although it may not have been funny at the time. Even this act was already splitting up, but George's optimism was organic. He had yet another idea—"a talking mixed double"—which meant a comedy act with a woman. He had already posted notices at both the National Variety Artists Club and the vaudeville union, The White Rats. That was how a vaudevillian found a partner.

Burns and Lorraine's final booking was in Union City, New Jersey, and so was George's final booking as a second-rate song and dance man. For at this time, which was the winter of 1923, his stars were in perfect alignment.

On the same bill was an unusual low comedy act called "Rena Arnold and Company." It was an unusual act because a low clown was usually male. Women in comedy acts played sexpots and served as "feeders," serving up straight lines to the comedians. They were not supposed to get the laughs, but this act was different.

Rena Arnold was a boisterous young woman, and between shows she got to know George and Billy. One night, her roommates, Mary Kelly and Grace Allen, both of them actresses, came "back" (show talk for backstage) to visit. Rena knew that Grace was looking for a partner and suddenly grabbed her hand.

"Grace," she cried. "These boys on the bill are breaking up their act! Billy Lorraine is looking for a new partner. Why don't you talk to him?"

Grace stayed for a second show and took another look

at Burns and Lorraine, after which she came back and introduced herself. "Mr. Lorraine, I'm a friend of Rena Arnold's and I understand you're looking for a new partner. So am I."

Billy Lorraine was so shy that the hardest thing for him to pronounce seemed to be his own name. Intimidated by Grace's beauty, he could only stammer, "A-a-a no, my name is Burns. Th-th-th-that's Lorraine over there." He nodded in George's direction.

Grace turned to George and held out a hand. "Miss Arnold said you were looking for a partner, Mr. Lorraine."

"I am," said Burns, who was always interested in pretty girls. "Why don't we have lunch tomorrow and talk it over?"

He liked her hair, her skin, her voice, and her two-different-colored eyes. She liked him better than Billy Lorraine because Lorraine stammered. At least, that was Burns's story, and so the next day, back in Manhattan, they met at noon in front of the Palace Theatre.

They walked around the corner to Wiennig and Sberber's, a restaurant just off Times Square. It was a hangout for actors, songwriters, prizefighters, and journalists. Hanging out had been Burns's main occupation, so he was familiar with the place.

As they sat down, he rolled out his raconteur charm, beginning by telling Grace about the restaurant's two owners, both of them eccentrics. If you asked Mr. Wiennig a question, he said, the old man would give you the answer to the last customer's question.

"I walked in one day and said, 'Hello, Mr. Wiennig. Have you seen Manny Mannishaw?' He said, 'Look on the floor, maybe it fell down there.'"

Perhaps Wiennig said it that way or perhaps Burns put a shine on it. Either way, it was wonderful material. George's problem was that he could not use this material onstage. The humor was too oblique.

Sberber, he said, was no better. "He once told me he'd seen *La Bohème* so many times he knew it by heart. When I asked, 'How does it go?' he said, 'Good.' "

Grace always would be his best audience. She never tried to be funny offstage and was not hungry for a spotlight. She was warm but ladylike. Her giggle was contagious, but so high-pitched that Burns was already worrying about her singing voice. That would turn out to be fine, her dancing would be even better, and she was also a dramatic actress.

In short and in total, she seemed flawless. She was small (five feet, 102 pounds), fair-skinned, and extremely beautiful, a seventeen-year-old *shiksa* goddess with long, curly, thick blue-black hair and eyes that only seemed to be two different colors. In fact, one was green and the other had lost its coloration in a frightful childhood accident, when she had knocked over a storm lamp and sprayed glass all over her face.

When she was eight years old she had another painful accident, this time at her grandmother's home. Since there was no electricity, kerosene lamps were used. One was knocked over, searing Grace painfully with the hot oil as it splattered across her left shoulder, arm, and upper wrist. She was left with injured tendons and permanent scars. None of this was seriously disfiguring, but it was enough to trouble a young woman. Throughout her life, she would cover that arm, either with high gloves or long sleeves, as it was covered at that first lunch with George.

"We talked over the act," he remembered, "and it was very pleasant. She certainly was very pretty. An hour later, we had made a rehearsal date. Two days later, we started to rehearse."

Unable to resist a punch line, he added: "Three days later, I told her to stop calling me Lorraine."

Grace called him "Nat," as everyone did. It would become "Natty," a term of endearment reserved for his closest friends. And he called her "Gracie."

George Burns and Gracie Allen could hardly have come from more diverse backgrounds. As Burns wrote in *Gracie: A Love Story* (G. P. Putnam's Sons, 1988), she was an Irish Catholic from San Francisco. Her father, George Allen, had been a performer. In the early days of variety, before there was such a thing as vaudeville, he had been a clog dancer in saloons and in storefront honky-tonks, working up and down the California coast.

Grace Ethel Cecile Rosalie Allen was one of five children, including a boy, George, Jr., and the four girls—Bessie, Pearl, Hazel, and Grace, who was the youngest, born July 26, 1908. The family lived in San Francisco, in a big white stucco house at 668 Fourth Avenue.

George Allen taught all of his children to dance, and by the time Grace was three, he was encouraging her to perform in public. After teaching her how to do an Irish jig, he volunteered her for a church social. It must have been hard to resist a three year old wearing a pint-sized top hat, a full set of tails, and, tied under her chin, the bright red whiskers that were the trademark of Irish comedians.

As soon as little Grace heard her downbeat, she strutted onstage, yanked off the whiskers, and began the jig as her dad watched from the wings.

Two years later, he walked out on the family.

Grace's mother, Margaret, was a devout Catholic, at least until she got a divorce and married a policeman named Edward Pidgeon. That was how she got the nickname "Pidgie." It was the name that Grace called her mother.

Divorce or not, all of the Allen children went to Catholic schools. Even so, by the time Grace was seven, like Nathan Birnbaum on the Lower East Side of Manhattan, she was in the show business.

Whatever the mysterious source of little Nathan's stage

fever, Grace had a father to inherit it from, as did her sisters. In fact the oldest of them, Bessie, had become a professional singer as well as a tap dancer, and was already touring on the Sullivan and Considine time. Grace was six years old when Bessie played San Francisco, and naturally, Pidgie took all of the children to see their sister perform. Like many youngsters who are not accustomed to seeing family on the stage, Grace thought that when the audience laughed at Bessie's material, they were laughing at Bessie—and she wept for her sister.

But as soon as they were old enough, Hazel, Pearl, and Grace followed Bessie onto the stage, and the four girls formed a harmony quartet. It was of a somewhat contrasting ethnic color to George's old Peewee Quartet. That group had comprised Nathan, Toda, and the two Weinberger boys, all from Jewish immigrant homes. Grace's quartet was "The Four Colleens." They not only sang Irish favorites but also worked in Scottish kilts, lining up to do a synchronized Highland fling, which certainly was not the dance of the moment in George's Lower East Side neighborhood.

There was another difference. In contrast to the sporadic nature of George's so-called professional career, Grace and her sisters stayed together for ten years. In short, while George Burns was always a flop, Grace Allen never was.

Her act folded when Pearl decided to quit and open a dance school in San Francisco. That left Hazel, Bessie, and Grace with a three-girl Irish quartet, which they kept together for a while, dancing with Larry Reilly as "Reilly & Co." But when Hazel and Bessie also gave up, going home to teach dancing in Pearl's school, "Reilly & Co." was reduced to Reilly and Grace.

They toured eastward while she grew increasingly unhappy, and when they got to New York, she decided to quit vaudeville and enroll in a school of stenography. But it was a tough transition. Her background was in the show business, her friends were in the show business, and, inevitably, so were the boys she met.

A girl as beautiful as Grace soon had a beau. His name was Benny Ryan, and he was a talented young Irish dancer in the successful act of Ryan and Lee. Ryan also wrote sketches and songs, including the hit "When Frances Dances with Me (Holy Gee)." But he was on the road as a dancer, and although they were already discussing marriage, Grace was looking for work—and not as a secretary. Stenography school had taught her only that she wanted to go back on the stage. That was when she met George.

The "talking mixed double" that he wanted to do, he told her, was a "flirtation" act. It was a variation on a "street corner" routine. All that meant was a man and woman standing at center stage exchanging courtship-oriented jokes.

Grace, he made it clear, would be the straight man. Although he had never in his life been a talking act, he was now not only going to talk. He was going to be a comedian.

4

As they began rehearsing the new act, George was not yet divorced from Hannah Siegel. In various memoirs, he dismisses this marriage with a joke ("I didn't sleep with married women"), rather than dealing with it as a youthful mistake, or even simply as a curious event in his life. The closest he gets to talking about it is, "I know nothing except it didn't work."

Better to turn the twenty-six-week episode into comedy material. "She was a lovely girl, but I wouldn't have married her for a sixteen-week booking."

George, certainly, was not an emotional exhibitionist. In later years he kept his feelings to himself, and he probably did the same as a young man too. Perhaps at bottom an act really *was* more important to him than a marriage, and the only kind of divorce that may have meant anything to him was breaking up an act.

Gracie, as he now called her, seemed satisfied that she was in love with Benny Ryan. George moved in with his younger brother, Willie, and seemed satisfied to be in love with show business. Besides, he had more serious concerns. He was a failed song and dance man who was now going to try to be funny.

His material did not help. He borrowed most of it from two joke collections, *Captain Billy's Whiz Bang* and *College Humor,* even though he could be funnier over lunch at Wiennig and Sberber's. He was more worried about Gracie than about himself. She was having difficulty learning her lines, and her readings were ill at ease, as if she were unable to shed her real-life self. In time he would realize that Gracie was essentially a dramatic actress, and like many actresses she came into her own with the performance itself.

After rehearsing for three weeks, they were ready for a test. George wangled a three-day booking as fill-ins at a small-time, four-a-day vaudeville house in Newark.

Costumes were a big part of any act because they advised the audience of a performer's intentions, and performers needed all the help they could get. Gracie chose a dark dress and high heels. George made sure that his clothes shouted "comedian." There was an old show business story about a performer who tore onstage with a red nose, a blue wig, green makeup, teeth blacked out, baggy pants, a funny hat, a loud vest, an outsize checkered coat, a polka-dot bow tie, and a long watch chain. An actor watching from backstage said to the stage manager, "By the looks of that guy, he must be a very funny comedian."

The stage manager said, "That's the straight man."

Burns wasn't quite that broad, but he did dress "funny," with shortened trousers and a turned-up hat, none of which convinced the sparse audience that anything he said was amusing. Yet the conservatively dressed Gracie was getting laughs *with her straight lines.*

Many years later he remembered rummaging through his mind for explanations as he followed her up the spiral metal stairs backstage at the Hill Street Theatre after the first show. A straight man basically asked questions, and sometimes merely repeated the comedian's first line. ("I went to see a chiropractor yesterday." "Why did you go to see a chiropractor?")

What made unfunny straight lines into gags when Gracie said them? And why were his punch lines falling flat? One explanation might be that the content of a joke is not necessarily the funny thing about it; equally important is who tells it and how it is told. In fact, the joke itself does not have to be funny. But the person who tells it has to be.

There was something about Grace that was even more important than being funny. As Burns says in *Gracie: A Love Story,*

> Some kind of magical transformation had taken place. As the act progressed, I realized that the audience felt it too. They loved her, I could feel it. It was the most amazing thing, and it happened just like that.

In the few hours before the second show began, he excitedly rewrote the act. "I didn't have to be a genius to understand that there was something wrong with a comedy act when the straight lines got more laughs than the punch lines." The jokes he added were not much better than the ones replaced, but this time he gave some of the funny lines to Gracie, and took straight lines for himself. "It broke my heart but I was young and hungry and not a dope."

GEORGE
Who was that guy I saw you kissing backstage?
GRACIE
Oh, I don't know.
GEORGE
You mean, you kiss a guy and you don't know who he is?

GRACIE

Well, I was standing in the wings and he said, "How about you and me having a bite tonight?" And I said, "No, I'm busy tonight, but if you'd like I'll bite you now."

This made the routine a cross between a flirtation act and a "Dumb Dora" act, which was yet another standard routine. There was nothing standard, however, about Gracie's line readings. "What made her different," George said, "was her sincerity."

He was grasping the quality in her that the audience was responding to. He would prove to be a natural writer for this character, perhaps any character. He would probably have made a good playwright.

He was also a natural director, and he told her to play the sketch as a dramatic scene, interacting with him— actually facing him—rather than playing to the audience. This made the spectators feel as if they were watching a real person.

While playing the second show, Burns kept an ear to the audience. "No matter how funny you think a joke is," he believed, "if they don't laugh, take it out. The audience tells you what's funny."

At the end of that show, he knew for the first time in his life that he was in a smash act. The audience might as well have been rising up from their seats and taking Gracie Allen into their arms. Perhaps he was not funny, but the act was, and that was the only thing that mattered.

Gracie had given him an awesome gift, a kind of miracle: she made him a success at the only thing he wanted to be. He would receive several such critical gifts during his life, and that did not happen by chance. There was a magic about Burns, and it was related to his vitality, his determination, his optimism, and his extraordinary ability to relate to another person.

Grace had invited her roommates to see the show. George also brought a friend, Jack Benny, a fellow vaude-villian he had met on the road.

Two years older than Burns, Benny was already on the medium time and was part of a new generation of gentlemen-monologists. Gone were the funny clothes and aggressive style of the old clowns. These were gentlemen-comedians wearing suits and ties. They stood at stageside with one hand in their trousers pockets, and spoke with casual confidence in well-modulated voices.

That was quite a change from banging around with slapsticks and punching out corny, scattershot jokes in fractured foreign dialects. These monologues were longer, the stories were anecdotal, and one led to the next in connection with an overall theme.

Jack Benny was reserved offstage too, and so, while he was the same age as George, he seemed more mature. It was really just shyness, and he was as inhibited as his neck was in that tight, starched collar. It was buttoned so high that his chin seemed to tilt upward, as if he were playing the violin, which he did in his act.

In all of these respects, Benny was an unlikely person to be an entertainer. George was more like it, Mister Slick, a dandy from stickpin to spats. He waved a cigar, he flashed a ring, and he shot his cuffs. This was show business.

A difference in background explained some of this. Jack, although Jewish as well, was from a comfortable home in the Midwest, far from George's scrappy New York side-walks. Benny had never struggled, either personally or professionally. And he was as buttoned up as he looked, while George was and would always be an independent spirit, adventurous and open to new ideas.

Despite the differences, these two young and energetic fellows had a centeredness in common. They were both doing something they loved to do and it reflected their *themness*—they were very much who they were. There was a kind of sanity in that. They also loved to be funny with each other, and as the friendship blossomed it was expressed through their common language of humor.

One afternoon, they ran into each other in Times Square and Jack asked whether George had any bookings. Burns said, "I just saw Fitzpatrick and all I got was his drawer routine." He explained what he meant by mimicking someone opening and closing desk drawers, looking inside and hunting for anything, just as long as the actor would get the point and go away.

Benny started laughing. Burns did not think the subject of Fitzpatrick was a particularly funny one. The ruse with the drawers was familiar enough.

"What are you laughing at?"

Jack couldn't tell him. He was laughing too hard.

Burns stopped a man on the street.

"Do you know why this man is laughing?"

The fellow shrugged.

He asked another pedestrian, "Do you know why this man is laughing?"

The man asked, "Don't you?"

"By this time," George would remember, "Jack was screaming."

Passers-by stopped to watch and when Benny saw them, he laughed even harder. "Finally," Burns said, "he fell down on the ground . . . and just lay there, gasping."

This was not the Jack Benny that vaudeville audiences saw. That fellow was a sedate gentleman who seemed to have wandered into a stage spotlight. The best of that genre was a tall, slender, handsome red-haired Irishman named Frank Fay. Fay had everyone in vaudeville talking. He was admired by both George and Jack for his quick, understated wit and his dry, ironic manner. It was in that direction that Benny was moving. "He came from Fay's school," Burns said. "Everybody came from Fay's school," but unlike Frank Fay, Jack Benny wasn't an egoist. They were both "light" comedians—meaning, in Burns's definition, "they didn't 'press' "—but what made Jack special was his gentleness, his sweetness, his benign self-deprecation. That was unique, and it was Jack.

In private, he didn't even try to be funny, but he seemed to think that his friends were. That was his sense of their humor.

Jack, Rena Arnold, and Mary Kelly came to see the new Burns and Allen act at the late show, that day in 1923 when the team first performed in Newark, New Jersey. Afterward, George took them all to midnight supper.

They were a rowdy and warm group. The girls had been raving about the Burns and Allen act from the moment they went backstage. Benny had privately felt, when the act began, that "George and Gracie were as nervous as any vaudeville actors were when they tried out new material before an audience." But by the time they took their bows he thought they were "sensational," and now he honestly told them so.

Sitting at the table in that restaurant, George had Jack in stitches. Everything he said seemed to make his friend hysterical, and that was a great thing in a friendship because everyone feels good when they feel funny. Jack, being so safe with his ego, was able to do something that was unique for a comedian—he was able to make other people feel that they were funny. There was a lot of laughing at that table.

The laughs stopped, however, the moment that Jack exchanged special glances with Gracie's friend Mary. There was a reason why people called her "Pretty Mary Kelly." As Benny himself described her, "She was tall and had golden blond hair. Her face was beautiful."

He was even more of a loverboy than George. "In the early days," Burns remembered, "Jack played on the Orpheum circuit and slept with every girl from coast to coast." But after one exchange of glances with Pretty Mary Kelly, he was lost for the night.

As he himself admitted, "Mary Kelly looked over at me. I looked into her eyes. Our glances joined. We felt a kind of magnetism pulling us."

While the magnetism was pulling them, the newborn comedy team of Burns and Allen played out their Newark engagement. It was so successful that by the time they came back to New York, they had an agent and another booking. This time it was for a full week at a theatre in Boonton, New Jersey.

Burns developed even more material for that engagement, and they were a smash all over again. In fact, with each performance, he learned more about the character Gracie was playing. "The audience found that character," he said. "They loved the character so she played it."

He continued to refine her "illogical logic," as he would call it.

GRACIE

Where do you keep your money?

GEORGE

In the bank.

GRACIE

What interest do you get?

GEORGE

Four percent.

GRACIE

Ha! I get eight.

GEORGE

You get eight?

GRACIE

I keep it in two banks.

Just as there had been a "magical transformation" when audiences first discovered Gracie's character for him, he was having a magical transformation of his own. This one is sometimes called growing up. He realized that George

Burns was not a good act. He realized that he would always be a small-time song and dance man. But he also appreciated what he was. "I knew show business, especially vaudevillle. I knew all the ingredients involved in putting an act together. I knew exits, entrances, how to construct a joke, how to switch a joke, where the laughs were going to drop, how to build an act to a strong finish.

"And most important, I knew the zany, off-center character Gracie Allen played onstage."

In her sincere silliness, she was delivering an accessible version of his own quirky, amiably perverse sense of humor.

And so, even more important than his role as the straight man in the act was the new role as a writer, a director, and perhaps as a Svengali. He was the medium through which the audience perceived and appreciated Gracie. She was now free to act, to read her lines straight and seem to have no idea that what she said was funny. She never dropped that facade, and that was their pretense.

The audience believed it, and he respected that belief. For instance, he sensed that the audience felt protective of her, so he learned never to seem mean to Gracie, or raise his voice to her. He would not touch her during the act, not even with affection. If the people laughed when she said she used a short electric cord on her vacuum cleaner in order to save electricity, he understood that the laugh included appreciation. They liked Gracie for being a housewife, and an economy-minded one at that. Everyone thought they knew somebody like her.

He also realized that audiences didn't laugh when she was sarcastic. They did not want her to be a wise guy. The audience finds your character for you, he said. "The audience finds everything, and you cannot be a star unless the audience makes you a star."

They certainly were making Gracie a star. George always would say that the only thing he had to do was ask her,

"How's your brother?" and he would just stand and listen for the rest of the act. But she could hardly do it without that "rest of the act" being written by him. Yet, one newspaper reviewer wrote, "Miss Allen can extract oodles of mirth from the most commonplace remark, and there's no telling how far she could go if she worked alone."

But she did not work alone. Burns's droll style counterbalanced her sweetness, his sanity safeguarded her lightheadedness. In brief, if she was the angel, he was the realist, the audience's earthbound surrogate.

When things go well, they go well fast. Even though Burns and Allen signed on as only a "disappointment," or replacement act, a new, six-month deal with the B. F. Keith vaudeville circuit brought them closer to show business success than anything George had ever done. He negotiated the contract himself; agents notwithstanding, he would always be on top of the Burns and Allen business dealings.

Being available as a replacement act meant living with bags packed. "It seemed," George remembered, "we were always on a bus or a short-hop train." Other acts were canceled often enough for them to be busy most of the time, but even on the Keith circuit on the medium time, theatre conditions were not luxurious. "We dressed in boiler rooms, bathrooms, and closets."

Since Gracie's beau, Benny Ryan, was also traveling, the couple had little time together. Even so, she told George—"Natty"—that she was now engaged. It introduced a new feeling for him: jealousy. He didn't know until then that he had been falling in love with her.

He began to take Grace dancing in the evenings. It was a way to be sexy and romantic while still being proper. George knew he was a smooth dancer—after all, he had been a professional. All his life he would have a professional's confidence on the dance floor. That was one place where he could really be romantic. But if Gracie was responding to him at all, she certainly did not show it. As far as she was concerned, she was still engaged to Benny Ryan.

George was good at being a friend, and one he made was Luther Adler, the son of the famous Jacob P. and Sarah Adler, icons of the legendary Yiddish Art Theatre. They were known as "the Barrymores of Second Avenue," and reigned over a family of celebrated Yiddish actors. Luther was a young scion of this royal family, but their lofty reputation did not deter him from being an adventurous young man.

George might have looked like a flashy vaudevillian, and he certainly talked like one, but he was actually a rather naive young man. Luther Adler, on the other hand, was worldly and daring, and he showed George a side of life he'd never seen.

He even took George to an opium den.

Burns remembered only that the "den" was an apartment, that it was dark, and that mattresses were spread on the floors throughout the place.

He was given a pipe and shown how to inhale the sweet fumes. After he did, he stretched out on one of the mattresses. Beyond that, he remembered nothing of the evening.

It was one story he never tried to revise into vaudeville material.

At the start of 1924, a historic event took place. George Burns finally broke into the medium time, not as a replacement but in a regular booking. It was a Sunday concert, just one show, but the booking was at the big Hurtig and Seamon Theatre on 125th Street in Harlem. The only shadow cast on that splendid afternoon was Gracie's pounding migraine headache. She had suffered such headaches before, but not to this extent. She went on, but with discomfort. Apparently her sacrifice was worth it, for as George recalled in *Gracie: A Love Story,*

We were struck by that wonderful wave of feeling that comes up when you have a great audience. It's what keeps performers alive. If your audience is good, the hotel you're staying in is good, the food is good, everything is good.

If something can make a person feel that good, he should do it. This is how to make a living, and Burns understood it all his life. Now, with every engagement, he had a stronger sense of what the Burns and Allen act was all about. So he refined and polished.

> GEORGE
>
> Did the maid ever drop you on your head when you were a baby?
>
> GRACIE
>
> Don't be silly, George. We couldn't afford a maid. My mother had to do it.

He turned to the audience. They laughed and he looked, and he looked and they laughed.

He introduced continuity, so that one funny exchange followed from the last and related to the next. Burns and Allen gradually moved upward, earning $300 a week at a time when that was a fair amount of money. Nat must have figured that if they were paid that much, the act must be good enough to show his mother. And so, when they were called in as substitutes for a balancing act at the Greenpoint Theatre in Brooklyn, not far from Dora Birnbaum's apartment, he invited her to see the show.

As Burns related in *Gracie*, after the show he took his mother to dinner and introduced her to Gracie. When Dora complimented her on the performance, Gracie asked, "But what about Natty? Wasn't he terrific?"

"To tell you the truth," Dora Birnbaum said, "I think sometimes he acts like a relative got him the job."

By 1925, the act had the chance to play ten weeks on the

Keith-Orpheum circuit, which was the mammoth wheel resulting from a merger of the B. F. Keith theatres in the East and the Orpheum theatres in the Midwest. Although this was a step up in class, on the brink of the big time, Gracie told her pal Mary Kelly that she was quitting the act to marry Benny Ryan.

That is so unfair, Mary said. "You're not only breaking up the act, you're breaking Natty's heart."

Mary and Nat had become like brother and sister, now that she and Jack had gotten serious about each other. For Benny's part, the womanizing young comedian had dropped every other girl and, he remembered, "I began seeing her [Mary] all the time."

They had problems from the outset. Mary Kelly was a devout Roman Catholic, more so than Gracie. Jack was already daydreaming about marriage, but marrying out of his faith was inconceivable to him. In fact, it was so nasty a subject that he could not even talk to George about it.

Mary Kelly had similar problems. As Jack related it, she told him that marriage to a non-Catholic was out of the question. Perhaps she might have reconsidered if he complied with church requirements, but apparently he would not entertain that possibility.

They seemed to talk incessantly about the dilemma. "We didn't think we would get serious when we started going out," Jack said. Like so many young people, it was precisely when they were starting to get serious that they began to say they were not going to get serious. Perhaps the gods' seeming to be against them had made it all the more romantic.

"From being stuck on each other," he remembered, "we went on to become crazy about each other. We decided life was unbearable unless we could be with each other constantly."

Their romance was all the more attractive for being part of a foursome of friends. Since George and Gracie were also an interfaith couple, they became two sets of mirror images. Fraught as the Jack-Mary romance was with reservations, they might well have seen the Burns and Allen act as an idealized, stage version of their relationship. And so they wished for George and Gracie what they wished they had themselves—easy sailing.

Of course Natty and Gracie were not having a romance, at least Gracie wasn't. Nat, however, was hooked and Mary Kelly knew it. But she seemed to feel, or hope, that her friend was unknowingly in love with him too. Since Gracie indicated no such thing, Mary said to her, "Listen, if you are going to break it up, at least give him an excuse."

Before Grace could think of any, Mary suggested that she refuse to sign the Orpheum contract unless they got more money. "It's better than saying, 'Goodbye, I'm breaking up the act and getting married.'"

So Grace told Nat that she wouldn't go along with the Orpheum contract unless they were paid $400 a week, which was $50 more than they had been offered. Being an unrequited lover, he was a suspicious one and immediately thought that this was only a subterfuge. He promised to make a pitch for the raise, but "I only knew," he remembered, "that it was the end of Burns and Allen"—as an act, and as a couple that never was.

Mary Kelly took no chances. She made a telephone call to a friend in the Orpheum management, a fellow who was sweet on her. Nat got the extra $50 and Gracie had no choice but to accept it.

The Ryan-Allen nuptials were postponed, and Burns and Allen moved up to the medium time.

5

Nat said that Gracie was playing "the dizziest dame on earth," but hers was a charming dizziness.

> GEORGE
> This family of yours. Did they all live together?
> GRACIE
> Yes, my father, my uncle, my cousin, my brother, and my nephew used to sleep in one bed, and my—
> GEORGE
> I'm surprised your grandfather didn't sleep with them.
> GRACIE
> He did. But he died and they made him get up.

The dialogue makes a kind of loony sense, and it is economical, rhythmic, and hard-edged. The great Irish playwright Samuel Beckett doted on such short, rapid-fire exchanges as relief from the florid, symbol-laden language of the classical literature. Beckett, a disciple of James Joyce but also a reader of *Variety* and an enthusiast of the English music hall, incorporated the language of vaudeville into his great play *Waiting for Godot*. Centered on a pair of Chaplinesque tramps in an existential limbo, the play is written almost exclusively in vaudevillian short takes.

> ESTRAGON
>
> I'm hungry.
>
> VLADIMIR
>
> Do you want a carrot?
>
> ESTRAGON
>
> Is that all there is?
>
> VLADIMIR
>
> There might be some turnips.
>
> ESTRAGON
>
> Give me a carrot.

Gracie Allen's "illogical logic" could easily have fit in with Beckett and the other absurdist playwrights. That would have amused Nat Burns. On the other hand, some knowledge of dramatic structure might have helped him, for there was no form to his routines. Despite his intention to write material that had continuity, the rapid-fire exchanges didn't go anywhere and a joke was the end of the line, usually three lines:

> GRACIE
>
> My sister had a baby.
>
> GEORGE
>
> Boy or girl?
>
> GRACIE
>
> I don't know, and I can't wait to find out if I'm an uncle or an aunt.

Moreover, while the writing was superior to generic comedy material, and well tailored to Gracie's stage character, it remained the stuff of all "Dumb Dora" acts, written to the standard form of a straight man and a comedian. Jack Benny tweaked George about it, a gentle way of urging him to do better. "He repeats everything," Jack said, "just like every other straight man. Now the other day, I said to him, 'George, how's your brother Willie?' "

There was no tricking George. He knew this game too well.

"He said, 'How's my brother Willie?'"

"Then *I* had to think of a funny answer. Sometimes you could stand that way for days."

Nat began to write longer exchanges, and as Gracie's character evolved, the exchanges became short scenes. He even gave the routine a title, "Dizzy," because of her breathless line, "I'm glad I'm dizzy boys like dizzy girls and I like boys and you must be glad I'm dizzy because you're a boy and I like boys."

George always described Gracie not as a comedienne but as an actress. He said that she was the only person in the auditorium who didn't know that her lines were funny. "She was able to block out an audience," he said. "She would deliver a line, I'd look at the audience, and when they stopped laughing, I'd look back and Gracie would still be looking at me."

This led the audience to identify with him and believe in her; to watch as if at a play, with Gracie a character in a story and George a participant in that story, yet also a part of the audience's reality.

He added a prologue to sweeten the act's flirtatious aspect. Now, they walked onstage hand-in-hand. She stopped, glanced over her shoulder, and called, "Yoo-hoo," into the wings. Then a man strolled out and kissed her.

GRACIE

Who's that?

GEORGE

Who's that? You mean to say you kiss people you don't know?

GRACIE

Sure.

GEORGE

Well, if you kiss people you don't know, what do you do with people you do know?

GRACIE

People I know I don't kiss.

George had been kissing her on the cheek after the show, or when he said good night after a late supper. Now, when they toured, he not only took her dancing; he kissed her lightly on the lips. She didn't say no, but he was cautious.

The torrential passion was left to Jack and Mary Kelly, and they were in the throes of it. One day they might be soaring along joyously and then the next, they would be tossed by interfaith panic, sending them plummeting into despair.

Jack blamed it all on Mary. "She was so dramatic," he said. "She oscillated from one extreme to the other. At one moment she was convinced she couldn't live unless we were married. I would say, let's do it right now—let's go to Waukegan, meet my father, and begin planning our married life. Then, likely as not, she'd fly into a temper. She'd say we could never marry. We were of different faiths. She could never marry a person of my faith."

While this implied that Benny had no qualms about an interfaith marriage, in fact it was Mary who took him home to meet her parents. The Kellys lived in Chicago, not far from Jack's family in Waukegan, Illinois. "They were wonderful people," Benny remembered, before punctuating the thought: "One of her brothers was a priest."

That seemed to say it all for him and it was all he had to say on the subject of her family. He certainly never brought her home to meet his own parents, and George would later say that it was not Mary Kelly but Jack who was to blame. "He didn't have the nerve to marry a Catholic."

There were no such melodramatics with George and Gracie because she seemed oblivious to his deepening feelings. Their life together was the act, and on the road George roomed with his younger brother.

Willie Burns (he changed his name too) was a combination of manager, traveling secretary, and dresser. He read the contracts, scheduled bookings, arranged interviews, and made travel arrangements. "He ran interference for me," Burns said, "so I didn't have to worry about anything except writing and performing."

Willie also took care of personal details and occasionally made suggestions for the act. If nothing else, he had gone to school longer than Nat and could write better. George could barely read or write at all.

Meantime, the team of Burns and Allen was becoming smoother and more popular.

GEORGE
I'll take you home if you'll give me a kiss.
GRACIE
All right. If you take me home, I'll give you a kiss.
[As he started walking her across the stage, he stopped abruptly.]
GEORGE
Wait a second. Is your mother home?
GRACIE
Sure she is, but my father won't let you kiss my mother.

George was now using his cigar as a prop. "It was something to do with my hands." Some performers are self-conscious about their hands, as if there were fins at the ends of their wrists. "Jack," Burns said, "had terrible hands. That's why he was always folding his arms or touching his cheek. He needed someplace to put his hands."

George needed his right hand to adjust the microphone, so he held the cigar in his left hand. But he had to be careful about not bothering Gracie. "When I smoked on-stage," he said, "I had to find out which way the wind was blowing and sometimes I had to change where I was standing so the smoke wouldn't go in Gracie's face. The audience wouldn't stand for that."

Gradually, his admiration of her work and his appreciation for their success began to transmute into feelings of love. There is no other way to put it: *He loved her as he loved the act.*

He started proposing in 1925. The first time he did it, Gracie said, "Oh, Natty. Don't be such a kidder."

Unlike Jack and Mary, there was never any discussion of religious differences. But there was no discussion of marriage, either. Gracie insisted that she was in love with Benny Ryan, that she was engaged to Benny Ryan, and that she was going to marry Benny Ryan.

If she wanted to discourage Natty, rejection was not the most effective approach. This was the George Burns who had not been discouraged by twenty years of being a flop. If one measure of emotional stability is the ability to cope with rejection, he was a paragon of sanity.

So he kept proposing while they kept moving up in vaudeville. Along the way, they collected friends. For instance, they started spending time with Jesse Block and Eva Sully, who did a similar "Dumb Dora" act. George took to Jesse immediately, and Gracie brought Eva into her little circle with Rena and Mary. The George-Gracie-Jack-Mary foursome was now a sextet.

Nat and Gracie also took to a singer named Blossom Seeley, who was already a headliner. "Bloss" was a voluptuous, full-bodied young woman. Burns loved it that as a hot seventeen-year-old in a tight dress she had been billed as "Baby Blossom." Now she was a star and she performed lustily, snapping her fingers as she stepped over the footlights to mix it up with the customers while she sang "Dardanella," "Darktown Strutters Ball," and her signature song, "Toddling the Toddle-O."

Bloss had divorced a baseball player, Rube Marquard, to marry a song and dance man named Benny Fields. Unlike his wife, who had a voice that could rattle the rafters, Fields was a subtler performer. He worked in top hat and tails and sang through a megaphone in the new style called "crooning." An act frequently reflected its owner's personality, and that was certainly true in this case. Benny Fields tended to fade into the background alongside his bombshell wife.

They, too, joined the gang along with George, Gracie, Jack, Mary, Eva, and Jesse.

That year, Burns and Allen got their first booking on the big time, with its luxurious schedule of only two shows a day. They were called in as a replacement act at the Fifth Avenue Theatre near 12th Street in New York, and the engagement went so well that it led to a sixteen-week booking in many of the better theatres of the Keith-Orpheum circuit.

At the top they started at the bottom. Playing the Orpheum Theatre in Brooklyn, they were slotted eighth on the bill, which was last, right after the star. Number eight was as bad as the number two slot because either way, the audience was preoccupied and not paying attention, either still arriving or already leaving.

A vaudeville bill was ritualized and every spot on it had unique significance. A standard eight-act program began with a "dumb" or non-speaking act precisely because of the noisy, incoming audience. This would be an acrobat, or a bicyclist, or an animal act. The second spot was the worst "talking" spot on the bill, and it was usually filled by a newcomer or a minor comedian. That was followed by something elaborate, either a "tab" (tabloid) act, which was an abbreviated version of a recent Broadway success, or else a "flash" act with a big company, fancy sets, and costumes. A flash act did not have to be glamorous—a schoolroom act with a lot of youngsters (moppets) would qualify, like "Fun in Hi Skule."

The fourth and fifth spots were major ones, filled with an established comedy or dance team, and sixth was close to the cream of the show. Then came the headliner, always billed seventh.

Playing the eighth spot on the bill at the Brooklyn Orpheum Theatre, then, while still the big time, hardly meant that Burns and Allen had arrived.

The contract on the Orpheum circuit was taking them across the country, first to Chicago and then west to Portland, Seattle, and Vancouver. From there, they were to go south to Oakland and then into Gracie's hometown of San Francisco. The bus days were over. They traveled strictly de luxe, by Pullman coach, and there was a fitting rhythm to it. Perhaps most people would not want to live a trouper's life, but for a vaudevillian this life of packing and unpacking, moving in and out of hotels, handing their music to conductors in one theatre and then the next, was *the* life, the only life.

While they traveled, George worked on a new act. He called it "Lamb Chops" because of the opening lines:

GEORGE

Do you like to love?

GRACIE

No.

GEORGE

Do you like to kiss?

GRACIE

No.

GEORGE

Well then, what do you like?

GRACIE

Lamb chops.

High praise in stage writing is often related to its economy. Burns's writing was achieving such spareness. To be sure, it was not all his own. A New York writer named John P. Medbury worked with him.

Medbury, like many comedy writers, was an eccentric. He rented a hotel room and kept a wooden Indian for company. The Indian was named "Chief" and Medbury tried out the material on him. Nat would get used to writers like this.

For a working vaudevillian, new material was treacherous territory. An act that had been played and proven was a living, it could even be a career, because with so many theatres, a year or two could pass before the same one was played again. Naturally, "that seventeen minutes," Burns said, "was your life savings. You couldn't gamble with that."

Yet Nat Burns, who would go out of town to try out a mere three new jokes, was now embarking on a whole new act.

Johnny Medbury wrote drafts of "Lamb Chops" in New York and mailed them out to wherever they were booked. With Willie as a sounding board, Nat reshaped the material, polishing it to suit Gracie and the act. Then the pages went back to Medbury, and so it continued. For an uneducated man, Burns's response to language was literate and his taste assured, and the project may have helped distract him from the one-last-time-and-that's-it wedding proposal he was planning to make in San Francisco.

Jack, meantime, had not seen Mary Kelly for months. He was on the road while she was finishing her own tour on the way back to New York. They poured their hearts into love letters—"almost daily," Jack remembered. As Natty and Gracie rolled west, Benny came east, and when his train arrived in Pennsylvania Station, Mary was there to meet him.

She didn't look as happy as he was feeling. He remembered that he "couldn't wait to kiss her," but she appeared to be drained.

"I can't marry you, Jack."

That was a welcome home.

"We don't have to get married," he pleaded.

"Everything is over between us," she said bleakly. "I can't stand this torture any longer. We have to forget each other."

What was this but pure romance? After months of ardent letters, she was meeting him at Penn Station to say good-bye!

"We sat on a bench," Benny later wrote in notes for a memoir. "We talked it over, heart to heart. She showed me why we had to break it up. I promised to put her out of my mind. I would never call her again. I would never write her another letter. We were finished."

They were finished, in fact, for a couple of days.

"I miss you so much, honey," Mary said (or, as Jack put it, "her velvet voice said") on the telephone.

"I gotta see you. Just once more. Then we'll break it off forever."

Natty at least had no problems with Grace's Catholicism. His only problem was that she was engaged to Benny Ryan, and after he made the one-last-and-that's-it proposal—in the house on Fourth Avenue where she had grown up—she was still engaged to Ryan.

But if George Burns had proved anything in his short but peppy life, it was his doggedness. He kept proposing as they continued the tour, now on the eastward leg. By the time they got back to New York it was Christmas, a very emotional season.

As if they were in some vaudevillian Forest of Arden, all of these young people—Jack, Mary, Nat, Gracie, and Benny Ryan—were now in the throes of a pregnant lovesickness. Ryan's mistake was always being out of town. Burns was playing Santa Claus. It was Mary Kelly's party. Gracie was miserable. She didn't know whether to choose Benny Ryan or Natty, and, as young men did, both fellows were demanding that she make an immediate decision. Ryan's ultimatum expired at midnight of Christmas Eve. Natty gave her a couple of extra days.

Shortly after twelve, Ryan telephoned and Gracie told him that she didn't love him any more. Soon afterward, she called Nat at his apartment, for he had gone home early, a heartsore Santa.

"You can buy the wedding ring," she said.

"You'll never be sorry," a relieved Natty replied, and the next night, they made love for the first time. At least, so he said, and there is no reason to doubt it.

The way it looked to Jack Benny, "George and Gracie . . . were in love . . . their emotion . . . was so strong." The way that Gracie was going to behave over the course of a thirty-eight-year marriage, it would truly seem that when she fell in love with Natty, it was profoundly and forever.

It was ironic that after a slow-developing love, Nat and Gracie could make a prompt decision about marriage while their ardent friends were still, as Jack put it, "on the merry-go-round of frustration. Maybe," he said about Mary, "she liked tormenting herself and me." It never struck him that he had anything to do with the problem.

Once again, they went their separate ways. Mary's act, Swift and Kelly, was booked into Chicago, while a "heartbroken" Jack went west to California and then Vancouver. Natty and Gracie hit the road too, heading for Canton, Ohio, where they were going to try out the new "Lamb Chops" act.

New acts were tested with supreme caution. One slip and an entertainer who had laboriously achieved success could plummet through the ranks to the bottom. Life could be rocky for months until the act was fixed. And so Natty gradually blended "Dizzy" into "Lamb Chops," easing the new material past the old. When that was done, they could think about their wedding date. They set it for Cleveland.

Engaged or not, when they got there, Nat took a room with Willie as they checked into the Statler Hotel. Even show people respected propriety (as a matter of fact, vaudeville was priggish and there were strict rules against the use of "such words as devil, cockroach, spit, etc.").

But in anticipation of a legal relationship and something to celebrate, he checked Gracie into a suite.

Mary Kelly took the train out to be the maid of honor. Willie was the best man, and a justice of the peace performed the ceremony on January 7, 1926. Gracie must have been an independent-minded Catholic because she did not insist on a church wedding and would never let this unsanctified union keep her from attending mass.

As for the psychology of the couple, Natty was ten years older, which was a great difference at the ages of twenty and thirty. His name was George, the same as her father's, who had deserted her when she was a child. Like George Allen, too, he was an entertainer, a dancer who taught her an act. He took a paternal role as her mentor and would continue to do so as her husband. The dynamics of the couple set him in the dominant, caretaking role. This, obviously, was a stereotypical father-figure relationship.

It was the relationship that also lay at the center of their act. The real Grace Allen was not as absurdly dumb or naive as the "Gracie" onstage, but she was definitely vague (to employ an oxymoron) and there was a vulnerable goodness about her. In a cynical world, that played as dumb and naive. Burns was the envoy from that world, the audience's agent, asking their questions and expressing their surprise. He did not necessarily share in any conclusions about her stupidity but he raised the eyebrow.

In short, he understood why the audience laughed at Gracie, but he also spoke Gracie's language and knew what she meant. He was surprised by her, he was bemused by her, he was her protector. And so the Burns and Allen stage routine was a reflection of the Burns and Allen personal relationship, only exaggerated and made into a cartoon.

Sleeping together can be more intimate than sexual relations, as they soon learned. On their wedding night, Gracie could not conceal her scarred left arm from him. Sleeping together also meant that she could shake him awake in the middle of the night.

"Natty? Would you say something funny? I can't sleep."

All he could think of was, "Googie, googie, googie." It was supposed to be a joke, but it became his pet name for her. From then on, Gracie was "Googie" (as in "boogie woogie") not only to him but to their close friends.

With both of them at last asleep on their wedding night, the telephone rang. The call was from Vancouver.

"Hello, George? It's Jack. I'm calling to congratulate you and Gracie."

Burns was never too sleepy to fool with Jack, and said, "We would like breakfast at ten o'clock. Up in the room. Scrambled eggs, bacon, toast and marmalade."

"But—"

"And a big pot of coffee."

Then he hung up.

A few moments later, the telephone rang again.

"I know it's late, Nat, but it's me. Jack. Why did you hang up? I wanted to congratulate you and—"

"And don't forget the orange juice," George said, hanging up again.

Only after the third call did he let his pal finish congratulating him. By then, Jack almost couldn't get it out, for laughing so hard.

He didn't resent or envy Nat and Googie's happiness; in fact, he was encouraged by it and began to fantasize about such good things happening to him and Mary too. "We also would get married . . . we would start a new vaudeville act . . . Benny and Kelly."

But there was only more of the old argument about her Catholicism and his being Jewish, and it was an argument without a solution. Mary would not agree to a civil ceremony, and Jack refused to be married in a Catholic church. And that was just the beginning. While Nat had no qualms about promising Gracie that any children they might have would be brought up as Catholics ("It didn't make a difference to me. My religion was show business"), Jack could not make such a promise.

So he and Mary would break it off again. He would go out on tour and swear not to write, insisting she do the same. And then there would be a telegram from Mary, waiting at his hotel.

CAN'T WE BE FRIENDS? THE LEAST YOU CAN DO IS WRITE TO ME.

For George and Gracie, being man and wife was the best thing that could have happened to Burns and Allen. "Some people have to choose between their marriage and their career," he said, "but our marriage was our career."

The new material from "Lamb Chops" was so well received in Cleveland that George replaced virtually all of "Dizzy" and even gave the old act to his friends, Block and Sully.

"Lamb Chops" played to a thrilling reception in Detroit. They were kept onstage for an astonishing thirty minutes. In Syracuse, the next-to-last stop on the tour, they arrived to find their names in lights on the marquee:

THE ORPHEUM WELCOMES
MR. AND MRS. GEORGE BURNS

It was a wedding present from Rena Arnold and Mary Kelly, and it made the couple feel almost as good as the cheering audiences did, for the B. F. Keith Theatre in Syracuse was the final test of "Lamb Chops" before bringing it to New York.

The final booking was in New York's big Jefferson Theatre on 33rd Street, and the reward there was a new, five-year contract with Keith-Orpheum, two performances a day on the big time. It guaranteed them an annual salary that would pass the $25,000 mark, which was a lot of dollars in 1926.

But money was only numbers, and a drab way of quantifying the great thing that had happened. They had been married six weeks, and if it had been good times so far, the rest of the way was going to be strictly on the big time.

"Nothing," George said, "but two-a-days."

6

The first big-time tour opened in Chicago, as so many tours did. The theatre was the Imperial and the great Frank Fay was the master of ceremonies. He introduced the performers, and after their acts, sent them off with words of appreciation. In the number seven spot he did his own monologue.

Fay never looked anything less than the matinée idol. His clothes were superbly tailored, his wavy red hair glistened in the spotlight, and his voice was a musical instrument. He was an orator, beautifully articulating every word. It was a style he had pioneered and "nobody did it better," according to Burns. "He even had beautiful hands."

A big part of any act was its look, and Fay's denoted total confidence, which he substantiated with a sharp tongue and a wicked wit. "He was a fabulous performer," Burns remembered, "nobody could touch him—and there was nothing about him that you could like."

That was an unusual thing for Nat to say. It was against his principles to bad-mouth anybody.

Fay's specialty was the barbed remark, and he wasted no time tossing one Burns's way. It happened while Nat and

Gracie were standing in the wings waiting to go on. The preceding act went into its finish. As Burns was straightening his tie, Fay leaned over and whispered, "I'm going to listen to your diction."

It was a calculated remark and Nat knew it. "My *diction*? He was a mean son of a bitch." But he shrugged it off as Fay strolled onstage to introduce them. That, however, was not the end of this introduction to Frank Fay. Even as Nat and Gracie were taking their bows, the comedian stepped through the curtain at the center of the stage. He stood beside Burns, and began to tell Gracie how wonderful she had been.

He praised her for being a great comedienne. He told her that she was a superlative actress. "He even told her that her hands were great," Burns remembered, and for every compliment, she thanked him as Fay knew she had to. But he would not let it end.

Burns could only smile, unable to interrupt such praise for his partner. Standing in the middle and left out of the conversation, he looked back and forth, from Fay to Gracie.

As the compliments continued, Fay began to lean forward, now in front of Burns. That resonant voice took on a confidential tone so that Gracie had to lean forward. Soon both heads were in front of Burns, "with my face," he wryly remembered, "covered in the middle.

"After about a minute of this," he said, "which is an eternity onstage," Fay stopped. Then he said to Gracie, "Where did you get the man?"

The audience roared. Nat didn't. "I'm *standing* there," he remembered. "*Where did you get the man?* I could have killed myself, but that was as big a laugh as I ever heard in my life.

"Fay was great," he repeated, "but he was a mean son of a bitch."

Meanness is at its worst when touching a nerve, and sadists look for those nerves. Short shrift was the straight man's curse—and Frank Fay knew it. Nat joked about their reviews ("Burns was all right too"), but it was a black humor. The emotional part of him was hurt even as he intellectually believed that "my work was not onstage. My work was at home. I knew what to do but I couldn't do it. Gracie couldn't write it but she knew how to do it. So that made us a good team."

If the sadist in Frank Fay knew that Burns felt unappreciated, the professional in Fay understood that the comedian without a straight man was a con man without a shill, a one-man tennis match. Fay also knew that an act didn't write itself. But as a mean-spirited man, he knew how much audiences and reviews meant to a performer.

As the tour proceeded, the road life did not seem to wear on either Gracie or Nat. In her free time between shows she shopped for clothes, and hotels apparently were home enough for her. She seemed to have no great interest in having a house of her own. Even when they were in New York, they stayed in a hotel.

They had been keeping a two-room suite at the Edison Hotel just off Times Square. Success was now taking them to the thirty-sixth floor of the Essex House, with a panoramic view of Central Park.

Some of their friends were already there, and the hotel was beginning to resemble a theatrical boardinghouse for stars. Jack Benny rented an apartment, and so did Jesse and Eva Block, as well as Blossom and Benny Fields. Actors liked to mix with actors, and Nat and Gracie's crowd expanded to include Eddie and Ida Cantor, Fred Allen and his wife Portland Hoffa, Jack and Flo Haley, Harpo and Susan Marx, and one non-performer, the writer Goodman Ace and his wife Jane.

Money and success did not seem to change show people the way it did civilians. Perhaps it was because an actor's life was so precarious. Rich only meant rich today. Anyone could be broke and unbooked tomorrow. Too, an actor could not feel socially snobbish, as the profession had traditionally been considered disreputable. Perhaps some of them socialized only with performers who were at their level of success, but Nat and Gracie seemed to have no need for status, or any patience with snobbery. Success became them, and their friends remained their friends, whether great stars like Jack Benny or medium-timers like Jesse and Eva Block.

Burns was also a helping friend. Jesse and Eva were still playing "Dizzy," the old act he'd given them. Now he suggested that they try "Lamb Chops" as a movie short. He even wrote the screen adaptation for them, and offered it to Jesse for $500. The price was nominal, and just for the sake of Jesse's dignity, but he wasn't interested.

Because the whole gang worked on the road, their social life continued around the country. Some pal was always closing just before they opened, or opening after they closed. More than a couple of times, they ran into Jack that way.

One of those times, Nat called Benny from his hotel lobby. Jack was still in bed, having arrived late the night before.

"Come on up," Benny said. As soon as he put down the telephone, he leaped from the bed and stripped out of his pajamas. Naked, he waited until there was a tap at the door.

"Who is it?"

"It's me. It's Nat."

Benny took the Gideon Bible from the night table and put it on his head. He grabbed a flower and held it in one hand, a glass of water in the other.

"Come on in," he cried.

When the door opened, it was the maid who came in. Natty stood behind her.

"I told you," Natty said to her, "the man's just crazy."

Friendship is so much easier than ardor. Alas, Benny's

careening romance with Mary Kelly had ended painfully, as so many of that thrilling kind do, but at least the torture was over. Within months, she would meet another vaudevillian and marry him.

Jack met somebody else too, actually for the second time. Five years earlier, in 1921, he had been playing Vancouver on a bill with the Marx Brothers. The least zany of the guys was Zeppo, their straight man. He would ultimately quit the act and become an agent. He invited Benny to a Passover seder, for there were Marx relatives in Vancouver.

A cousin of Zeppo's at the seder was a fourteen-year-old brunette named Sadie Marks (presumably a spelling variation on the family name). Five years later, in 1926, Jack ran into this girl while he was playing a vaudeville date at the Orpheum Theatre in Los Angeles.

Sadie had grown up to be a slim and lovely young woman, with thick black hair that she wore in long curls and tied with a red ribbon. She had moved to Los Angeles and was working for the May Company department store on Hollywood Boulevard, in the hosiery department. It wasn't odd for Jack to be shopping for hosiery. He had lots of girlfriends.

They started seeing each other, and while he never spoke of her with the sweeping emotion he expended on Mary Kelly, they immediately began talking marriage. Perhaps he was on the rebound, or grateful for the calm, or relieved to be with a Jewish girl.

Sadie Marks's father was a Romanian immigrant who had settled in Montana, of all places. That was far from the teeming ghettos in the port cities along the East Coast where most of the East European Jews had landed and stayed. He met Sadie's mother on a business trip to Denver and they moved to Seattle before settling in Vancouver.

For a time, Sadie's sister Babe [Ethel] had been part of a vaudeville act. That encouraged Jack to invite Sadie to appear onstage with him. It would only be a four-minute sketch in the middle of his act, and he might have been trying to make her into another Mary Kelly. But all that the two weeks in vaudeville did for Sadie Marks was terrify her. "She shook so much," Jack remembered, "that she had to hold on to my arm when she spoke." It was the beginning and the end of her vaudeville days.

Sadie was eager to get married and Jack was ripe. First it had been Gracie and Nat; then Willie Burns married Louise Serkin. Now it was Jack's turn.

"Looking backwards from the vantage of wisdom," he said about Mary Kelly, "I can see we weren't in love. We were infatuated with each other. [George and Gracie's] emotion was contagious. You can catch love by picking up love microbes from being around a man and woman who are in love. That's what Mary and I caught. A disease. A bad case of love."

It was a sad denial of what had been a rare and true passion as Jack played the depressive to Nat's manic. And it was a gloomy revision in contrast to the clown's face that Burns painted on life's frowns. Perhaps it was true, as Nat said, that Jack hadn't the nerve to marry a Catholic. Perhaps, too, it had been inevitable that this lovely but submissive man would gravitate to a dominating woman.

More cheerful things were happening to Burns and Allen. Their contract with Keith-Orpheum provided for a booking into the circuit's top house, and that provision would be fulfilled in 1928. They were going to play the Palace, and in the number four spot.

George's mother knew that she could not be there, for she was profoundly ill. Having become a vaudeville aficionado, she appreciated what "playing the Palace" meant. She even understood the difference between a number four spot, which was the place of a featured act, and a number one, or opening act ("That's for acrobats"). She certainly knew that playing the Palace meant hitting the jackpot.

Such success had surely softened the shock of Nathan's marriage to a Gentile. Ordinarily, in that time and place, such an event would have been calamitous. Even as a fourteen year old, and hardly likely to marry, when he brought home a Christian date, Dora told the girl exactly where to go, albeit in Yiddish.

With intermarriage, some Jews actually declared the transgressor dead, and even formally mourned the death, sitting *shiva* for the deceased child.

Dora had met Gracie before they were married, but at that time she was only Nat's partner. Now, with the marriage an accomplished fact, it was too late to declare a son dead. And evidently Dora had no inclination to do so anyway. Far from being devastated, she was proud of this marriage. She seemed smitten with her son's glamorous career, and charmed by his beautiful wife. It is not likely that she welcomed a Roman Catholic daughter-in-law as enthusiastically ("with open arms") as Natty claimed, but she certainly never acted as if she regretted her son's choice of Gracie Allen for a wife.

By this time, Nat and Gracie were the family stars and there was a gathering of brothers, sisters, and children whenever they came around. Nat's brother Izzy, whose name he had borrowed and whom he called "George the First," would even come in from Ohio when they were playing New York, just to see them.

The Birnbaum family gatherings were usually hosted by Nat's sister Mamie. Her home, on Empire Boulevard in Brooklyn ("right across from where the Marx Brothers grew up"), had the most room because her husband, Max Sallis, was a dentist and they had a double apartment, half of it his office.

The group was smaller when Gracie and Nat visited Dora in her own apartment on Carroll Street, also in Brooklyn. Then it was restricted to her grown children. On those occasions, Nat and Gracie would sometimes put on a show especially for his mother. The family squeezed onto the sofa, the armchairs, the bridge chairs, and the floor of Dora Birnbaum's living room. Then the golden couple sang and danced and did bits and pieces from their act. So Dora had to be very sick indeed to miss Burns and Allen playing the Palace.

The first performance of any vaudeville engagement was the Monday matinée. At the Palace, that was the show for people in show business and the performers' friends. With Burns and Allen making their debut at this mecca of the variety entertainment world, a cheering squad arrived en masse—Jesse and Eva, Bloss and Benny Fields, Willie Burns and his wife Louise, Jack Benny, and of course Gracie's former roommates, Rena and Mary.

Jack and Mary Kelly had little to say to each other. They were married at last, but not to each other. Mary's thoughts are not recorded, but Jack remembered thinking, "She's as unhappy now as she was with me." He made no mention of how unhappy he was.

As the stage card was changed for the Burns and Allen spot, the orchestra leader ("Professor") raised his baton and struck up the team's music. For some time now it had been "The Love Nest," a song that Louis A. Hirsch and Otto Harbach wrote for a flop musical comedy called *Mary*. Nat had seen the show in 1920, three years before he'd met Gracie, and he remembered this tune. He had a wonderful memory for old songs.

The big spotlight hit the side of the stage and he and Gracie strolled out from the wings, arm-in-arm and smiling. As usual, she seemed to walk straight out of the rotogravure, a beautiful, perfectly dressed young woman, her lustrous black hair shining in the stage light. He was beaming at her.

After a year of performances, "Lamb Chops" shone with confidence. Such polish was the payoff for years of doing, redoing, revising, and finishing an act. It had not only taken that long to get to the Palace and what it represented; it had taken that long to deserve it. By now, George understood Gracie's character, and she understood exactly how to play that character.

It was actually a trio. The audience was part of the act, catching the wink as Burns threw it, for as Gracie played to Natty, he played to the house. Wasn't she grand, he seemed to be asking, wasn't she great?

GRACIE
A funny thing happened to my mother in Cleveland.
GEORGE
I thought you were born in Buffalo.

Light music came in under those closing lines. They eased into the soft shoe dance that they had started, a few steps at a time, over the final sequence of jokes. Now the music rose fully from the orchestra pit, and they danced off.

As the applause swelled, the gang sitting down front pushed out of the row of seats and rushed down the aisle to the stage. They seemed to be handing up armfuls of bouquets. Cheers came cascading down from the huge theatre's balconies. But of course Burns and Allen were a smash.

The only shadow across their landscape was Dora Birnbaum's health, for she was grievously ill. When their stint at the Palace ended and they returned to the road, they kept looking over their shoulders; whenever there was a break between engagements, they came running back even if it was all the way from the West Coast.

"Look," she said from her sickbed, addressing the crowded room. All of her children were crammed in, flanking the family stars. "You are here because you think I am dying. I am not dying. I am not dying because I am not ready yet. When I am ready I will let you know. Now you should all go back to your business. I'll be up to see Nat and Gracie play the Palace—I missed the first time but I won't miss the second."

The next time they played the Palace, Nat hired a limousine and sent his brothers Sammy and Willie to bring his mother from Carroll Street in Brooklyn to the Palace Theatre in Times Square. The young men carried Dora from the car outside, through the theatre lobby, and down the aisle to her front-row seat. It was as if she had been hanging on to her life just long enough to catch Burns and Allen at the Palace. Then, she said, she was ready to die.

Dora Birnbaum was such a commanding woman that at death's door, she began to direct her own period of mourning. To the youngest son, Willie, she said, "You and Sammy and the rest of the children should sit *shiva* seven days. . . . Nat has a show to do . . . you could tell him, though, it wouldn't hurt to pray a couple of days."

As Burns's nephew Lou Weiss said, "My grandmother was a great lady."

With success becoming familiar to them, Nat and Gracie began to talk about possibilities beyond vaudeville. The contract with Keith-Orpheum, once so secure and exciting, began to feel constricting, for it left them with no time to work elsewhere or try new things. For instance, because of the five years of bookings, they were unable to accept an offer to succeed Fred Astaire and his sister Adele in the Gershwin musical *Funny Face.*

Good enough to replace the Astaires, that was how well Burns and Allen danced. They might have been flashing their taps and whirling across the big stage of the Alvin Theatre, singing such wonderful Gershwin songs as "He Loves and She Loves," " 'Swonderful," and "My One and Only." Alas, they could not do the show and, in fact, never would play the legitimate theatre.

Yet life might have been worse. If they were not in a

Broadway musical, they were going to England for a six-month tour of London and the provinces.

Life was certainly worse for many Americans, including a number of their friends, who lost huge amounts of money in the 1929 stock market collapse. Blossom Seeley and Benny Fields both lost their life savings. Stars like Cantor and Jolson lost millions. Gracie and George were among the few in their crowd who were spared. "It's not that I was smart," George said, "I didn't know anything about money." Of course he was smart, and he would always be smart about money; certainly smart enough to realize "I didn't understand the stock market well enough to risk investing."

In later years, a trip to Europe would be as ordinary as a ride in a taxi, but in 1929 it was a heady event. Then, just as they were preparing to sail, Paramount Pictures asked them to substitute for Fred Allen, who "fell out" (withdrew) from a ten-minute movie, a short subject. The movies were not yet glamorous. Headlining at the Palace was more impressive. It was only as a favor to Allen that they agreed to do the short.

Conveniently, a script was already sitting in Burns's desk drawer: the movie version of "Lamb Chops" that he had written for Jesse Block. It was simple luck that his friend hadn't bought the script for $500. "Had I sold the short to Jesse Block," Burns later said, "I would have had a problem."

Now Paramount was paying them $1,700 to do it, and for the first time, Burns and Allen would be able to see what their act looked like.

In one respect, a moving picture was no different from a still picture: No one liked the way they looked. Gracie was especially unhappy about how she photographed, but Nat was delighted with the results. Using perhaps the most common phrase in his vocabulary, and surely the favorite one, he said, "We were a smash," and Paramount Pictures was pleased with *Lamb Chops* too. In fact, the studio asked them to make ten more shorts when they came back from England. The William Morris Agency negotiated the deal. The agency president, Abe Lastfogel, was now taking personal charge of Burns and Allen, and first of all, he got the fee doubled to $3,500 for each short.

So they were financially comfortable. They were also international headliners, stars of the vaudeville big time, and movie actors. They were close to the pinnacle, yet even as they were peaking, their show world was on the brink of evolution. Fast approaching were two new media, radio and talking pictures, poised to threaten every vaudeville performer with extinction.

Sailing on without any sense of approaching the brink were the acrobats and jugglers, the dance acts, the ventriloquists and magicians, the comedy teams and singers, blithely believing that greasepaint and follow spotlights would endure, that life would always be what life had just been.

7

Early in 1930, movie audiences got a glimpse of George Burns and Gracie Allen in the newsreel between pictures. They were strolling down the gangplank of an ocean liner, home from England after six months abroad. Nat was wearing a beret, the better to cover his thinning hair.

Their tour had gone well enough, although some said it could have gone better. Humor is parochial and seldom travels well. Gracie felt that the British were too literal-minded, "They took us too seriously."

Burns, who never would be an enthusiastic traveler, was positive-minded as usual. He told the reporters greeting them at the dock that he was pleased about how well they had fared on British radio, and he was not merely putting on the cheer. It had been their radio debut and the new medium was already capturing the public's imagination.

The BBC had engaged them to do five short spots while touring from London to Bristol, Manchester, Brighton, and Blackpool. For Burns, these broadcasts served as out-of-town—out-of-the-country—radio tryouts. He couldn't know how the listeners were responding; for the first time, he had to manage without an audience to help with the timing and offer a hint of how he was doing. But that was exactly what he was learning to do without. Happily, this learn-as-you-go method was not dangerous, as the experiment was carried out safely away from America.

In transposing their act to radio, all he'd deleted was the dancing, and the experiment convinced him that Burns and Allen were not bound to the stage. Radio was poised to change the fabric of American life and the act was ready.

When they got back there was still a year to go on their contract with Keith-Orpheum, which now was called RKO (Radio Keith Orpheum). Burns and Allen played almost all of that remaining time in New York, an unprecedented booking of seventeen consecutive weeks on Broadway. Nine of those weeks were spent at the Palace, the other eight at the Paramount Theatre. It, too, was a Keith-Orpheum house, but the Palace was still the Palace.

Frank Fay was also still Frank Fay, and he was not only the master of ceremonies for part of this stretch, he was more impressed with himself than ever, having married a glamorous movie star, Barbara Stanwyck.

Fay was also still wickedly funny, which Burns respected and appreciated. One week, a comedy and dance team called "Barry and Wootledge" was on the bill. Nat watched from the wings as they took their bows, while Fay strolled onstage to see them off.

They had prepared for the moment. With Fay's first remark, Wootledge topped him. Fay came back with a quick riposte and this time it was Barry waiting with a topper. Burns watched in amazement as, next, Wootledge did it.

"Three times," he remembered with awe, "they topped Frank Fay."

Then Wootledge said to the legendary master of ceremonies and putdowns, "Do you mind if we go?"

To Burns's way of thinking, Fay's response was an acerbic classic. "Without looking at them, and looking at the audience as if these guys were nothing, he said, 'If you will.'

"You never heard such a goddamn laugh in your life. You can't explain it. These are '*no jokes*.'

" 'If you will??!' "

His admiration for Frank Fay's talent was unlimited, but it was peppered, almost pained, by disgust with the man's cruelty. Backstage gossip had it that Fay was physically abusive with Stanwyck, which Burns could not abide. That was reason enough to dislike the man, but there was more: Fay was an anti-Semite.

During the long run at the Palace, while Burns and Allen remained, the rest of the bill kept changing. One week, a popular new comedy act, "The Ritz Brothers," was booked. And if Frank Fay did not like Jews generally, he did not like the Ritz Brothers in particular.

At their opening show—the famous Monday matinée— Burns remembered, "They weren't just a hit. They were a riot."

As usual, Fay strolled out as the act was taking its bows. He stood at the side of the stage and looked on while the three rowdy comedians trotted in and out of the wings, taking bow after bow. Their faces beamed while the applause kept rolling in from the darkened theatre. The audience would not let go of them.

"Fay hated one Jew," Burns said, "and this was three Jews, and by now he is hating the audience because the Ritz Brothers are such a smash.

"He's looking at them, he's staring at them. And Jimmy Ritz told the audience how happy they were that they did so well, especially on Monday afternoon."

Fay was quiet. Handsome as ever, beautifully groomed as always, he stood in his own spotlight at stageside while Jimmy Ritz continued talking.

"Jimmy told them," Burns recalled, "that it meant so

much to the three of them because 'Mr. Fay'—and Jimmy smiled in the great monologist's direction—'had not been so sure we would do this well.

" 'So,' Ritz said, 'this means so much to us.' "

The applause resumed, the cheers still greater.

With Jimmy Ritz "almost crying," Burns remembered, "the three of them left the stage.

"Fay let the applause die. Then he ambled—not walked—*ambled* down to the footlights. When he got there, he said, 'Ladies and gentlemen, the next act is Lillian Chalk.' He never said a word about what had just happened. Never *mentioned* it."

Fay's unfortunate combination of talent and cruelty seemed to particularly rankle George Burns. Otherwise, Burn's rule of political silence was all but inviolate.

Married couples learn from each other and Gracie became as close-mouthed as Natty—in one painful instance, even more so. One night, during the Palace engagement, they went as usual to their separate dressing rooms. In Gracie's, the telephone rang. It was the man at the stage door—by stage tradition, they are all called "Pop." He said that a George Allen was there to see her.

Gracie had not seen her father in eighteen years; not since he'd walked out on the family when she was five years old.

"He wanted to talk," she said, "so I let him."

Nat looked at her.

"What'd you say?"

"Nothing. He had nothing to say to me when I was growing up, so I had nothing to say to him."

She didn't even tell Natty about the brief visit until years later. She evidently neither forgot nor forgave. Even years later, when her children asked about their grandfather, Gracie did not mention that he had once come to see her, backstage at the Palace.

•   •   •

Perhaps Nat and Gracie considered that this might be their last stand at the Palace, for they left without signing a new contract with RKO. If so, it was their last stand in vaudeville, for if they didn't plan to play the Palace, they were not likely to play anywhere else.

Apparently, they were taking the biggest step of their career, for in effect their vaudeville days were numbered. They would have shuddered to know that so were the Palace's.

The last weeks of their engagement, the bills were studded with stars. In addition to Burns and Allen, and Frank Fay, the fabulous theatre offered Eddie Cantor, W. C. Fields, and George Jessel. No one could have imagined, or would have wanted to imagine, that it was the last big finish.

The day after their Keith-Orpheum contract expired, Nat signed with Paramount Pictures to make movies. At the same time, he and Gracie began to work in radio, at least Gracie did. Eddie Cantor—the first vaudevillian to make the successful transition to the new medium—borrowed her for his program. George agreed as long as he could write her material. It was actually Burns and Allen material with Cantor reading George's lines, and the routine went so well that Rudy Vallee, the crooner-bandleader, offered them a regular spot on his show. With these broadcasts, Burns was faced by the new medium's constant, harrowing need for fresh material. He drew from both "Dizzy" and "Lamb Chops," knowing that unlike the vaudeville days, once a joke was told to a national radio audience, it could never be told again.

On early radio, most programs were built around bandleaders. Burns and Allen moved on to the Guy Lombardo Show for several guest appearances. Now George had to write a five-minute sketch every time they did a show, and what was worse, they had to perform it untested. He found that it could be done, even done well, but could it be done indefinitely?

They were extended on the Lombardo Show for a year, and the smart dumbness of Gracie Allen played as beautifully to a national home audience as it had on the Palace stage.

Nat understood this character as if she were alive. "She puts salt in the pepper shaker and the pepper in the salt shaker," he said, "because then if she gets mixed up she's right. And she always drives with the emergency brake on so if she runs into an emergency she's ready for it."

Although the Guy Lombardo program was broadcast from New York, it didn't conflict with their movie assignments. The wizardry of broadcasting technology miraculously enabled them to do their Lombardo segment from Los Angeles while the rest of the program was happening in a New York City studio. Just a telephone wire hookup, it was the period's equivalent of a communications highway.

Making movies did call a temporary halt to the fun George had been having with Jack Benny. Laughter can give life to any relationship, but it was the soul of theirs. In a sense, they were mirror images. Nat was always funny except onstage, and Jack was always serious except onstage.

Burns had Benny's number, though, and could make him laugh virtually at will. It had become commonplace in any of their conversations for Benny to collapse in a heap of laughter, pounding the floor with his fist in a plea for mercy. As far as Jack Benny was concerned, Nat Burns was the funniest man in the world. The curious thing was that the public didn't know it. He didn't know how to deliver his humor to them.

What, indeed, was funny about hanging up in the middle of a telephone call? Jack was the only one who got his joke. Perhaps that was a good definition of a best friend.

No matter how often Nat hung up on him, Jack fell apart. He was talking about it to a vaudevillian named Benny

Rubin, who shook his head in disbelief that Burns would do such a thing.

"I bet you," Rubin said, "if you call Natty right now, he won't hang up on you."

After they settled on the amount of the bet, a cocky Jack Benny picked up the telephone and dialed Burns's number. They talked and talked—and talked. In the midst of the conversation, Jack covered the mouthpiece and whispered to Rubin, "I can't understand why he isn't hanging up."

Finally, he had to ask, "Natty, why aren't you hanging up?"

Burns replied, "Because I have half of Benny Rubin's bet."

Laughing yet again and sliding down to the floor, Jack couldn't win, and surely didn't want to.

The first short movies that Burns and Allen made were film versions of their vaudeville routines. They drew on whatever of "Dizzy" and "Lamb Shops" had not yet been ransacked for radio. When George strayed from the original formula, he got into trouble. *Pulling a Bone* in 1930, for instance, made Gracie a smart aleck. That was supposed to be against George's rules, and for good reason.

The sketch is set in a coffee shop.

GEORGE

What is that hair doing in my coffee? A straight hair. What is that?

GRACIE

What do you want for a nickel. A permanent?

That would never happen again. The next year's short, *The Antique Shop*, went directly to long-proven vaudeville material and the exchange about Gracie doubling her interest by splitting a deposit between two banks.

With *Let's Dance*, a couple of years later, George again

tested himself with the writing of new material. This short is tantalizing because it shows these two supreme dancers in each other's arms. Alas, it is only an undemanding fox-trot. Gracie's hair is a lustrous coal black, and as always she is beautifully dressed. She is wearing a close-fitting gown, its sleeves long and full to hide her bad arm. Nat, for no particular reason, is in a sailor suit. Neither it nor the dancing has anything to do with the routine.

"Say," he starts, "how is your sister Alice? What is she doing?"

"Well, you know," Gracie responds, "she was offered a forty-dollar-a-week job but she wants to save money so she didn't take it."

His line was the usual straight man's repeat.

"So she didn't take it?"

"No. She took a ten-dollar job instead."

"She did?"

"Yes, because she figures if she loses a ten-dollar job instead of a forty-dollar job, she's still saving thirty dollars."

Perhaps this was newly written, but it was bread-and-butter Burns and Allen. His every line was a questioning repeat, and her responses were simultaneously reasonable and silly.

But that same year, another of George's scripts showed crisper rhythms and a smoother flow. This was *Once Over Light*.

GRACIE

What's the difference between an umbrella and a pickle?

GEORGE

You're making this up?

GRACIE

Yes.

GEORGE

What's the difference between an umbrella and a pickle? (Thinks for a moment.) I give it up.

GRACIE

Oh? I give it up too.

GEORGE

I thought you said you made up riddles.

GRACIE

I do. I make up riddles. I don't make up answers.

Back in New York, Jack was appearing in the Broadway revue *The Earl Carroll Vanities*. That was prestigious, for unlike vaudeville, Broadway was the *legitimate* theatre. However, Jack was not enjoying it. The theatre liked to think of itself as the most sophisticated genre of show business. Some of the sketches in his show were sexy. In vaudeville, risqué ("blue") material was not only forbidden, it was considered the desperate resort of a second-class entertainer.

The off-color material in the *Vanities* was hardly the stuff of pornography, but Benny considered it "smutty," and he felt uncomfortable being associated with such a show. When the engagement ended, he declined an offer to tour with the show and instead agreed to start his own radio program.

In 1931, George and Gracie had begun work on their first full-length picture, *The Big Broadcast*. It was more like a series of shorts than a feature movie, and it was only an hour long. Intended to capitalize on radio's booming popularity, it was in fact set in a radio station and merely offered a series of vaudeville acts hosted by Bing Crosby. Burns and Allen played themselves and did a brief routine. The picture is notable only for Gracie's first appearance as a blonde. The director thought her beautiful black hair was too dark for the black-and-white film. She would soon be permanently blond.

With all of this movie work, they found themselves spending more time in Los Angeles than in New York. Gracie was not domestic by any stretch of the imagination, but she was eager to have children. After five years of marriage, however, she was still unable to become pregnant. And she was convinced that she never would.

George was not unhappy about that. He worried aloud about the effect of a pregnancy on a woman so petite. In *Gracie: A Love Story*, he says that "Gracie couldn't have children," but perhaps she could. Certainly, if he was sterile, as he later told a friend, then that would have been a reason why they were childless. His sterility, he said, was an after-effect of his teenage case of "Cupid's eczema." It was caused, he added, by either the gonorrhea or its cure. Apparently George never told Gracie about it, because she continued to talk about possibly becoming pregnant.

In 1932, they made the film *International House* with W. C. Fields and began their own radio program. It was called "The Adventures of Gracie," and if that slighted George, the movie gave him an entire scene without her. It is a hilarious sketch, set in a men's clothing store where the inimitably raffish W. C. Fields is a clerk.

BURNS
(Entering the shop) I'd like to buy a sweater.
FIELDS
A sweater. (He looks around.) Sweater? Sweater? (He picks up a derby and offers it to Burns.) Just to give me an idea of the size, try this on. (He places it on the head of a scowling Burns.)
BURNS
A little too tight.
FIELDS
(Examining the hat and trying it on) That's funny. It fits me perfectly.

BURNS

(Icily) I'd like to buy a sweater.

FIELDS

I could give you that (the hat) in black. (He picks up a pair of cowboy boots.) Here's something in a larger size.

BURNS

Listen, I came in here to buy a sweater.

FIELDS

(Pushing him into a chair) Sit down. Try one on. How does that feel?

BURNS

(Trying on the boot) It's a little loose.

FIELDS

You're rather difficult, brother.

This was writing of a higher order, and it is fair to assume that Burns had something to do with that, especially since a similar improvement was evident in the writing of the new radio show.

"The Adventures of Gracie," sponsored by the General Cigar Company, was aired by CBS at nine o'clock on Tuesday evenings. On the show, they were not married, but were simply Burns and Allen, a vaudeville team. The opening music was their old theme song, "The Love Nest," and from the first radio broadcast at the start of 1932 to the last television show, filmed on June 4, 1958, every Burns and Allen program concluded with the classic lines

GEORGE

Say good night, Gracie.

GRACIE

Good night.

That kept him the boss but, at the end, left her straightforward and decent. It was short, sweet, and truthful.

Because of time differences, two broadcasts were necessary every week, at six o'clock for the East Coast and then again at nine for the West. Gracie had mike fright for both of them. "Mike fright" was George's expression for stage fright on the radio, but it was just the same. In vaudeville, she had always played facing Nat because the act worked best that way. She grew accustomed to not looking at the audience. But in radio, she had to face forward as she read the script into a microphone.

Burns insisted that for her sake, there be no studio audience for the show. He even had the glass doors covered so that station employees couldn't stand outside and watch. He admitted to missing the sound of laughter, but whether there was an audience in the studio or at home, he was a dedicated pragmatist. "The audience is the answer to everything. You have a hit show, the audience makes it. You have a flop show, the audience makes it. You do well in radio, it's the audience. You get a rating, you're a smash."

But after the show had been on the air for a year, it wasn't a smash. The network and the advertising agency convinced George to go along with some revisions, for instance, changing the title to "The George Burns and Gracie Allen Show," and airing it a half hour later.

His solution was not to change the premise of their comedy but to do something about the audience's understanding of it. Together with his brother Willie and the writers Johnny Medbury and Sam Perrin, he cooked up an elaborate publicity scheme. It was based on Gracie's fictitious brother, the fellow who was always referred to in the act. Burns had always said that all he had to do was ask Gracie, "How's your brother George?" and she would do the next eighteen minutes of the act. There was a real brother, George Allen, Jr., and the publicity scheme came to be known as "The Hunt for Gracie's Missing Brother."

It began with her surprise appearance on the Eddie

Cantor Show on Sunday, January 4, 1933. Cantor was in the middle of a joke when he stopped abruptly and said, "There's a crazy woman here." Gracie replied, "Oh, no. I'm Gracie Allen. I'm looking for my brother."

After a brief exchange she left, to show up a half hour later on Jack Benny's show asking, "Have you seen my brother?" She proceeded to walk through the Sunday evening CBS lineup and into shows on the week's schedule. She cropped up on dramatic shows, mysteries, and musical programs, and in the daytime she walked in on soap operas. Wherever she went, she was looking for her brother, finally taking the search beyond the radio dial and onto the playing field at Yankee Stadium.

By then, all of America got the joke and fell in love with Gracie's amiable dizziness. Perhaps it was tonic in the depths of the Depression. National magazines came in on the prank. In the halls of Congress, politicians discussed the whereabouts of Gracie's brother. The police, maybe not as busy as today, brought Fred Allen in for questioning, and in San Francisco, they questioned one of the Allen sisters. Private detectives were put on the case. Gracie even showed up in a newsreel looking for her brother, and her brother George was watching it in a movie theatre in San Francisco.

The woman next to him said, "She'll never find him. She's too dumb."

It went on for weeks, an entire country appreciating the newfound sense of this humor, which George Burns, first of all, had perceived in the reasonable reading of an unreasonable statement. The search for the missing George brought CBS more than a quarter of a million letters from amused and even concerned listeners. As Natty said, "Gracie was becoming the biggest female star in radio." But the real George Allen was not so amused. Besieged by the press, he pleaded with a photographer, "I'm not funny at all. I'm just an accountant," and eventually he had to go into hiding. He wired his sister Gracie, "Can't you make a living any other way?"

Then he fled, actually becoming her missing brother. According to one national magazine, a chastened Gracie Allen "tried to cool down the hunt," but it had already taken on a life of its own. "It wouldn't die," the article continued. "It took weeks to kill."

With that, her brother finally went back to his job as an accountant for a San Francisco oil company; but for months, anyone could get an easy laugh just by introducing him as Gracie Allen's missing brother George.

With order restored, "The Burns and Allen Show" emerged as one of the most popular programs in radio. And Natty recognized that their popularity was greater than any they had ever known in vaudeville. They had become national stars.

8

If Gracie had become, as George believed, the most famous woman in radio, then the most famous man was surely Jack Benny. His program, broadcast Sunday evenings at seven, was consistently the top-rated show in the country—and for good reason. It was beautifully written, it was beautifully performed, and it was hilarious.

Benny was the Mozart of comedians, and his deadpan manner seemed to be invented for radio. There had been a time when his humor could be elusively dry. A fellow vaudevillian remembered, "Jack would look off into the wings and make comments that would have us hysterical with laughter, but the audience wasn't laughing."

They were laughing now. Radio seemed to have been created for him. Its intimacy, a few million home theatres with several people in each, allowed listeners to close in and concentrate on his subtext—on what he *didn't* say— and then his style of understatement became familiar. Audiences looked for and recognized it.

He patiently impressed a complete character upon them—a vain, miserly, hapless and inept, eternally amiable fellow who could survive any embarrassment. It would enable him to spend a career capitalizing on his listeners' foreknowledge of these foibles and quirks. Implicit was an almost noble modesty. Jack Benny came across as not only a uniquely hilarious man but also a deeply decent and sensitive one, and these qualities were not assumed. They were his own. Moreover, by grace of confidence he understood that he didn't have to be funny. His show had to be.

His program was a situation comedy about the Jack Benny radio show. Its company of actors portrayed fictitious versions of themselves. Just as he played the invented character of Jack Benny, so the singer on the show played a singer on the show, the bandleader played a bandleader, and even the announcer figured in the situation.

But one of the characters was totally invented. This was "Mary Livingstone," the seventeen-year-old president of the Jack Benny Fan Club in Plainfield, New Jersey. When the actress playing Mary failed to show up at the final rehearsal, Jack asked his wife, Sadie Marks, to try on the role for size. It suited her so well that she continued in it. Moreover, when any female voice was needed, the writers used the character of Mary Livingstone to fill it. There were no more references to her being seventeen years old, and the girl from New Jersey would sometimes show up as Jack's secretary, or even his occasional date.

Sadie Marks handled the assignment capably. She wasn't on the air every week—it was a part-time part and she would never be more than a part-time actress, but then she never wanted more. She was on the show often enough, however, to become one of its family of characters. She even bleached her hair blond like Gracie's, and changed her real-life name to Mary Livingstone.

Marks or Livingstone, she didn't fit in with "The Gang," as Jack's old friends called themselves. A few lines did not make her an actress, and certainly not a vaudevillian.

The rejection was mutual. She treated them as vaguely disreputable, from her lofty status as the wife of the most popular comedian in radio America. Sadie was not yet the social climber she would become; she was more of a social incliner. Like most snobs, the inclination preceded the ascent. At the moment, the best this daughter of a scrap metals dealer could do was, as a member of her family said, "treat her sister Babe like a poor relative."

The attitude of The Gang toward this second Mary seems to have been a blend of clannishness, loyalty to Mary Kelly, and impatience with the Livingstone social pretensions. Nat and Gracie, Blossom and Benny, and Jesse and Eva were an earthy lot. When they weren't calling themselves "The Gang," they were "The Home Folks," because their idea of fun was getting together in one of their apartments, having a few drinks, talking about show business, and doing old routines. This happened informally, frequently, and easily, as they all lived in the Essex House.

Jack and Sadie lived there, too, and Burns had to reconcile his love for Jack with his dislike of Mary Livingstone. One evening, all four of them were going out to dinner. Nat met Jack in the hotel lobby while the ladies dressed. Suddenly, Benny started laughing.

George asked, "What are you laughing at?"

"I'm laughing at you."

"I'm not doing anything."

"But you're not doing anything *on purpose*," said Jack, falling into an armchair in the hotel lobby and holding his sides with laughter.

Gracie finally appeared but there was no Sadie, and Nat urged Benny to go upstairs and hurry her up. He came along for protection.

"She was up there," Burns remembered, "in a slip, staring at a closetful of clothes. She didn't know which black dress to wear. She must have had fifteen black dresses.

"Gracie had only one."

Whether or not this demonstrated inordinate materialism, it does suggest Burns's attitude toward Sadie. Caught in the middle between his friends and his wife, Jack tried to balance himself gracefully. He was good at it, a master of grace, but some of his friends felt there was a touch of the meek in the balancing act.

In 1934, Benny agreed to a brief vaudeville tour. His huge radio audience wanted to see him in person, and he still enjoyed the stage. A troupe was assembled and special material was written for the show. One of the ideas was that a trio of funny-looking girl singers would satirize the popular Boswell Sisters.

The approach was painfully typical of the period: the young women would sing funny (badly) and look funny (fat, skinny, homely). "They would be rotten singers," Jack said, "who thought they were marvelous. The moment these ridiculous-looking girls came out, I figured the audience would laugh."

Mary Kelly showed up at the Chicago auditions, looking to be one of the singers. She was in such bad shape and had so gone to seed that he didn't even recognize her. The once tall young woman with the "beautiful face" was now fat and slovenly. Her "golden blond hair" was dirty and disheveled, and the harshness of her voice betrayed a shackling and shabby alcoholism.

When she introduced herself, a stunned Benny saw that "her eyes were still sweet." But he was aghast at her condition and devastated by her downfall. He certainly did not want to hire her for the role she wanted, as the fat girl in the singing group.

"How can I do this to you, Mary?" he asked. "We've been sweethearts. Once we cared for each other. How can I go out and make fun of you now? I can't do it. Please don't ask me. I can't."

She pleaded desperation. Her marriage had failed, she had gone home to Chicago and had no money. "I've got to have the job, Jack. I'm down on my luck."

He was miserable about the dilemma, but ultimately he gave her the job, and tried to look the other way when she performed. As it turned out, "she was sensational," he said. "She still knew how to get laughs. She mugged and sang out of tune and shook her fat body like she was a mound of jelly."

The audience loved it.

"I didn't," he wrote in a memoir that was not published until long after his death. "I'm supposed to be a comedian," he said with uncharacteristic bitterness. "They paid their money to laugh. Mary Kelly was sure earning her salary. [But] I was crying inside. I was crying for Mary Kelly and for myself."

Gracie had concluded that she was never going to become pregnant and applied to the Evanston Cradle, a prestigious Catholic adoption agency in Illinois. Within months, she and George were notified that a newborn girl was available. They decided to name her Sandra Jean, and Gracie asked Mary Kelly, who was down and out in Chicago, to meet her in Evanston and help bring the infant back to New York.

Help was hardly necessary since Gracie was bringing along a private nurse. What she needed was a gin rummy partner and, not incidentally, she was trying to save her friend's life. So while the nurse saw to the three-month-old baby, Mary and Gracie played cards all the way back to New York on the Twentieth Century Limited.

Only months later, Jack and Sadie—now Mary Livingstone—adopted a baby girl too, but not from the Evanston Cradle. That was because the Cradle's policy required the child to be raised as Catholic. Many Jews of Burns's generation would have had difficulty with this requirement, but friends remembered that it did not bother him. As usual, he just turned complications into comedy material: "I'm the only Jew in the family."

Jack was not formally religious, but he had more of a

Jewish identity than Nat; it had been enough to prevent any marriage to Mary Kelly. Mary Livingstone was from an Orthodox Jewish family, and while they never would be practicing Jews (for instance, there would never be a Passover seder in their home), she did go to a Jewish adoption agency. The baby, also a girl, was named Joan Naomi.

Mary Livingstone had no biological reason to adopt a baby, but adoption had become fashionable in Hollywood. Many movie stars were doing it for reasons of work and vanity. It might also have been another example of doing everything that Gracie did, the way Mary's bleaching her hair had been. In fact, not just imitation but outdoing Gracie would sit at the center of Mary Livingstone's relationship with Gracie Allen.

Her relationship with George was another matter, a competition between two strong people. Mary seemed to feel competitive with him for Jack's ear, his trust, and his affections. She might also have felt that Nat would have preferred Jack to have married Mary Kelly. Finally, what others perceived in Burns as impish or naughty must have seemed exactly the independence that Mary did not want to find in Jack. So, Natty was a bad influence in general. These were all reasons for Mary to keep a certain distance from him.

But it behooved both of them to be polite to each other. That was easy for the politic, close-mouthed, and courtly Burns. Years later, after both Jack and Mary were dead, he would only say, "I don't think that Mary was ever a really happy person," or, "I often wondered if Jack knew Mary had very little talent." Their relationship was characterized by a cool distance. There was detente between these two, the dislike being tacit, and mutual.

And the issue of other women hadn't even come up yet.

It probably didn't help that Mary Kelly had gone with Gracie to pick up the new baby, or that Nat hired her to be Gracie's stand-in. There was hardly any reason for a radio stand-in, but Burns said that Mary could work with the writers, reading their lines back to them, which radio writers did need. Of course the real reason for hiring her was to provide some stability in her life, give her some money, keep her off the booze, in short, rescue her. They even invited Mary to move in with them. There was plenty of room in the big triplex apartment they had just leased in the elegant Lombardy Hotel on East 56th Street.

They never would move into that fancy apartment. The networks were switching broadcast operations to Los Angeles, and Nat and Gracie were already commuting to California to make movies under a contract with Paramount Pictures. They had just finished *We're Not Dressing,* and two more pictures were scheduled in the year ahead, *Love in Bloom* and *Here Comes Cookie.*

Perhaps because of all these movie scripts, Burns hired a private tutor to instruct him in elementary reading. He had quit school after the fourth grade and at that level his literacy remained. The tutor seems to have served him moderately well, but he continued to find reading a slow and painful process.

None of the Burns and Allen movies were for the ages, and few even for the moment. For instance, *We're Not Dressing* was a relentlessly mediocre shipboard musical comedy, notwithstanding the presence of such wonderful stars as Bing Crosby, Carole Lombard, and Ethel Merman. Merman was the key to this pathetic imitation of Cole Porter's *Anything Goes,* in which she had just starred on Broadway. As for Burns and Allen, they were sandwiched into the movie doing a five-minute routine that was entirely irrelevant to whatever story wasn't there.

Depression-era audiences had to be profoundly depressed to sit through such turkeys. Evidently they were, and Paramount Pictures must have been thrilled about it. There were plenty of these pictures for Nat and Gracie to do, and they seemed to do every one. They made three in 1933, and three more the following year, although this was not as strenuous as it sounds. They had no roles in any of these pictures, merely doing self-contained sketches that seemed arbitrarily inserted in the pictures.

But it certainly was lucrative. By the time they filmed *The Big Broadcast of 1936,* they were being paid upward of $75,000 a picture. They should have realized earlier that there was too much work on the West Coast for them to live in New York.

Breaking the lease on the triplex before they even moved in, they rented a huge house on Sunset Boulevard and while they were at it, applied to the Evanston Cradle for a second child. This time they chose a boy, and named him Ronald Jon.

Inevitably, Mary and Jack followed them in the move to California, but emulation is a catch-up game, and Gracie always seemed to be one step ahead of Mary Livingstone. She was already having a house designed, to be built at 720 North Maple Drive in Beverly Hills.

It was not going to be grand; in fact, it was downright modest compared to the mansions in the neighborhood. There wasn't even going to be a gate at the end of the driveway. Anybody could walk up the front lawn and ring the doorbell. George or Gracie might well answer it themselves.

The house was going to be a simple, two-story, wood and brick box that was vaguely Spanish thanks to black wrought-iron railings that ran the length of the second floor. There would only be four bedrooms upstairs, two of them quite spacious with adjacent sitting rooms and dressing quarters. But the children's bedrooms were children's bedroom size, and there were no grand wings. Downstairs, the living room was ample enough, but the dining room was not even a formal one, simply an open area. Off the kitchen there was a small suite for the couple working in the house, and that was it. Even the swimming pool, when it was built several years later, would be medium-sized. In short, it was a house, and it wouldn't have looked out of place on a middle-class residential street in the heartland of America.

Within a year, Mary Livingstone was also building a house in Beverly Hills. She hired the same architect who had designed Gracie's house and had him replicate it, only bigger. It also had a fancier address, 1002 Roxbury Drive, which was movie star territory. Within two blocks were the houses of Eddie Cantor and Jack Haley.

While the Benny house was still being built, the Burnses moved into theirs, bringing along Mary Kelly and Gracie's ailing sister Hazel. This was the way decent folk did things. Their social security, their sound egos, and their fundamental intelligence served to sustain their perspective. As the actress Benay Venuta said, "George and Gracie were everyday people. If you didn't know they were Burns and Allen, you wouldn't guess."

Venuta was a Broadway actress who had married the movie producer and Sears, Roebuck heir Armand Deutsch. Benay and Ardie Deutsch were on Hollywood's social "A" list, and Nat and Googie were added to it. So they were getting around, and who they didn't know they got to know.

George was meeting people at the Hillcrest Country Club, which was located on the south side of Pico Boulevard, east of the Avenue of the Stars. It faced the 20th Century-Fox studios, which would later be razed to make way for the building of Century City, a business/apartment complex.

Hillcrest was established because Jews were excluded by the elite Los Angeles country clubs. Its members followed the example of their detractors, sinking to the same level and barring Christians.

That didn't mean Jewish food at the club. "No gefilte

fish, or anything like that," one of its members said, mildly horrified by the very idea. The club maintained a delicate balance of modified Jewishness. Certainly, Hillcrest was closed on the high Jewish holidays, although Burns was surprised when he found out about it, as if he were barely aware that there *were* high Jewish holidays.

Los Angeles being a company town where the company was show business, the pride of the Hillcrest Country Club was its celebrity membership. Burns was immediately admitted into that caste and took his seat at the Round Table—a big table in a corner of the Men's Grill—where the funnymen met every day for lunch. There was no procedure for admission. One was supposed to know if he belonged (unlike Hillcrest itself, the Round Table was strictly male). If he did not belong, it wouldn't take long for him to find out. It was a sorry interloper who caught the venom of Groucho Marx; his was a verbal version of the hook that used to drag losers off the old amateur shows.

When George first sat down at the Round Table, it was a New York stage club within the country club. In addition to Groucho Marx, the regulars included his brother Harpo, Al Jolson, George Jessel, Edward G. Robinson, Eddie Cantor, and the three Ritz Brothers. Sometimes, movie producers were accepted too, David O. Selznick, for instance, or Armand Deutsch, and there was even the occasional civilian. It must have been a curious table that included the Ritz Brothers, a couple of the Marx Brothers, and financier Bernard Baruch.

Much as Burns enjoyed lunch at the Round Table—and he would be there almost every day for the next sixty years—he did not restrict his friendships to the movie community. To start, he and Gracie had their old pals. When any of The Gang visited from New York—Blossom Seeley and Benny Fields, or Eva and Jesse Block—they would stay at the house and go wherever Nat and Googie went. "They really didn't fit in with the Beverly Hills crowd," Benay Venuta said, "but they were George and Gracie's friends and they were taken to all the parties."

As for the Burnses' own parties, these were intimate affairs similar to the old ones at the Essex House with The Gang. Nat called these evenings "sociables" because it was a good old word and nostalgia was already his hobby.

Nat could get risqué at these dinners, something he would never do onstage. His language was always proper, but the tone was naughty and Gracie played to it when he started.

"Gracie," he'd say, and she would reply, "Yes, George?" As soon as she called him "George" instead of "Nat," it was a signal to friends that they were in character and doing a little routine.

"Gracie—would you like to feel my 'D'?"

"George!" she would cry in mock disapproval. "Don't talk that way!"

In fact, he would never use "dick," or any other scatological language when women were present. Evidently, saying "D" made it funny and acceptable.

"Just a touch," he would say. "My 'D' could use a nice little touch."

"Stop it! Nat-tie!"

After dinner, somebody would invariably get up to perform alongside the grand piano in the living room. That would start the singing and the comedy routines and the soft shoe dancing.

But the closing act was always the same, Natty Burns singing vaudeville songs. Even with Al Jolson in the house, he would sing his heart out, and the songs were always the same vaudeville ditties, "Tiger Girl" or "In the Heart of the Cherry" or "Syncopation Rules the Nation" or "(So I'll Buy a Ring and) Change Your Name to Mine," but especially he would sing "The Red Rose Rag."

When Jolson, "the world's greatest entertainer," asked if he could sing a song, Nat said, "Just one." The great Jolson had a legendary ego and stalked off with it.

George's singing ego, on the other hand, was either secure or nonexistent, and that was a good thing too, because when he was finally cast in a movie musical, he didn't get to sing at all. Gracie did, and those songs were not novelties like "The Red Rose Rag" or "In the Heart of the Cherry." They were great songs by George and Ira Gershwin, for this was the movie that introduced "A Foggy Day" and "Nice Work if You Can Get It."

It was called *A Damsel in Distress,* and in effect, Burns and Allen were taking the place of Ginger Rogers. She had decided to quit her popular series of movies with Fred Astaire, and prove that she could be a serious actress. While she was occupied with drama, George and Gracie had the pleasure of being joint partners with Fred Astaire, the greatest of all popular dancers. In a way, this might have made up for their lost chance to succeed the Astaires on Broadway.

A Damsel in Distress (1937) is set in London, where Astaire is an American dancer on tour with his press agent—played by an unusually robust Burns. George's secretary is the very trim and very beautiful Gracie. Thus, they are for once cast as characters other than themselves. The acting opportunity, however, is a limited one. George has several scenes with Astaire in which he reads lines ably enough, but Gracie is relegated to her "Dumb Dora" mode. In these Burns-and-Allen-type exchanges, the screenwriters Ernest Pagano, S. K. Lauren, and P. G. Wodehouse only proved how important George was to the act. Without his hand, the material doesn't scan. Gracie is seldom funny and (or because) George is sometimes unpleasant. He comes across as angry with her, rather than exasperated but awed.

There was compensation at hand, however: Astaire's leading lady, Joan Fontaine, was a beautiful *klutz*. In the one dance number she was allowed, she nearly crashes into a tree. The choreographer, Hermes Pan, mercifully spared her any further risks to life and, excuse this, limb.

Instead, Astaire dances with George and Gracie, and their dancing is concentrated in a unique twenty-minute sequence. Here is a truly classic stretch of musical moviemaking.

It starts with rhythmic patter, a repeated chant of "Why I've just begun to live." This is pure vaudeville; in fact, rhythmic patter was the way the old Burns and Lorraine act began. Even more vaudevillian is the "whisk-broom dance" that follows.

In it, Astaire, Burns, and Allen dance while slapping and brushing their shoulders and thighs with whisk brooms, substituting the sound of hand slaps with the whoosh of the straw whisks.

The number was George's idea, motivated, no doubt, by a wish to dance in the movie. Drawing upon his encyclopedic memory of old acts, he remembered a vaudeville team that did this unique dance routine: "They were out of work, so I sent for one of the guys and I said, 'Teach me and Gracie the whisk-broom dance.'"

After learning it, they got a pianist and demonstrated it for Astaire. "If you want it for the movie," George generously said, "you can have it," devilishly aware that it was not a solo.

According to George, Astaire's response was, "Are you kidding? I'd love it," and that is not surprising, for Astaire was always attracted to novelty dances.

In the "whisk-broom dance" as it was finally performed in the movie, Astaire, Burns, and Allen sparkle through a series of difficult steps with cheerful synchronicity. The number is set to Gershwin's light incidental music, with both the music and the dance highlighted by the catchy swooshes of the hand brooms. The trio moves through a room, ducking under each other's arms, as if in a square dance. They face the camera in the style of stage performance. The number conjures up how wonderful Astaire must have been in the theatre, and alas, how wonderful George and Gracie would have been. For their footwork is deft, their turns and spins are casually confident, and their presence is altogether theatrical.

Nat and Googie keep up with Astaire's sudden stops, his syncopated pauses, his off-the-beat starts; they stay with the fleet and nimble dancer almost every step of his way. It is true that they don't try to duplicate the float of his arms, but some things were best left to Fred Astaire.

The fabulous whisk-broom dance is only a scene away from Gracie singing an all-but-forgotten Gershwin song called "Stiff Upper Lip." At first, her voice is as high as her speaking voice—and that was an octave above her real voice. But as she digs into the catchy tune, her timbre drops to a comfortable theatre (or "chest") voice.

"Stiff Upper Lip" is but the introduction to an extraordinary twelve-minute amusement park sequence. In a white, very thirties and very Astaire-movie fun house, the merry trio sails into a Tunnel of Love, loops through turning tunnels, hoofs along on rotating turntables, and then taps in front of distorting mirrors, until they slide down a flight of stairs that turns into a chute.

Most of this appears to be photographed in one continuous take as George and Gracie flawlessly replicate Astaire's airily murderous style. Even these two not-so-youngsters (George was thirty-nine, Gracie twenty-nine) seem to handle Hermes Pan's intricate choreography without looking exhausted. Throughout the number, however challenging the choreography may be, Gracie remains Gracie. As the fine dance critic Arlene Croce wrote of this scene, "Gracie could even *dance* in character."

Nearing the end, she breaks into an exaggerated trot that brings the sequence toward a cheerfully zany conclusion.

This kind of trotting in a circle had become popular as a quirky bit of stage business. Bea Lillie, the great British comedienne, liked to do it. Groucho Marx adapted it for his slouch-walk. Fred and Adele Astaire trotted in many of their Broadway shows, and Burns and Allen did it in one of their old acts. Gracie's trot brings this magical and exhilarating sequence to a blissful conclusion.

The series of amusement park dances in *A Damsel in Distress* won Hermes Pan a deserved Academy Award, but it is hard to imagine this great number without the chemistry of Astaire, Burns, and Allen. The warmth of their personal friendship, palpable throughout, is what elevates it from choreography to dance.

As Croce wrote, George and Gracie "are like ministering angels in this film." The scene itself is heavenly for sure.

George was a businessman, too, and a businessman has an office. He took three adjoining rooms on the fifth floor of the Hollywood Plaza Hotel, which sat on the fabled corner of Hollywood Boulevard and Vine Street. He went there every day with the writers of his radio program and his brother Willie.

It was more than a place to get work done; it was a place to go to, a way to structure a day, and not incidentally, it was both an alibi and a convenience, for where there were hotel rooms, there were other hotel rooms.

Burns had been married for eleven years. He was restless, and when his brother was around, women were often the subject. Willie was articulate, good-looking, and charming. As one of his relatives said, "He loved the ladies and was always involved with women." He and Nat had looked for ladies when they were on the road together in vaudeville, and they still did.

The radio show was more popular than ever, and some of Gracie's remarks were becoming catch phrases, such as

"I'll bet you say that to all the girls." A guaranteed laugh was an invaluable asset, but too often comedians were greedy and abused their catch phrases. Burns doled out such lines carefully. His control over the Gracie Allen character was more comfortable and complete with every season, and the two of them functioned like a single entertaining entity. Because of that, their careful and disciplined work would appear spontaneous and easy. They never developed a long-run drone. Moreover, there was now a studio audience to add to the vitality.

That ice had been broken when they broadcast from the stage of a theatre during a brief vaudeville engagement. After that, Gracie accepted the contribution a live audience could make.

One radio routine had a special ring of truth, for it was about the Burns and Allen act itself. Inspired by the first time George had ever worked with Gracie, it was an homage to her. This was his demonstration of how Gracie Allen, even playing straight man, was the funny one.

GEORGE

If I should say to you, "Why are apples green?" all you have to do is repeat the same thing. You say, "I don't know. Why are apples green?"

GRACIE

I get the idea. I repeat what you say and then you tell the answer.

GEORGE

That's it. Well, here we go. What fellow in the army wears the biggest hat?

GRACIE

I don't know. Why are apples green?

GEORGE

Now don't be silly. When I say, "What fellow in the army wears the biggest hat?" you must say, "I don't know. What fellow in the army wears the biggest hat?"

GRACIE

Oh, I got it. Yeah, you're the comedian.

GEORGE

All right now. What fellow in the army wears the biggest hat?

GRACIE

The fellow with the biggest head.

GEORGE

I certainly am the comedian.

This is flawless writing. Gracie announces exactly what a straight man is supposed to do: "I repeat what you say and then you tell the answer." The straight lines that follow serve to set up not only the jokes but the audience. The short sentences are used for flow—"I get it," or, "That's the idea." Finally, there are double edges to such lines of Gracie's as "Yeah, you're the comedian." A wised-up Nat must ironically note, "I certainly am the comedian," for he realizes (as he did back in Newark) that come what may, Gracie will get the laugh.

But there was nothing funny about George hitting the tabloid headlines in December 1938. It was the first and only scandal of his career.

The saga began two months earlier when the Treasury Department was notified of illegal valuables at the Park Avenue apartment of former Supreme Court Justice Edgar J. Lauer. The informant was Lauer's German maid, who, according to the *New York Daily News*, "became insulted when she overheard disparaging remarks about Adolf Hitler."

As a result of the tip and the ensuing raid, Lauer and a man named Albert N. Chaperau were arrested for bringing undeclared jewelry into the country. Chaperau was a confidence man straight out of Central Casting: he looked elegant and claimed he was a Nicaraguan consular attaché. The tabloids wasted no time in exposing the worst, describing him as not only a "former convict" but, equally evil, an "international film promoter."

Lauer and Chaperau's records incriminated Burns and also Jack Benny, both of whom had bought contraband jewelry from him and still had it in their possession.

George was booked and fingerprinted at the U.S. Marshal's office in New York. He claimed that Chaperau had sold him a $5,000 ring and a $3,000 bracelet with a diamond "G" (an especially wide bracelet for Gracie's scarred wrist) without letting him know that the pieces had been smuggled into the country. In December, he was allowed to plead guilty to smuggling $4,885 worth of jewelry, and on January 30, 1939, he received a suspended sentence of a year and a day. He paid $8,000 in fines, along with civil penalties of $9,770.

Considering that Burns's income was estimated at $11,000 a week in an era of minimal taxes and the Depression, perhaps the greater punishment was the publicity. His radio sponsor did not thrill to such headlines as the *Boston American*'s

GEORGE BURNS IS FINED $8,000. IS GIVEN SUSPENDED SENTENCE

Jack was not as nonchalant as George, who admitted to friends that he'd known perfectly well the jewelry had been smuggled into the country. Mary Livingstone had made a serious mistake when she copied Gracie this time, pressing Jack to buy her something from Chaperau too. And now Benny, like all worriers, began to panic. "The executives at NBC, General Foods [Jell-O], and the advertising agency were in a state of hysteria," he remembered, assigning the panic to them. "I was probably the single most popular radio star in the country. They finally decided to take a chance and continue sponsoring me."

He promptly aired it out. On the first broadcast after the headlines, Rochester (his sassy valet) warned him during a hiking trip, "Look out, boss. There's a rattlesnake."

Benny replied, "Listen, rattlesnake, would you leave me alone? I'm in enough trouble as it is."

But he wasn't. Instead, his Crossley rating jumped from 37.4 to 40.1. Being more idealistic than Burns, and less pragmatic, he rejected a similar plea bargain when it was offered him. He was adamant about his ignorance of the illegality of the $2,131 gold bracelet he had bought for his wife. He entered a plea of not guilty, which posed the possibility that Nat might be called to testify as a witness against him.

Finally, Benny's lawyer, William J. ("Wild Bill") Donovan—later director of the OSS—persuaded him to plead guilty. He paid a $10,000 fine and was given a six-month suspended sentence.

This ending was happy enough. But at the other end of the smuggling transaction, where Chaperau had bought the jewelry in the first place, those bargains had come at the expense of terrified Jews who were selling their valuables at any price in a final, desperate effort to buy their way out of Nazi Germany. Neither Burns nor Benny would have been proud to know where the trinkets had come from.

9

It was never "Gracie" at home. There, she was always "Googie," and that was appropriate. At home, Ronnie Burns insisted, his mother was nothing like she was on "The Burns and Allen Show," "although she did once ask me, 'How old were you when you were born?'"

There would always be an element of the stage Gracie in the real Gracie, and sometimes more than just an element. She was an attentive mother, a doting mother, and a loving mother, but she was not maternal. For instance, she never changed the diapers or heated the formula. There was a nurse for that, and when the kids were older, a governess, and then George's secretary, Gerry Broggio, ferried them to school or parties.

"They were good parents," a couple friendly with the Burnses said, "but they didn't have a lot of time for the kids. They just weren't your hands-on parents so much."

Googie wasn't a homemaker, either. She didn't have the time or the inclination for it. Working full time could do that to anyone. Someone could always be hired to do the decorating, the food shopping, the cooking, the laundering, and the housekeeping.

She and Nat not only worked a lot, but of course they worked together, and so both of them were out most of the time. Because of their mutual career, they were first of all devoted to the world of each other. Burns once pointed out that most people have to take time off from their careers to work on their marriages, "but we didn't have to because our marriage *was* our career."

For a show business family, the Burnses maintained a very un-show-business home. To start, as Sandy said, "Having stars for parents wasn't particularly unusual in Beverly Hills. Most of our friends were children of stars." And because both her mother and her father were stars, there was no lone ego lording over the house. "My mother and father were equally famous, so both of them seemed the same."

It meant a lot to Sandy and Ronnie that life at 720 North Maple was down to earth, even if it also meant modest weekly allowances and reasonable nightly curfews. There were family meals, family trips, and regular visits with the extended family of aunts, uncles, and cousins. The world of the house was casual, with no grand staff of servants. There was a live-in couple, a houseman, and a housekeeper/cook, but that was all—except for a while after the Lindbergh kidnapping, when there was a watchman.

The one special touch was not material. It was the constant laughter around the house. Ronnie and Sandy agreed that their father was probably the funniest dad anyone ever had. "Things were fun at home," Ronnie said. "It wasn't like other households because of that—there was a lot of humor, so much laughing. It was always around us."

Sandy had much the same memory. "My dad was constantly funny at home, but nothing like the way he was on the air. He never told 'jokes.' He just said funny things. It just burst out of his mouth. Which my mom never did."

Instead, Gracie treated herself to the laughter that was

forbidden her during the act. As Ronnie said, "That would have been out of character. She wasn't supposed to know she was funny. But at home she would laugh plenty, and she was funny too."

Still, there was a difference between her and Nat because he was not only a professional comedian, he was a professor of comedy. When the family went to a funny movie, for instance, "all of us might be roaring," Ronnie remembered, "but Dad would be one step ahead of what was going on. He would be looking at it from the point of view of construction."

In short, Googie was "just a regular mom," as Ronnie put it. She wasn't impressed with her own celebrity even though she was besieged by autograph seekers whenever she was in public. "Show business," he said, "just was not as important to her as it was to Daddy." She was more interested in going to Hollywood Park racetrack, or playing gin rummy and mah-jongg with girlfriends like Bea Benadaret, from the show, or Susan (Mrs. Harpo) Marx; or just going shopping with them.

She took time, when there was time, to visit her sisters in San Francisco, and when the kids were old enough, she brought them along. More often, Bessie and Pearl came down to Los Angeles to see her and Hazel, and when they did, the children seemed to bask in the attention. Long into adulthood, Sandy remembered her aunt Bessie teaching her to dance the Irish jig. It was when Bessie was fat and jolly, and before she turned prematurely senile, as Alzheimer's disease was then described. That would happen to all three of Googie's sisters, which scared her. Even though she was not quite thirty-five, she worried aloud and fearfully about it.

Googie would also drive over to see Willie's wife, Louise, or go down to San Diego to visit Nat's sister Goldie. As for Willie himself, both of the children adored their uncle. "Uncle Willie was fabulous," Ronnie remembered. "If there was anything to take care of, Daddy would say, 'Talk to Uncle Willie.' " And for Sandy, "He was my favorite person in the whole world."

Willie's daughter Julie, the eldest of three girls, was Sandy's best friend the way Fred Astaire, Jr., was Ronnie's. Yet when George organized a sociable, Uncle Willie and Aunt Louise were rarely invited. A dividing line seemed to be there.

Willie had to be careful when he walked that line. His relationship with Nat was evolving, his responsibilities taking a turn for the servile. There was no longer any pretense of his being a writer on the show. He was billed as the producer, which according to one of the writers merely meant "the man with the stopwatch." He would time the script readings and keep track of when there had to be commercial breaks. There was no director as such.

Sometimes, too, Willie's job seemed to be to take the heat when Burns did not want to blow off steam at anyone else. Willie accepted the role stoically, although one time he rose up in offense.

"Listen, Nat," he said, "I don't have to take this from you."

Burns glanced up and eyed his brother coolly.

Willie dared push it no further. "I could go back to doing what I was doing before I came out here."

"And what was that?" George asked.

"I was sitting back home in Brooklyn and you were sending me twenty-five dollars a week."

As one of the men in the office said, "It wasn't easy being Willie Burns."

He also had to do a certain amount of dirty work. One afternoon, all the fellows in the office were having lunch at the Brown Derby, which was across the street from the hotel where they had their office. The Derby was a show business hangout.

Eddie Cantor was sitting in one of the booths, and as the

Burns party came in, the little comedian leaped up to embrace Nat.

"George! You've got to help me out."

"What's the problem?"

"I don't have guests for my show next week. Will you and Gracie be my guests?"

Burns replied, "Of course, Eddie. Of course," and they hugged some more.

When the Burns group was settled in its own booth, George turned to his brother. "Willie," he said, "get me out of that."

But basically, Willie Burns had become his brother's coat man. A "coat man" was derisive talent agency jargon for a flunky, an agent who runs errands, makes hotel reservations, and, in so many words, helps the star get into his jacket.

As in most comfortable families, the Burns children had to take lessons after school. They studied piano and tap dancing, but unlike most tap students, they had a mother who had danced in the movies with Fred Astaire. Googie was still able to flash fancy footwork, and if she was a little tipsy on champagne she occasionally did it in public, at least at a sociable.

"Mom would dance in the house when we were kids," Ronnie said, "and the rest of us would have to keep up with her."

As for the music lessons, the living-room piano was put to better use when George and Gracie had company. The kids would tiptoe out of their bedrooms and sit at the top of the stairs, listening to George Gershwin accompany Fred Astaire's singing and dancing. There was no sense trying to compete with that.

Their upbringing was Catholic, in accord with the adoption agreements, and they went to Sunday mass at Good Shepherd Church, although Googie herself did not. "Mother would go to church with us on the holidays," Ronnie remembered, "but she didn't take communion or go to confession. [Mom and Dad] always said to us, 'When you reach eighteen you can make your choice.' She told us, 'If you want to stay Catholic or you want to become Jewish or whatever you want to be, go ahead. But now you're going to be raised as Catholics.' "

The children's Catholicism did not seem to bother Burns, as it might have some Jews of his generation. He would joke about eating meat on Friday nights while the rest of his family had fish. But the truth was, he liked fish, so there was no point in not eating it. In other words, it was of no practical importance to him that his wife was Catholic.

"Mom did wear a gold cross," Sandy remembered, "and occasionally she would cross herself for good luck before going onstage." But that seemed to be the functional extent of her parents' religious differences. What could indeed bother Burns was an ostentatious Catholic like Frank Fay, who would cross himself every time a recent death was mentioned; or the gossip columnist Louella Parsons and her husband, "Doc" Martin, who brought a priest with them when they came to dinner.

As for George exposing the kids to Jewish lore, he told them stories about his own father—how Louis had been a cantor, and how he had taken Nathan to the steambaths on the Lower East Side ("All I remember was beards—that's all I saw"). But Burns never went to synagogue. He was as uninterested in Judaism as he was in Catholicism.

Sometimes, Nat and Googie brought the kids along to watch the broadcast. The show had moved from CBS to NBC, whose studios were at Sunset Boulevard and Vine Street. That was only a two-block stroll from George's three-room office at the Hollywood Plaza Hotel. Walking distance was a novelty in Los Angeles.

It was important to Sandy that even when she was at a

broadcast and her parents became the famous George Burns and Gracie Allen, they still acted like a mom and dad, "holding my hand and telling me where to sit.

"So they were just my parents."

The Burnses' first big, Hollywood-style party was given in 1936 to celebrate the completion of Jack and Mary's new house. A tent was put up in back and the swimming pool was covered with a dance floor. Some 250 of the movie community's most glamorous were invited, from Astaire and Bob Hope to Edward G. Robinson and Ginger Rogers.

Hollywood party though it was, the guest list reflected a partiality for vaudevillians. There were such former Palace headliners as Eddie Cantor, the Marx Brothers, Blossom Seeley and Benny Fields, Ted Lewis and Fanny Brice. It was like a giant version of a sociable with The Gang, and they all entertained for hours. Bloss strutted through "After You've Gone," and even Jack Benny, who was the evening's master of ceremonies, announced that he was going to sing.

As soon as he said it, Nat's voice rang through the tent. "Check, please!"

That was it for Benny. He reeled with laughter and nobody ever did hear him sing in public.

At the end of the party, a giant cake was wheeled out. "The cake," George wrote in *Gracie: A Love Story*, "was a perfect replica of the Bennys' new home, which in fact was a replica of our new home."

Mary hired Billy Haines, the popular Hollywood decorator, to do the place—just as Gracie had hired him. The bedroom suites were gigantic, and Jack and Mary slept in separate ones. "As far back as I can remember," their daughter Joan said, "my parents had separate bedrooms."

Mary's was the master suite at the front of the house, with its three windows looking out over the lawn. Jack's faced the back lawn, but even at that distance, his violin practicing annoyed her. Mary finally made him play behind the closed door of his dressing room.

She began organizing Hollywood-style parties with glittering guest lists. "My mother," Joan Benny remembered, "had this terrible problem of trying to pretend that she was to the manor born. She had to be seen at the right restaurants, driving the right car [Rolls-Royce], shopping in the right stores, and wearing the right labels. She had to be seen with the right people as well. You could never remind her that she was once Sadie Marks. I think she never really got away from being Sadie Marks to herself . . . a shopgirl from Seattle, a woman with no credentials, little sophistication or experience. Her insecurity knew no bounds."

She did have the Hollywood look, from upswept, blond hair and a bobbed nose to closets full of the most expensive clothes and shoes. Her best friends were Barbara Stanwyck and Claudette Colbert, but Joan thought "she looked more glamorous than any movie star."

She engaged a staff of servants. "In the Hollywood homes of the 1930s and 1940s," Joan Benny recalled, "staffs varied from the grand to the grander to the grandest. My mother's staff was medium grand." Mary hired a European cook, an English butler, an upstairs maid, a downstairs maid, a nanny for Joan, a laundress, and a gardener. Under her officious rule, servants came and went. Cooks were particularly transient. Whenever a new one was hired, she was given specific test meals for the first three days. If she passed, she stayed. "My mother was as tough with them," Joan said, "as she was with me," and Mary Livingstone was a very tough lady.

When Joan was in grade school and came home in midafternoon, "the very first thing I had to do was go to Mother's room for a kind of command performance. She'd be sitting up on her side of the queen-size bed. I'd go around it, give her a kiss, and then settle down cross-legged on the other side."

"Your hair looks terrible," her mother would say, or, "Why did you wear that ugly dress?" or "When are you going to stop biting your nails?"

Joan was required to stand up whenever her mother entered the room, and had to wait for permission to be seated. The rule became so ingrained that she obeyed it as an adult, and continued to do so until her mother's death.

"I don't think I could have *not* stood up."

Jack was equally intimidated by Mary. He loved sweets but as a diabetic who required regular insulin injections, he had to watch his sugar intake. At a baseball game with a friend, he said, "I'm going to have some ice cream, but for God's sake don't tell Mary."

The friend said, "Well, I won't tell her, but don't you think it'll show up the next time you go to the doctor?"

"I'm not worried about the doctor," Benny replied, "but I'm scared to death of Mary."

He learned to be proficient at keeping out of her way, and it frequently took him in the direction of other women. "I think Jack cared about his wife," one of his writers said somewhat cynically. "He wasn't faithful to her but he cared about her."

That was a common attitude. Whether a marriage was unpleasant, like the Bennys', or complex but adult and close like George and Gracie's, these men took infidelity as an entitlement. They saw no conflict or inconsistency between unfaithfulness and marital honor. They were boy-men who demanded indulgence, and perhaps some of their wives accepted that in exchange for an expensive way of living. The privileges and perquisites of being married to a celebrity were considerable. Some wives may even have welcomed freedom from sexual demands. Many of these elements were present in the tacit arrangement between Jack and Mary.

But if anyone doubted who was running this household, the matchbooks in the guest room said it all: they were inscribed "Mary Livingstone."

Jack was now making movies at Warner Brothers with such beautiful actresses as Priscilla Lane and Ann Sheridan.

He was particularly smitten with Sheridan and some suspected that they were having an affair. Jack certainly had
the time for it—especially on Friday nights, when he and
Nat supposedly went to the fights.

Some Friday nights, Burns confided to a friend, they
actually did go to the fights. When they did, "Jack and I
compared notes about our girlfriends."

Their friendship, and the laughter that signified it, was at
least as important to them as the girlfriends. One Friday
night, Milton Berle was seated opposite them, on the other
side of the ring. Between rounds, he tried to impress his
party by waving familiarly to Burns and Benny. Nat got so
irritated with this that he waited until Berle was engaged
in conversation with his friends. Then he waved in the
comedian's direction.

A beaming Berle stood up and waved back. That was
when Nat shook his head impatiently. "No, not you," he
cried out. "Him!" and he gestured toward a man sitting
behind Berle.

Jack was the "Uncle J" in Ronnie and Sandy Burns's life.
Sandy saw more of him than Ronnie did, because Joanie
Benny was her age and they had sleepovers. But the
Burnses and the Bennys were frequent dinner guests at
each other's homes.

These were family dinners with Sandy and Ronnie and
Joan Benny, and they all remembered the meals as being
like track meets. Joan thought that "George and Gracie's
cook should have had roller skates" because her father and
Nat ate so quickly that by the time the cook got around to
serving the rest of the table, they were ready for their next
course.

The men would begin by taking off their jackets—
George's toupee was already off, it was always off at
home—sitting down at the table, and eating as soon as
they were served. "No waiting for the hostess," Joan
remembered. When dinner was at the Bennys' house and

Mary was the hostess, she would sit straight up in her chair and delicately cut her food into little pieces. As she did, "those guys ate like vacuum cleaners," Joan said. "Maybe it stemmed from when they did six shows a day and had to grab a bite in between."

And Jack and George, like a couple of little boys forming a bond with their quirks, would both demand that the soup be served boiling hot. At home or in a restaurant, if the soup wasn't bubbling, Burns sent it back.

"I don't know how they didn't burn their mouths out," Joan wondered, "and how they could even taste the soup. . . . But if it wasn't boiling, then it was too cold, and they were adamant about that."

Ketchup often went into it, a habit George had retained since childhood, and Jack's taste was no fancier. Even though his wife engaged a first-class chef, "he preferred diner food," Joan remembered. "His favorite food in all the world was chicken-fried steak."

With such earthiness and laughter between them, the families might have seemed like great pals; most outsiders assumed as much. All four were circumspect and they were perfectly polite with each other, but Joan was quite aware of Gracie and George's true feelings. "They loved my father," she said, "so my mother was there and there was not much they could do about it."

Gracie started to put her foot down when Nat and Jack suggested that they all go on a Hawaiian vacation. It was an unusual display of temperament because she always did what George wanted and rarely complained about anything, not even her migraine headaches, which were getting worse. But knowing how much time the men would spend together on such a trip, Googie protested that she would be stuck with Mary. In fact, at the outset she simply refused to go, which was truly unusual since Nat was the boss in that family.

•　　•　　•

Gracie finally agreed to go to Hawaii with Jack and Mary, but only because she was exhausted from her "presidential campaign."

The presidential campaign was a Gracie Allen phenomenon which began early in 1940. She announced on the air that she was going to be the nominee of the "Surprise Party" as an alternative to both the Republican candidate, Wendell Willkie, and the President, Franklin D. Roosevelt, who was running for a third term. What began as a few political jokes on "The Burns and Allen Show" turned into invaluable publicity and four months of unusual fun—unusual because, dizzy as Gracie's character was, she was never as ridiculous as American politics. As for the fun part, it was mostly George's.

Like the 1933 search for her missing brother, this stunt took off with her unexpected appearances on other radio programs. The big break was the city of Omaha's offer to host the Surprise Party's nominating convention. Then the Union Pacific Railroad offered to make a train available, so that she might run a whistle-stop speaking campaign while traveling from California to Nebraska.

Speaking to crowds of people from the rear deck of a train was not the best of ideas for a woman who was uncomfortable in front of audiences. But it struck Burns as a good idea at a time when their radio ratings were starting to fall. In fact, there was already talk of canceling the show.

Grace was never able to say no to him, whether he was being the object of her adoration, a dominating type, the master of the house, or playing Pygmalion to her Galatea. When Nat wanted Googie to do something, she invariably did it. He promised to have the campaign speeches written by Sam Perrin, who had replaced Johnny Medbury as the show's head writer. Then he offered to bring along both her sister Hazel and Mary Kelly for gin rummy games. Mary was no longer Gracie's stand-in. She was her secretary now, a job with a salary but no responsibilities.

Googie finally capitulated, but her headaches were growing in frequency and fierceness.

Neither Burns nor Sam Perrin was a political creature and Burns never would be. (Some years later, another of his writers would say, "He probably voted for Nixon and Reagan because they were nice to him, they invited him.")

Burns and Perrin certainly weren't satiric in the Will Rogers tradition. Most of the stuff they put in Gracie's speeches was Dumb Dora material with a Washington wash. It could as well have been written for the radio program. She would call for bigger farms so that asparagus could grow lying down. On the subject of a living wage, she said, "It should be paid because wages aren't very good when you're dead," and speaking of the Neutrality Bill, Gracie figured, "If we owe it, let's pay it."

She gave press conferences and she visited with Eleanor Roosevelt. The newspapers were always grateful for an excuse to report something funny. Her campaign train drew the most attention. Making more than thirty stops, it played to a quarter of a million people. By the time it pulled into Omaha for the May "convention," Gracie had learned to be at ease when facing an audience. Sometimes more than a thousand people showed up to watch her stand at the back of the train and say a few Gracie Allenisms.

When it was over, she was more popular than ever, but the show's ratings had not improved. The gains achieved by the publicity were apparently offset by the lapse in the show's quality during four months on the road, with scripts written on the fly and constant remote broadcasting.

They came home exhausted. To make matters worse, Mary Kelly had started drinking again. Not wanting her around the children, Gracie had to ask her best friend to move out. Within a year, Mary was going to die.

At this point, the Hawaiian vacation must have looked like something a doctor had ordered. Mary Livingstone or no, Gracie went along with it, and the trip was evidently a success. When Gracie was asked how she enjoyed Hawaii, she said that they had all walked up a tree. It was a tree, she explained, Gracie Allen-style, that grew sideways.

Nat went to work improving their program, beginning with a new staff of writers. One of them was a young man named George Balzer, who found "The Burns and Allen Show" basically sound. Like the Benny show, its cast played exaggerations of themselves. Here, the announcer, Bill Goodwin, was a ladies' man; the conductor, Paul Whiteman, was a hifalutin' classical musician; the singer, Tony Martin, was shy and sweet (actually, Martin was a former saxophonist who was so shy he wouldn't sing unless he was wearing his saxophone).

Burns and Perrin agreed that something drastic had to be done. The program had been on the air for eight years, and it was definitely stale. George and Gracie were playing a couple of vaudevillians living in Los Angeles. On the first show of the 1940–41 season, George casually informed the national radio audience that they were not only married but had been married for fourteen years and had two children, a six-year-old daughter named Sandy and a five-year-old son, Ronnie.

It was possible to do this because the tone of the show had always been truthful. Just as the vaudevillian George and Gracie were extensions of the real George and Gracie, in radio, too, any references to family were drawn from the actual histories. This made the show entirely different from any other in radio. While most comedians used their own names—Eddie Cantor, Jack Benny, Fred Allen—in their situation comedy shows, everything was fictitious. But everything about the Burns and Allen program was rooted in fact: she was from San Francisco, she had a brother named George and three sisters named Hazel, Bessie, and Pearl.

Likewise, George on the radio was based on the real George, with a brother Willie and a childhood act called the Peewee Quartet. The facts were exaggerated, yes, and of course restructured for comedy, but at the core they were the facts. And this foundation of truthfulness would continue through all their work together and later into George's work alone.

In other words, the line between history and stage material, between show business and real life, was a blur from the beginning. There was always a colorful lie, there was always an essential truth.

And the ratings rebounded.

10

Kisses were not common between the Burnses. Although they had started out as a flirtation act, the team played as a platonic couple. This did not change in their movies, where they were invariably cast as themselves rather than as characters in the story. Sometimes their presence wasn't even explained and the routines they performed were brief and irrelevant. Gracie was still winsome in a featherbrained way, which added up to innocence. George was the eternally patient know-it-all. There was nothing romantic between them. That did not change when they became a married couple on the radio, because American popular culture rarely depicted married couples as romantic.

Sometimes it seemed as if this sexual antisepticism carried over into their personal life. None of their friends seem to have ever seen Nat and Gracie kiss, or even embrace. At home, Ronnie remembered his parents hugging occasionally, but Sandy thought "Daddy was not a very loving man." Her mother was more demonstrative, but when it came to plain warmth, her uncle Willie was the coziest of the Burnses.

"If I was in really deep trouble, like wrecking my car," the daughter remembered, "I'd talk to Uncle Willie first, to break the news to my dad and sort of smooth the way. Uncle Willie was wonderful. He would always go to my parents for me."

It wasn't that George was cold. He simply did not show any emotion, one way or the other. He was never tough with his daughter. "He was easy to talk to," she said, "if I needed money." But in terms of affection, Nat and Googie were preoccupied with their life as a team. They lived their life as a dual persona, and it was an identity they could not escape. Every time they walked out the door, they were a joint celebrity. Burns and Allen were *always* Burns and Allen. This identity kept them aloof from their children.

"And they both were vain," Sandy remembered. "They were performers, they had to take care of themselves." Her father even used facial cream to keep the wrinkles away. "They looked pretty good," Sandy said, "but they had no plastic surgery. I grew up seeing Mom's arm and I never even realized that she covered it. To me it wasn't badly scarred. She could have had it fixed but she didn't."

An actor's appearance is not always a matter of vanity. It is also a professional concern, and clothes were important to Burns and Allen as actors. George had been a dandy from the outset, but Gracie was equally meticulous about her appearance. "She always looked like she stepped out of a magazine," their nephew Lou Weiss remembered. "I never saw her with one hair out of place, or less than perfectly dressed and manicured."

The tradition of the era was that the maintenance of a man's clothes was his wife's responsibility. Grace instructed the housekeeper to check George's wardrobe regularly and to send out whatever needed cleaning. One day, while emptying the pockets of one of his suits, the woman found a package of condoms.

Diplomatically, she placed the foil envelope on the night table between the twin beds in the master bedroom. And that was where Gracie found it.

But Nat did not use condoms. There hardly was a need for them when the couple had been unable to conceive a child. Rather, as Gracie had to be thinking at the awful moment of discovery, he did not use condoms *with her*. In fact, as he told an intimate, the reason he used condoms with others was that, thirty years after Cupid's eczema and the case of the swollen testicles, he had no intention of contracting gonorrhea again. Whether or not Googie knew that history, she certainly knew that the condoms were for extracurricular use only.

There were no witnesses to their confrontation on the matter, but soon afterward, Natty gave Googie a mink coat as a conciliatory gesture and a symbol of retribution. Although she apparently told nobody how she found out about her husband's infidelity, she did say to one of her pals, "I wish Natty would find another girlfriend. I could use a silver fox jacket."

The line got around and even Ronnie Burns heard it, although George and Gracie made certain that the children did not hear about the reason for the fur coat—the case of the confiscated condoms. As far as Ronnie Burns knew, "There was never any kind of a domestic crisis about infidelity." He would have been surprised to learn why the condoms proved that his father was philandering.

For the kids knew nothing about their father's sterility. As far as Ronnie understood, he and Sandy had been adopted for the same reason as so many of their friends. "Mom was never pregant," Ronnie said, "but probably, like most of the actresses, she didn't want to go through pregnancy because of their figures and working time. Mom worked every week. The only one of that level that I can remember having her own baby was Lucy, and then [she and Desi Arnaz] brought it into the show.

"But usually, if you had both parents working and they wanted kids, they would adopt."

George and Gracie, however, had to adopt, and as for their own sex life, outsiders speculated that there was little of it. If true, that wouldn't have been unusual after being married for some fifteen years, but of course, nobody really knew. George told one of his lovers that he and Gracie had an arrangement which gave both of them sexual freedom. He even said that she had taken Louella Parsons's husband, "Doc" Martin, for a lover, but it is not a likely story. Gracie Allen does not come through as having an arrangement sensibility and she was too smart to risk the wrath of a powerful gossip columnist. Besides, Doc Martin was unattractive, a falling-down drunk. At one of the Burnses' own parties, he passed out near the swimming pool.

Parsons glanced down at him, looked around, and said, "Don't step on Dockie's fingers. He has to operate tomorrow."

Finally, Googie appeared too smitten with Natty to have an affair with Doc Martin or anybody else. More likely, Nat told the arrangement story to a semi-guilty girlfriend on the way to her bedroom. Perhaps he half believed it himself, the way he did some of his vaudeville fantasies.

Some might feel that the marriage was bad or unhappy because of his infidelity, and the untruthfulness that went with it. However, there is more to a marriage than its sex life, and as for dishonesty, some truths are cruel, accomplishing only hurt. There are worse disloyalties than sexual ones. Some sexuality is purely, sadly, and emptily physical. In Burns's case, there is not a shred of doubt that he loved Gracie with all of his heart. In Gracie's case, she was wise to overcome, if not overlook, what she knew, and was lucky not to know the rest. For she had Natty's love all of her life and even afterward.

•   •   •

George's daily routine had already taken on the strict and formal structure that would continue for the rest of his life. When he said, "My life is show business," he seemed to mean exactly and entirely that. He may have been the only adult in America who was utterly unaffected by World War II.

At forty-five, he was too old to be drafted, but while most of the stars, including Jack Benny, went on tour to entertain the troops, there is no record of Burns and Allen ever doing so. George claimed that it was because of Gracie's fear of flying, and he told a friend they did entertain servicemen domestically. If so, it did not happen often because there are no public records of it. Except for doing a few programs for the Armed Forces Radio Service, the nearest that George seems to have come to the war was the newsreel theatre down the street from the Hollywood Plaza Hotel. He would sometimes stop in with the writers.

A familiar face in those newsreels was General Douglas MacArthur. A corncob pipe was MacArthur's trademark, but when he took off his hat Burns noticed that his hair was styled in a "comb-over." It was parted at the ear, and then swept across the top in an effort to disguise his baldness.

"I guess MacArthur's a good general," Nat said, as the bunch of them strolled out of the movie theatre, "but he combs his hair from the hip."

Burns had baldness on his mind. He had lost so much of his hair that he had a toupee for movies and wore a beret at the radio studio, at the club, and even during work sessions.

Everybody knew somebody in the service, and most people had relatives who were in the war. Lou Weiss, the twenty-three-year-old son of Nat's sister Sarah, had enlisted in the

U.S. Army. Sandy Burns, at the age of seven, was smitten with this dashing, uniformed cousin.

The young man's connection to George Burns had given him a youthful yen for show business and his uncle had gotten him an entry-level job at the William Morris Agency. He already had a flair for theatrical gestures and the little girl fantasized that he would fly over North Maple Drive and send down a Japanese flag for her.

"I waited out there every night," Sandy remembered, "but it never happened." That was because Lou was in the Infantry.

Her room had two beds, with pink bedspreads, although Googie had not made the room especially frilly. Ronnie's room also had twin beds so that friends could stay overnight, but his bedspreads were a manlier plaid. As the male child, he was pampered, which tended to be the case in most families. Sandy was considered the family prankster. She was the one Gracie "lay waiting for when I got off the school bus" because of a shoplifting caper at the May Company department store (framed, Sandy insisted, by Lydia Minnevitch, whose father was in a harmonica act). She also was blamed for setting off the house burglar alarm. That was Ronnie's doing, but Nat and Gracie assumed that the mischiefmaking Sandy was guilty, and that Joanie Benny was her accomplice. "Ronnie was always 'Who, me?' " Joan remembered, "so innocent and sweet."

Ronnie's saintly reputation ended on the dark day his mother found a copy of *Playboy* magazine in his bathroom. A family friend tried to intercede, asking, "Gracie, what difference does it make? It's a natural thing for a boy." But his mother was outraged. "Oh, no," she cried, brandishing the wicked publication, and that was the end of Ronnie's saintly status.

Kindergarten through fifth grade, Sandy went to Marymount, a Catholic school. Then she went to Chadwick, a girls' boarding school, where she stayed through high school. "There were quite a few show business kids there," Sandy recalled. "Benny Goodman's stepdaughter, and Christina Crawford, though she was in the sixth or seventh grade while we were in high school, and Barbara Goetz—Edie's daughter."

The name of Edie Goetz came up a lot around Hollywood women. Married to the producer William Goetz, she was a daughter of Louis B. Mayer, who ran MGM, the most prestigious of all the movie studios. That was royalty in Hollywood, and it made Edie Goetz the queen of the movieland social world and keeper of the "A" list. If she sent her daughter to Chadwick, most mothers followed suit. Mary Livingstone sent Joanie there too.

Ronnie Burns also went to sleepaway school, the Black Fox Military Academy. He liked that—the uniform made him feel patriotic during the war. Both he and Sandy came home for weekends. Chadwick was only an hour's drive away in Palas Verdes, and Black Fox was right in Hollywood at Melrose Avenue and Wilcox.

Every morning, Burns went to the suite of rooms at the Hollywood Plaza and worked with the writers—Sam Perrin, Frank Galen, and Keith Fowler. On Mondays and Tuesdays, the days before and of the show, he took them to lunch in the hotel coffee shop, and they worked while they ate. He would always be a light eater.

The rest of the week, he went to the Hillcrest Country Club for lunch, and then played golf. He and Gracie were out most evenings, usually at parties, but even Hollywood was an Army town. There were uniforms everywhere and more young men were donning them daily.

In need of a replacement writer, Burns hired a young man named Paul Henning, who had been writing "The Rudy Vallee Show." Henning was a farm boy from the Midwest who would remain unspoiled through a successful career that included creating the television series *The Beverly Hillbillies,* and writing such sophisticated movies as *Lover, Come Back* (with Stan Shapiro, for which they were nominated for an Academy Award).

Henning noticed at once—it was hard for a writer not to—that as the scripts developed, all the funny lines went to Gracie and none to George. "The reason," he suspected, "was because Burns's vaudeville act hadn't been successful before Gracie and he didn't want to change a good thing."

Henning regretted it. "I don't think he knew how funny he was." The oddity was that although they were no longer an act, they certainly were a team, and the team's personality was based on the relationship that had originated with the act.

The show now had a policy of booking movie actors as guests. Such stars as Cary Grant, Clark Gable, Ronald Reagan, Shirley Temple, and of course Jack Benny were worked into the story along with the regulars. Bill Goodwin was still the announcer, Tony Martin was still the singer, and Meredith Willson had replaced Paul Whiteman as the conductor. Bea Benadaret played the lone fictitious character "Blanche Morton," who was Gracie's friend (as Bea in fact was).

No longer nervous before an audience, Gracie took part in the warm-up before the show. There was a regular routine that she and Nat did with Goodwin. The handsome announcer had started making movies.

"Now that you're a movie star," Gracie began, "you must get to kiss all those beautiful actresses."

Goodwin would mumble modestly.

"Come on, Bill," she continued. "Show me. Show me how you kiss them."

At last, he would oblige, stepping out in front of the script stands and microphones, taking her in his arms and leaning her over backwards in a dramatic embrace. Audiences invariably giggled.

"Gracie!" George cried. "Are you going to kiss Bill Good-win right before me?"

"Okay, George," she said. "You can kiss him first."

It was from their old vaudeville routine and it still worked.

Although the home audience was only exposed to the program itself, the performers' and writers' work experience started at the week's first meeting and continued through the script conferences, the writing by committee, the first readings, the rehearsals, the early show for the East Coast, the quick revisions, and the final broadcast. "Sometimes," Henning remembered, "the laughter we got for the first show wouldn't be there for the second one, or it would be more for the second one, and so we would have to cut or stretch . . . milk the laughs or talk faster."

Gracie was never involved with the writing process; she didn't sit in on conferences or suggest story lines, but it was noticed that on the rare occasion she made a suggestion to George, he went along with it.

She did do the first readings of the scripts for the writers, now that her stand-in and friend Mary Kelly was dead.

The death must have struck at the heart of the four-way relationship between George, Gracie, Jack, and Mary Livingstone. Kelly was one of the original Gang. She had bamboozled Gracie into staying with George rather than breaking up the act to marry Benny Ryan. And her split up with Jack led directly to his marrying Mary Livingstone on the rebound. Without Mary Kelly, their lives would have been altogether different; but while Nat, Gracie, and Jack seemed to have all the luck, Mary had none of it. And each of them must have had a personal reaction to her sorry end, including Mary Livingstone, who surely knew how the others felt. None of them said anything, although Gracie took over Kelly's job of doing the first readings.

She had always avoided that, but she did it well. As

George Balzer, another new writer, said, "We could hear what was working and what wasn't. Then she would be gone until the final rehearsal."

Sometimes, Balzer conceded, she didn't seem to know which of her lines were supposed to be funny. He came to believe that "she had to maintain that attitude if her character was to work. She had to read her lines in the most realistic fashion."

By 1941 Burns was wealthy and no longer had to work. His brother Willie Burns told young Henning that Nat was already worth $14 million because of excellent investments. And he was not yet fifty years old.

But he wasn't interested in grand homes or fancy cars. For him, work was synonymous with life, as retirement was with death. He had accumulated $14 million because he had good business sense, and because he took the advice of good businessmen, not because he liked money. That was the irony—even as a businessman, George was a smash; he was successful at everything he did, but only as long as it was offstage. As an onstage solo, he was always a flop. And he only wanted to be onstage.

If, as he'd always said, he had been a flop act before he teamed up with Gracie, then the corollary must have seemed equally true to him: If he broke up with her, he would be a flop act again. Where would his love of show business be then? It was a question he probably didn't want answered, and so there was tremendous danger attached to his indiscretions, for he was risking more than most. That was the down side of marriage being their act: no marriage, no act. If he was found out, or if he became romantically involved with one of his lovers, he might well lose both Gracie and the act in one sleazy headline.

For it would hardly do to have America's favorite couple disrupted by a cheating husband. Sweet, innocent, and vulnerable Gracie depended upon him. To betray such trust would mark George as a scoundrel who deserved exile. This was where his self-control came into play.

Every man who cheats on his wife seems convinced that he could never become involved. Burns had the edge on most, having his emotions under control and being disciplined in general. He knew that it would be senseless to destroy his professional and private life because he fell for somebody and so he would not allow that to happen.

A friend once took him aside in distress, confiding that he had fallen in love and was going to leave his wife. Burns's advice was short and tart.

"Don't think with your pecker," he said. "Because one look at it ought to tell you that it doesn't have a brain."

He certainly had plenty of time for getting into trouble. Gracie made a couple of pictures without him, *Mr. and Mrs. North* in 1941 and *Two Girls and a Sailor* in 1944. He always took advantage of opportunities and used these to seduce a string of young actresses in the rooms adjacent to the office. He made no effort to conceal these activities from the writers and relied on the conspiracy of males to keep his confidence.

Inevitably, there was gossip, but it was a funny kind of gossip tailored to the Burns and Allen image, as if life were being confused with the television series. The most popular rumor was about the fur coat that George had given Gracie, and her suggestion that he cheat again because she could use a silver fox jacket.

But every time this anecdote was repeated, it was changed. The "gift" George had given to Gracie became a wide variety of treats. For instance, Paul Henning reported that "after Gracie caught George cheating, he gave her a silver tea service to make her feel better. She told her friends, 'I wish Natty would do it again. I could use another tea service.' "

Others told the story with silver candlesticks instead of the tea service. The same anecdote went around with

George giving Gracie a brooch. It was told with the gift as a pearl necklace. And everyone who told the story insisted that it was heard directly from George or Gracie.

With the war ended, Army veterans were streaming home and there were many shifts and changes in the personnel of "The Burns and Allen Show." A writer named Sid Dorfman had been working with the program and told George he was quitting. "No hard feelings," he said. "It's just been a long time and I want to try my luck elsewhere."

Burns said, "Come on with me," and he took Dorfman into one of the adjoining bedrooms at the Hollywood Plaza.

"Sit down, kid."

The writer sat down on the edge of one bed.

"You know," Burns said, "I want you to think very carefully about leaving. Because you're much more than an employee to me. I mean, Gracie and I look at you as the son we've never had."

Dorfman was embarrassed—and surprised—by this kind of emotional talk. It was a side of Burns he'd never seen, and he stared down at the carpet, somewhat overcome. He continued to look down as George said, "You know, it's not just leaving the show; it's like you're leaving home. It's like our boy has grown up and is leaving us. Gracie and I feel a deep personal loss."

Dorfman continued to stare glumly, almost tearfully at the carpet.

"Sid," Burns said. "I can't work if you don't look at me."

If his humor flowed, his patience could run short. Herb Browar, who was going to be in charge of production at George's company, said, "He was so bright, he couldn't stand people around him who were slower. He had no patience for idle conversation."

He usually took the impatience out on Willie. If he was angry with any of the writers, he might yell and forget it.

He told an interviewer from *Look* magazine, "Sure I blow off steam. I scream bloody murder. Then I see the fellow ten minutes later, I forget I'm mad. . . . The only thing I can't tolerate is sheer stupidity. If something's wrong, I want to know it now, not Monday.

"Things are easy to fix the day they break. Everybody makes mistakes. The only people who don't are people who don't do anything."

He tended to spend his impatience on his brother. There was something vaguely snide in his frequent remark, "Willie was with me practically from the day I started doing well." He wouldn't let Willie forget that, or forget that he was a subordinate. Every day that George had lunch at Hillcrest without inviting him along was a reminder, and he had lunch at Hillcrest every day.

Sometimes, too, Burns was almost cruel to his brother in a way that didn't seem to be like him at all, calling to Willie in a stammer, "Hey, um—um—um—um," and then, as if he'd forgotten the name altogether, he would say, "Hey, you!"

Browar thought that "Willie contributed much more than George ever realized. Burns treated his brother as if he was taking care of him, giving him a job. He didn't treat anybody else that way. He never realized how much Willie contributed."

In the years after World War II, night life came back in Hollywood as it did across the country. A new spot in Los Angeles called the Mayfair became especially popular among those who were transplanted New Yorkers. It was an elegant place with a formal dress code and an entertainment policy that focused on Broadway veterans.

The Burnses and the Bennys were Saturday night regulars. They were especially excited when a Frank Fay engagement was announced, and they were there for the opening night of the great vaudevillian. "Blossom and Benny Fields came with us," Burns remembered. "Benny's tails were so long he kept stepping on them."

It was a glamorous audience, "and everyone," Burns said, "was doing well except Fay." The once triumphant comedian had fallen on hard times. Waiting to greet him was a room filled with colleagues who were still on top. That was the subtext as he strolled out to do his monologue.

"He got up that night," Burns remembered, "and he looked around."

His eyes flashed with the old contempt. All of his friends, competitors, and enemies were there, successful and looking it. "That was when he was at his greatest," Burns recalled with relish. "Sarcasm."

Fay began, but as he spoke, there was a stir in the audience. He stopped in midsentence and peered into the dark. Somebody had heckled him.

"Might I inquire who said that?" he asked with typical hauteur.

"A voice came out of the dark," as Burns told it. *"Groucho Marx."*

With snaky gentility, Fay said, "Groucho, come up here and we'll talk, you and I."

Marx was not such a fool as to go onstage during a professional comedian's act. He certainly was not going to walk out there and mix it up with a wise old cobra like Frank Fay.

After a wait, with no Groucho, Fay looked out at the audience, smiled, and in his most charming voice said, "You do need Zeppo, don't you?"

Zeppo Marx was of course the unfunny Marx Brother, the one who had quit the act to become an agent.

"That's how great Fay still was," Burns said. "At least Chico. Harpo. But not Zeppo. *'You do need Zeppo!'*

"That's Fay at his best. Or anybody at their best."

When the Mayfair engaged Frank Fay, it was a break for the once-reigning vaudevillian. He had already been down and then up again. First, radio had knocked him for a loop. That, George believed, was because of his arrogance. "He wouldn't hire writers. He thought he could do it all." Too, the medium's intimacy had revealed Fay's real character. As one of Burns's writers, George Balzer, said, "When you get out there, forget about that first laugh. That'll come, if you're a nice man."

Fay was a brilliant comedian but he was not a nice man. He was the dark side of George and Jack. He was the same performer without the benevolence.

Barbara Stanwyck had already wearied of his abuse, leaving to marry her fellow movie star Robert Taylor. That sank Fay lower. Then he had a second chance when he starred in a Broadway play called *Harvey*. The Mary Coyle Chase comedy won the 1945 Pulitzer Prize, and the critics gave him splendid marks as a stage actor. It revived his career.

But he was a self-destructive personality. Becoming obsessed with McCarthyism, he spent more time at anti-Communist rallies than he did performing as either a comedian or an actor. That knocked him down again, and this time he was going to be out for good.

Burns believed that Fay deserved what he got but wouldn't say so in public. When his manager told a writer that Fay's house was overgrown with weeds, George demurred. "He said that. I didn't. Maybe Fay likes weeds."

11

The Round Table at the Hillcrest Country Club brought together the country's best professional comedians when they were at their smartest, their fastest, and their most arrogant. For some thirty years, from the 1940s into the 1970s, this table for ten—twelve in a squeeze—was the site of a daily comedy tournament.

Like a group of people in any business or profession, they were bound by their common interest. What made this group slightly different from others was that their common business was monkey business.

They worked man against man at the table because a comedian always works alone against his audience. He stands in front of a curtain (in stage parlance, "working in one") and confronts the people he is paid to amuse. It is a dangerously solitary position, without the dramatic actor's protection of a story, a setting, a character to play, a costume to wear, or other actors for company. Nor can the comedian blame a playwright for his ill fortune. There is nobody but himself. He is alone and in person.

At the Round Table in the Men's Grill of Hillcrest, the comedians played to their equals, exercising and flexing their wits and their mouths. Funny was their art, their science, their craft; it was their offense and it certainly was their defense. They were the audience, the judges, and the judged.

In 1947, the regulars at the Round Table included Milton Berle, Lou Holtz, two of the Ritz Brothers, Jimmy and Al, and Al Jolson; George Jessel was considered best at the table for pure and fastest *funny;* Groucho Marx was the nastiest and Jack Benny the best audience. Danny Kaye was the freshest and Nat Burns the driest.

Lunch at the Round Table did not mean nonstop comedy. There actually was conversation, even if the only topic seemed to be show business. When they talked about anything else, it was invariably interrupted (or disrupted) by comedy. But there also was tension because everyone at that table was alert, awaiting a first serve. At any moment, a wisecrack could zing across the table, to begin a rally.

"There was a caste system at the Round Table," Joan Benny remembered. "First of all, it was a man's table, no women allowed. Top of the heap there was George Jessel or Groucho. My dad might be talking to Milton Berle and then Natty would show, so Dad would shut up because George had precedence. Then Jessel would come in, and George would shut up because Jessel had precedence."

Nevertheless, Benny was usually talking because he was such a *yenta.* He was always looking for the perfect something and did not need a cue. He might start out saying, apropos of nothing, "Nat, I've traveled all over the world. I've been everywhere at least once, and I've yet to find a good cup of coffee. Why is it you can't get a good cup of coffee?"

This would elicit quizzical glances all around, and chuckling, as if, "Is he serious?" He certainly seemed to be.

Or, he might ask, "Why can't you get a cold glass of water? No matter how much ice you put in a glass of water, it just isn't cold enough."

Occasionally, Benny would actually find an ideal, in which case, his appreciation could be boundless. He had to share such a discovery.

"Have you taken a shower today? The towels in the locker room are the *softest* towels I have ever seen in my whole life. You have *got* to go in there and take a shower. Come on, I'll go with you."

He dared to interrupt one of Nat's somber bridge games because something critical had happened.

"I've got to tell you that Sammy [the locker-room attendant] just gave me the greatest shoeshine I've ever had in my life!"

George Burns's strong suit was his intelligence, and perhaps that was why one of the things he liked best in Jack was the sheer goodness of his soul. This man had so much love to give, it seemed natural that he was born on Valentine's Day.

Brains and niceness do not often come in the same package. Smart people are usually too critical to be nice. Nat had the good sense to be well adjusted, diplomatic, independent, and ultimately wise, but his sheer intelligence seemed to work against such softer qualities as Jack offered—emotion, sensitivity, and warmth.

A second look at Benny, and another listen, might have suggested that all was not serious about the tasty coffee, the cold water, the soft towel, or the glossy shine. This humor might have been the driest of all, but the Round Table preferred to perceive Benny as an innocent.

He was talking about flying.

"You have got to be crazy," he said, "to get into an airplane."

The fellows at the table mocked his timidity, but Irving Brecher, a radio comedy writer ("The Life of Riley"), nodded in agreement.

"I don't care how safe they claim an airplane is," Benny

continued. "I say that anytime you go up there in a little metal thing, you're taking your life in your hands."

There were assorted snorts. Brecher finally said soberly, "Birds don't fly that high and it's their business."

Somebody pointed out that airplanes had become very sophisticated. The Boeing Superfortress had ended the war when it dropped the atom bomb. This plane, it was said, could go seven miles up and fly four thousand miles before refueling.

"The Russians will never build a plane like that," one of the fellows said, "and even if they did, there is no way that they are going to come up with an atom bomb."

George Jessel stepped in. "You think that just because the Russians dance sitting down, they can't invent an atom bomb."

That appealed to Burns's sense of humor, but not all of them considered Jessel the funniest. "Aside from Chaplin," Groucho said, "I'm probably the funniest comedian in the business."

"How can that be, Groucho?" Burns said. "Even I'm funnier than you are."

He meant it, and the feeling was mutual. The two men did not like each other, and Marx was capable of using Burns for a patsy.

"That's a nice suit," he said. "Do you think that style is ever going to come back?"

It was just an insult joke, which wouldn't personally bother Burns. What he didn't like was the mean spirit behind it. He would take aim with one of his cheap El Producto cigars, and blow the smoke in Groucho's direction. He knew that Marx had fancy taste in cigars.

"Don't you ever inhale?"

"Not while I'm sitting next to you, Groucho."

"That," Marx said, "must be a Lawrence Welk cigar."

George was willing to be a feeder for the sake of the

table. He provided the straight line, "What is a Lawrence Welk cigar, Groucho?"

"A lot of shit with a band around it."

The fellows laughed, but George kept puffing on his El Producto.

(When Milton Berle mentioned how much a good Havana cigar cost, Burns said, "Before I smoked it, I'd have to fuck it first.")

Of the Marx Brothers, he much preferred Harpo, who was a good man as well as a funny one. He did admire Groucho's professionalism, and they shared a fondness for old songs; but, Nat suggested, the man was nasty and a nuisance.

It was by the sea bass thing that he finally judged the man. Somebody at the Round Table had ordered sea bass for lunch one day and Groucho piped up, "If you can't sea bass every day, you can't see mamma at all."

This was a play on the old song, "If you can't see mamma every day, you can't see mamma at all," and it got a laugh.

The next time somebody ordered sea bass, Groucho used the same line. It got a fair laugh. He used it a third time, and then yet again, and naturally, there was less laughter each time he said the line. But Marx persisted, and it so irritated Burns that even when he felt like having sea bass, he wouldn't order it.

One day he had a yen for what these men called "a piece of fish." He motioned to Hugo, the regular waiter at the Round Table, and whispered that he would like an order of sea bass. The waiter straightened up and cried to the table, "If you can't sea bass every day, you can't see mamma at all!"

It became one of Burns's favorite anecdotes. Every time he told it, it let him describe Groucho as being tiresome without that seeming to be the point.

In 1948 Danny Kaye, who was the newest member of the

Round Table, had just returned from a dazzling triumph at the Palladium Theatre in London. It had lifted him to international status, a class that only Jack Benny had achieved. Other comedians were trying to emulate Kaye's success, and Red Skelton had followed him into the Palladium. Now, Burns and Allen were booked to play the fabled London variety house.

They brought the Hennings with them—Paul to write material if need be, and Ruth to take the teenage Sandra and Ronnie sight-seeing. They all sailed first class on the *Queen Elizabeth,* courtesy of Burns.

Ruth Henning was a busy radio actress and had seen a little bit of the Hollywood life, but she was dazzled by the glamour of the legendary ocean liner. Every passenger in first class had a reserved deck chair, she remembered. Afternoon tea was served by waiters wearing satin knee breeches and silk stockings. "They had those big epergnes [tiered silver serving dishes] filled with scones, cucumber sandwiches, and all sorts of pastries."

Formal dress was required at dinner every evening. They sat at the captain's table, which Ruth found almost as thrilling as dancing with George every night. "That was the most wonderful treat," she said, "because he was a great ballroom dancer."

She adored Gracie. "Her gowns were gorgeous, but they all had built-in boobs because she didn't have any. And because of the scars on her arms, they had long tight lace sleeves, or gloves made especially to go high up on her arm."

Everything about the trip was first class. They all stayed at the Savoy Hotel, one of the grandest in London and a favorite of theatrical people. There was a cocktail reception for George and Grace at the American Embassy, and an opening-night party at the Marble Arch home of Val Parnell, the managing director of the Palladium.

At the height of that party, Burns was taken aside by his

tough and burly but elegantly dressed host. Parnell had to raise his voice to be heard.

"Transatlantic call for you, Nat."

George took the telephone, and after speaking a moment, he turned to Parnell and said, "It's Jack Benny calling from California."

Then he hung up. He smiled at Parnell, explaining that he always hung up on Jack, it was a running gag. George Burns laughed out loud on selected occasions only, but that night became one of them when a door swung open and Benny strode in from another room to make his beaming way through the crowd, his arms open in embrace. He had finally pulled one on his pal. He'd set up the whole "transatlantic call" with Parnell, and come over himself just to be there with George and Gracie on their opening night.

The act Burns and Allen performed at the Palladium, Paul Henning remembered, was "stitched together from their old material." Some of it was plucked from the radio shows, and some from "Dizzy" and "Lamb Chops." The old dancing was worked into the act as well.

However, the Burns and Allen style of comedy, just as it had been the first time around, was not an Englishman's cup of tea. There was a different excuse this time. Paul Henning said, "Nobody knew them. Unlike Danny Kaye, they hadn't made that many movies and their radio shows weren't heard in England."

Whatever the explanation, "to be perfectly honest," Henning added, "they were not a smash."

After they got back home, Ruth Henning was having lunch with a cousin who was visiting from Missouri. The cousin had asked to be taken someplace where famous people might be seen. Ruth took her to Romanoff's. ("You could always see movie stars there.")

As they were eating, Jack came in and called to Ruth

from the doorway. "He cried out loud enough for the whole restaurant to hear.

" 'Ruth! Didn't we have fun in London?' "

She was thrilled. "Everybody including Gary Cooper and Greer Garson turned around to see who he was talking to." Speaking for herself, she said, "For a little Missouri girl, this was really glamour!" And she added, "My cousin was very impressed."

Jack certainly knew how to make a person feel good, and he enjoyed doing it.

George had returned from England to find that "The George Burns and Gracie Allen Show" was one of the prized items in a bidding war. The newspapers were filled with stories about the raid that the CBS chairman, William S. Paley, was staging on NBC in an effort to lure away the older network's biggest stars. Paley had already snared Jack Benny and Red Skelton, and now he was after Burns and Allen.

George telephoned Abe Lastfogel, the president of the William Morris Agency, and made an appointment to talk about it. The lucrative CBS offer was being brokered by MCA, which was the Morris office's arch rival, and a condition of the deal was that George and Gracie would switch their management to MCA.

Mr. Lastfogel was more than Burns's agent, he was a friend; after the war he had restored George's nephew, Lou Weiss, to his old job in the William Morris Agency mailroom. Yet Lastfogel advised Burns to "take the Paley offer. It's a good deal. I'm not going to stand in your way."

George was already a wealthy man, but this would secure it. The only one the deal wouldn't help was his favorite nephew, Louie.

"Holy cow!" was the way Weiss remembered his reaction. "The guy who brought me in just left the company. They could throw me out."

Gracie didn't want to go to CBS, or anywhere else. She wanted to retire. It was not merely that she was tired of performing, which she was. It was not only that she wanted to be a Beverly Hills lady who played cards and went shopping, which was what she wanted to be. Her migraine headaches were worsening.

But CBS was offering Burns more than a lucrative radio series. They were offering a television series too. The new medium had caught the American imagination, and every performer with a radio show was eager to make the switch. Moreover, the network was willing to make George the executive producer of his series.

Advertising was already available. At that time, radio programs were sponsored by a single company. The Carnation Milk Company, whose product was a condensed milk, had decided to make the leap into television and agreed through its advertising representative, Charles Lowe, to sponsor Burns and Allen at CBS. This decision had been made after its rival, the Pet Milk Company, announced its sponsorship of Fibber McGee and Molly on television.

They were a tremendously popular radio team, but Mr. Lowe was counting on Burns and Allen's vaudeville experience to make the difference in the new and visual medium of television. He was going to be proved right. Fibber McGee and Molly would falter on television while Burns and Allen would take Carnation past its rival.

Nat could always talk Googie into anything. She was crazy about him and it was obvious that Carnation wanted Burns and Allen, not just George Burns. Whenever he joked about owing his career to Gracie, it was clear that he was kidding on the square. "Nat was always aware," a friend said, "of the role that Gracie had played in his success."

Paul Henning was convinced that despite all of Burns's confidence as the brains behind Burns and Allen, he still thought of Gracie as the performing talent in the family business.

The television show was to be done in New York, live from the Ed Sullivan Theatre. With Gracie pleading exhaustion and George concerned about so much new material, the network agreed to drop the radio program, concentrate on television, and start with a twice-a-month schedule. Even so, the workload was going to be tremendous. The writing staff was expanded to eight, under Paul's benign leadership. This was going to be like producing, writing, and performing a new stage play twice a month, and Gracie's migraines were worse than she was letting on.

They moved to New York City for the duration, along with Willie, Paul, and their wives. Because Gracie was terrified of flying, and because she wanted partners for card games, everyone went with her on the great luxury trains, the Super Chief into Chicago and then the Twentieth Century Limited to New York.

As Ruth remembered it, "We brought along special food prepared by the Brown Derby. All the women were trapped in Gracie's Pullman room. We had to play gin rummy with her, not that anyone minded. The food was sent in. Coffee was sent in. Drinks were sent in. It was just nickels and dimes but she loved to play. We were only released when it was time to have dinner with our husbands."

In New York, CBS put all of them up in the Algonquin Hotel. Nat and Googie were back on the road, and on October 12, 1950, Fred De Cordova directed the first Burns and Allen television show.

They had met De Cordova years earlier while visiting George Jessel backstage after a Broadway show. It was a revue called *High Kickers*, which De Cordova had staged. He had gotten into television at the sound of the bell and so he was one of the few directors with any experience in the medium.

Burns sometimes called De Cordova "Freddie with a big 'D.' " This was his idea of a dirty joke. He rarely used scatological language, not from prudishness but out of leftover conditioning from the moral proscriptions of the old days.

The forty-year-old De Cordova was a tall, lanky, handsome fellow who might have been Ronald Reagan's double. The "big 'D' " joke was inspired, if that is the word, by his reputation as a ladies' man. He was likewise aware of George's reputation for womanizing. He'd also heard that Gracie had found out about it. The story had been retold so many times by so many people that it now came in high- and low-class variations—De Cordova's was high. "Nat bought her an expensive Tiffany lamp," he said, "to make it up to her. Gracie told her girlfriend, 'I wish he would have another affair. I could use the matching lamp.' "

The television version of "The Burns and Allen Show" had many of the same actors as the radio series. Hal March played the neighbor Harry Morton, while Gracie's friend Bea Benadaret was still playing his wife, Blanche. Bea was appearing on many shows and would have to commute from Los Angeles, where she was starting work on the new *I Love Lucy* series.

Burns wasn't worried about *I Love Lucy* making the actress's schedule indefinitely complicated. "Fellas," he said to De Cordova and Henning, "it'll never happen, it just won't work. Here's this redheaded American married to the Cuban. The public won't buy it."

As adapted for television, *The George Burns and Gracie Allen Show* was essentially the same as it had been on radio. If that didn't make George and Gracie feel at home, the setting surely did, for this living room was a replica of their own house on North Maple Drive.

However, the opening of the show was novel. George crossed through the set and then stepped in front of it, revealing it as scenery while he delivered a monologue straight into the camera. This was not only radical television but radical Burns, for—as Paul Henning recognized with pleasure—he was at last doing solo comedy. To be sure, Burns was tentative about it, and even if Gracie wasn't standing there onstage with him, he depended on her to get the laughs by talking about her.

The cigar he held while he delivered this monologue swiftly became his trademark, but it would take more than a cigar to establish George Burns as a solo comedian, particularly in his own mind. At this point, he had a consistently droll attitude, and a comedian needed a consistent attitude, but a comedian also needs to be funny. Droll without enough laughs was not funny enough.

The cigar worked well. Being an inexpensive El Producto, it burned continuously because its tobacco was loosely wrapped. As George often explained to friends and interviewers, a good Cuban cigar is tightly wrapped, which causes it to die out when it is not puffed.

He needed the cigar not only as something to keep his hand occupied. He needed it—needed it to keep burning—so that he could puff on it while waiting out a laugh, or even extending it. That was a variation on Benny's device of extending a laugh by staring at the audience.

Later, when Burns was working in nightclubs, he would depend on the burning cigar as well to time his monologue. He could tell how long he'd been on by how much cigar was left. It was better than looking at a wristwatch.

On television, the characters of the neighbors, Harry and Blanche Morton, were beefed up. There were occasional guest stars, and George got De Cordova to invite Blossom Seeley and Benny Fields onto the show. They weren't working much.

The series worked, the public liked it, and George persuaded Gracie to come back for another season. That was going to be an annual sell, but by the end of the first season the show had already moved to California, which made the first sell a little easier.

They came home to find out their seventeen-year-old daughter Sandy was eloping.

12

Sandra Jean Burns had always been a mischievous kid, so it shouldn't have surprised her parents that despite their hopes for her going to college, she announced her intention to get married. Her father dismissed the young man as "a surfer," but that was just a father's reaction. Jim Wilhoite was a surfing enthusiast, it was true, but he was also a UCLA student. Moreover, George and Gracie liked him; they just thought that at seventeen, Sandy was young to be getting married. After all, Joan Benny was one of her best pals and Joanie was young enough for a sweet-sixteen party. Much had been made of that.

The party was supposed to be for her friends, and there was a big crowd of them, some eighty young people. But, she remembered, "Mom turned it into a major Hollywood event." The guest list included Frank and Nancy Sinatra, Dinah Shore and George Montgomery, Stewart Granger and Jean Simmons, Cyd Charisse and Tony Martin, and of course Natty and Googie. Obviously, it was as much Mary's party as Joan's.

Late in the evening, after dinner and dancing, the huge group crowded into the Benny living room for the usual entertaining. At the back of the room, Mary Livingstone whispered to Joanie, "Come upstairs. We have a problem."

Mary closed her bedroom door. The problem, she said, was Benny Fields and Blossom Seeley, who were the Bennys' houseguests. "I don't know what to do," she said. "I completely forgot about Blossom and Benny. Should we ask them to perform? It would be rude not to, but your friends have never heard of them and it would be embarrassing if the kids didn't respond."

Joan suspected that perhaps her mother considered Seeley and Fields to be a couple of vaudeville has-beens, not good enough to sing with Frank Sinatra, Dinah Shore, and Tony Martin.

"Maybe we shouldn't ask them," Mary said. "But they're staying here, and, oh, I don't know. You decide."

Joanie wasn't sure what to say. The two sixtyish vaude-villians seemed "ancient" to her.

"Let's get Daddy to decide," she finally said.

When they described the situation to Jack, he didn't hesitate.

"What's the problem? Of course we'll ask them."

He stepped up to the piano and introduced Blossom Seeley and Benny Fields as two of the greatest stars ever to play the Palace. Fields sat down at the piano and plunged into the rollicking left-hand chords that rang with a vaudeville strut and swagger. Blossom strode to the piano, her elbows pumping and her big head of hair shaking as though it were still the era of two-a-day.

"They performed for an audience of Hollywood stars and us teenagers," Joan remembers. "Many of my friends were sophisticated show-biz kids who had never heard of them. But they were the hit of the evening."

When Blossom closed with her signature song, "Toddling the Toddle-O," "all the kids went wild," Joanie said, "including me. We all wanted more.

"Blossom and Benny wowed them, and a crowd of young

people went home that night having learned what it meant when they heard that someone had been a headliner at the Palace."

It was hardly the Nat and Googie style to give that kind of a sweet-sixteen party for Sandy, but elopement wasn't their idea of what was appropriate either. And elopement was the message they were now getting from her in Las Vegas.

Moreover, Joan Benny had gone along for the ride. It was as if getting married were just an end-of-summer, fun kind of thing to do.

The escapade had begun late the previous afternoon, when Sandy called Joan and said, without explaining, "Come over to the house." It was seven o'clock when Joan arrived at 720 North Maple. Nat and Googie had already gone out to dinner, and Sandy was in the house with Wilhoite, "a blond, good-looking beach type," Joan recalled. "The whole surfing thing."

They already were engaged, or had been. All four parents had agreed to that as long as no marriage date was set. But then Sandy broke it off, and now the young lovers were overcome by the thrill of reconciliation.

She grinned when Joanie Benny came in. "We're eloping to Las Vegas," she said. "You have to go with me."

"I'm game," was her friend's reply. They had a history of joint mischief.

Wilhoite's best friend was Marvin Mitchelson, and he was next to arrive. Mitchelson went on to become a prominent divorce lawyer, but at the moment he was an occasional date of Joan's, a college student, a co-conspirator—and a chauffeur. He had the convertible, and they made the drive to Las Vegas in five hours. It was after midnight when the wedding party rolled into the parking lot of the all-night, neon-lit marriage mill. This was hardly a Catholic church, and there were no postnuptial plans. "None of us had a lot of money with us," Joan remembered, "so afterward, it was, like, what do we do now?"

They didn't have enough money for a hotel. They couldn't even afford a midnight wedding breakfast, and Sandy was already distracted by other concerns, specifically, facing the music. Realizing what she had done, she now wondered what she should do. The teenage bride pondered when and how to tell her parents the latest.

At home, Burns was already worried, having come home from dinner to find his daughter unexpectedly out and her curfew at hand. He went upstairs to his son's room and "woke me three times," Ronnie remembered. "First at eleven, then at midnight, and finally at two in the morning." He kept asking, "Where's your sister?" and Ronnie kept replying in ever more earnest tones, "I have no idea, Dad," which was true.

In Las Vegas, the four revelers drove around aimlessly, mainly to delay the inevitable. As they passed the lighted marquee of the Flamingo Hotel, Sandy saw the billing and cried out in relief, "Tony's here!"

Tony Martin had for years been the singer on the Burns and Allen radio show. He had known Sandy all of her life. A lovely, gentle man, he was, Joan remembered, "a very good friend of both the Bennys and the Burnses. So we decided we'll go tell Tony and he'll tell us what to do."

The singer had finished his late show and was going to bed when the telephone rang in his room. As he opened the door of his suite, he was in his pajamas and robe. Facing him were four bedraggled youngsters, giddy no more.

"What are you doing here, Sandy?" the singer asked. "Joanie?"

"Well," Sandy said, "I'd like you to meet my husband."

"I'm calling your parents right now."

"*Please*, Mr. Martin," Sandy pleaded. "Can't we talk about this for a minute?"

"Look, come on in, all of you. Call room service and get something to eat. But I've got to call your parents."

When he heard what had happened, Burns was so enraged he refused even to speak with Sandy. He never could show anger with his daughter; but Gracie did not share this problem and when she got on the telephone, her conversation was one-sided and brief.

"Come home right now," she said icily.

"She was not happy," Sandy had to admit.

Ronnie was sixteen, like Joan, but boys tend to be less mature at that age, and at four o'clock in the morning, he was sleepy-eyed and confused as he stumbled downstairs to see what was happening. In the living room, seated side by side on the sofa, morose and silent as stone, were his mother and father, and Jack and Mary—all four of them in bathrobes and slippers.

His father gave him the news: "Sandy and Jim eloped. They're with Tony Martin."

Ronnie didn't much care. He turned around, went upstairs, and went back to sleep.

The sun rose in the desert behind the convertible as the wedding party glided toward Los Angeles. "We weren't exactly in a rush to get home," Joan remembered. Tony Martin had given them money and they stopped for breakfast, dawdling as much as possible. "It was about ten in the morning," Joan said, "when the four of us walked into Natty and Googie's house."

Wilhoite was, in Joan Benny's opinion, "a laid-back surfer and he wasn't intimidated by any of this."

Unfortunately, "Marvin Mitchelson was not the great lawyer he is these days."

As for the father of the bride, "George was positively apoplectic." Yet for all that, he could still keep his mouth buttoned up.

"My dad," Sandy said later, "just looked at me. He never

lost his temper with me—*ever*. But my mother got real furious."

Gracie wasn't furious about Sandy getting married in a civil ceremony instead of in church. She was just furious about Sandy getting married at all, and she launched into the girl, talking nonstop until her voice started rising. Ordinarily, she spoke in an adult alto, but as she grew angrier that morning, she began to sound like the Gracie Allen she played on the radio, the Gracie who spoke an octave higher.

Making it seem even funnier, at least to Joan Benny, was the difference in height between parent and child. Sandy was a tall girl, five feet eight, and she towered over the five-foot mother who was wagging a finger and craning a neck to berate her errant daughter.

Sandy turned helplessly to Jack.

"And Uncle J just gave me a look that said, 'Everything's okay.' "

A few weeks later, he and Mary threw a big party for the newlyweds.

While *The George Burns and Gracie Allen Show,* as it was formally called on television, was broadcasting from New York, Lucille Ball and Desi Arnaz were making a great success of *I Love Lucy.* They also revolutionized the medium of television by filming the series. This method not only allowed for retakes and editing; it raised the stakes tremendously, because a filmed program could be shown again, sold again, and, to use a new and lucrative word, it could be *syndicated.* Almost a half century later, reruns of *I Love Lucy* would still be sold and broadcast.

Desilu, which was Ball and Arnaz's production company, was going to become one of the financial miracles of the postwar era. A less miraculous technical innovation that went with it was a little black box that was invented to jolly up the final product. This was the machine that would associate every television comedy, from the classic to the banal, with the same inanimate and unamused laughter.

However George felt about canned laughter, he was quick to appreciate the possibilities of syndication. Following the example of the *Lucy* show, in the spring of 1951 he took space in the General Service Studios, at 1040 North Las Palmas in Hollywood. He organized his own production company and called it McCadden Productions, taking the name from Willie's home address on McCadden Street in the old Hollywood section of Los Angeles. And even though he would later tell Paul Henning how annoyed he was that he "blew the chance to buy General Service Studios," McCadden would still make his $14 million nest egg look like a pittance. This was the start of Burns's real fortune.

Even so, there was no syndication without a hit series and a sufficient number of episodes. Freddie De Cordova was now directing *The George Burns and Gracie Allen Show* with assurance, understanding that Gracie's character was the basis of its success. "The device of her being silly, a *daffodil*, which started in their vaudeville act, was the perfect way to make the humor. And she would always make things work out so that at the end, George could just look at the camera and shrug—as if to say, how can you knock it if it works?"

The show's schedule called for the actors to read the script aloud on Monday and Tuesday. Wednesday was used for camera set-ups, lighting arrangements, and general technical work. That day, too, the show was put on its feet, actors given their entrances and exits, movement blocked, gestures learned, and props specified. Late in the day, they filmed the show, and then on Thursday it would be shown to a studio audience of some two hundred people.

The man with the black box kept track of when this audience laughed, and that was where he put in his mechanical laughs. If they just giggled, he put a giggle on the laugh track, and if they laughed longer, or louder, the box laughed longer and louder. It was then mixed in with the real laughter, which was recorded along with the rest of the show. This procedure was called "sweetening," although souring seems the more appropriate word.

Friday was a day off, then the writers began anew on Saturday. By Sunday morning, George would again be sitting at his pool as his secretary Tommy Clapp read him the next week's script. That would begin the arduous process of learning his lines.

Gracie didn't have to memorize her lines. She could rely on cue cards, but George read too slowly for that. "It's important to read well," he explained, "with the cue cards, on television. I had very little school. I've got to rehearse. I've got to know it. I have trouble reading."

It was not for want of trying to learn. Once again, he hired a private instructor. "He had a tutor for years to teach him to write [and] to learn vocabulary," Ronnie remembered. "The tutor would sit with Dad for an hour or two at a time. She would teach him to read, to write."

But he never would be comfortable with either reading or writing. The office secretary would always type up his business correspondence and even his personal mail, including letters to girlfriends. And his signature would always remain a childlike scrawl.

After the next week's script had been read to him, he would sit down with the family at the dinner table that night, rub his hands together with pleasure, and announce, "Okay, here's the situation for next week's show."

And once more, Gracie would tense up. All week she studied the script in the upstairs sitting room, but here was the reason that she never tried to memorize her lines: Her character's illogical behavior made them virtually impossible to learn. There was no reasonable sequence to them. As the show's director, Fred De Cordova, said, there were too many non sequiturs.

George, on the other hand, was stimulated by the new medium, and soon learned how it worked. He believed that comedy should be directed as though it were drama. "After Gracie made a joke, the camera would stay on me until I reacted to that joke. Let's say the joke is, 'My brother's coming with pineapples.' Gracie would pick up an ashtray, put it on the other table, say the line, and walk away. The camera would show me deadpan.

"Now we show it to an audience. If that line doesn't get a laugh, we put back the piece of film where Gracie picked up the ashtray and put it on the other table. Then we put in a very small snicker [on the laugh track] and let it lay an egg.

"If it got a laugh, then my reaction would stay, but if not, then the camera would follow Gracie."

In the midst of the show's second season, Paul Henning asked for a meeting and Burns took him to Hillcrest for lunch. The writer had an idea for a comedy series to be built around the movie actor Robert Cummings. Henning wanted to produce and write it himself and told Burns that MCA—which was Cummings's agency as well as Burns's—was resisting the idea.

"If I could just get this thing on the air," Paul said, "I just bet it'll do well."

"Leave it to me," George said. "I'll see that it gets on."

He certainly did, and *Love That Bob* became the second series in production at McCadden Productions. Burns knew that in Henning he was losing a brilliant chief writer, but he watched Paul shape the Cummings show into a major success of the 1950s.

He didn't just watch. Having long supervised all the details of his own show, he now became the executive producer of a show that did not involve him as an actor. The director of *Love That Bob,* Rod Amateau, remembered Burns regularly stopping by to watch dress rehearsals. He would give pointers, but never make demands.

"I would do it this way," George would say, "but what do you want?" That was a tactful approach which both Amateau and Cummings appreciated.

"Everything George suggested," the director said, "was so apropos, so right, and just *tasty*. For instance, he would advise against two jokes in quick succession because one would cancel out the other. The logic of his suggestions was always obvious."

There was a different kind of obvious logic in putting his son Ronnie into *The Burns and Allen Show*. George had already given jobs at McCadden Productions to both of his children. Sandy had started as a production assistant and Ronnie as an assistant film editor. She was not especially interested in television as a career, and decided to begin classes at UCLA.

But by 1954, Ronnie had three years under his belt as an editor and was going to the University of Southern California at the same time.

Suddenly he was made an actor. The reason was the competitive *Ozzie and Harriet Show*, which was also a situation comedy about a real-life show business couple. When Ozzie Nelson and Harriet Hilliard's real children were brought into the show, its popularity boomed. David Nelson became a teenage favorite and his guitar-playing, singing brother, Ricky Nelson, was fast developing into a full-blown rock star.

"Sandy was too shy to be on the show," Ronnie remembered, "but I wasn't too crazy about school so I jumped at the chance."

It was an exercise in illusion, Ronnie acting as Ronnie. "I had to play myself, and how do you do that?" He also had to deal with his mother on the show as if she were not Mom but Gracie Allen. "It was all reaction, because you have to react to Mother's logic-illogic, which you didn't have at home."

Home life became strange too. George would be by the

pool, Gracie in the upstairs sitting room, and Ronnie in his bedroom—all studying the scripts in which they played themselves.

Ronnie had no special problems with learning his lines. "I didn't take that long," he recalled, "and my father, he would only work on his monologue."

Compounding George's reading difficulties was eyesight so poor that he couldn't read normal-sized print unless he held it up to his nose. Willie got the office a special typewriter that printed oversized letters, and it was used for George's script. This printing was big enough for him to read four feet away, which was exactly how he read it on the car seat as he drove. The double use of time seemed to compensate for the risk.

"But Mother," Ronnie said, "she just got very involved with the character. She would study the script for hours and hours and hours. Every time she got a new script, she had to work hard to make that script believable. She had a tough time doing it. You see, if she just read the lines naturally, people would say it didn't mean anything.

"She had to make it so that the audience says, 'You know? She's right.' "

Harvey Helm succeeded Paul Henning as the head writer of *The George Burns and Gracie Allen Show*. Some placed Helm in a rare subspecies of genius: he could not only write in the same language that Gracie spoke, but seemed to actually think in it. This freakish gift freed George to acquire a reputation as a television producer.

The William Morris Agency, having lost him as a client during the CBS raids on NBC, had been encouraged about recapturing him when Burns bought the Bob Cummings show over MCA's protest. The Morris people now came to him with an idea that they hoped might win him back.

It was not their idea, but the brainchild of a successful comedy writer named Irving Brecher. The notion was a television series to be called *The People's Choice*.

The Morris agency, hoping to lure Burns back, insisted that Brecher needed a producer to put up $27,000 for a pilot episode.

"But I don't *need* a partner," Brecher told them. "I've got the $27,000."

That was when the pressure was applied. As he remembered it, "The Morris people told me I had to have a partner and it had to be Burns."

George was behind his desk at General Service Studios and his brother Willie was seated in the corner of the office when Brecher walked in with the Morris representative. Brecher and Burns knew each other from Hillcrest. George tilted back in his desk chair, folded his arms behind his head, and said, "I hope we can do something together. What do you have in mind?"

"I've got this idea for a series," Irving said. "It's called 'The People's Choice.' The title won't mean anything until I tell you something about it."

Burns said, "Well, give me some idea."

"In the pilot," Brecher said, "Sock Miller is the name of the character. He's working for the National Bureau of Wild Life. He works in the woods, looking after the interests of wildlife, particularly birds.

"As he walks through the woods, he's followed by a dog with long ears—a basset hound. He stops at a tree and he carves a heart into it, with initials.

"And the dog looks at it and says—"

Burns interrupted, "The dog *says*?"

Brecher says, "That's right."

Burns turned to Willie and said, "Give him the money."

While Brecher would sourly observe that "it only cost Burns $27,000 to get half of my show and he made $500,000 on it," he also had to admit, "at that time, it was unusual for a star to have his own production company. On his own show, he supervised the writing and he was the boss of the show. It didn't take any genius to figure out that if you had an organization, it would be possible to do other shows with that same organization."

The genius part was figuring it out so early in the television game. Burns was the genius who had done that, first with *Love That Bob* and now with *The People's Choice.* George would let Brecher run his own show as producer/writer.

"Once in a while," an elderly and grouchy Brecher remembered, "I'd ask George to come in and watch a run-through to make a comment or suggestion. He was an easy partner, he was happy with our arrangement."

Burns's version of his contribution as a producer on *The People's Choice* was, naturally, a little different, and, naturally, funnier. "I would read a script," he said, "and know something's wrong. But I don't know how to fix it. So I go out to Hillcrest, I wander around the clubhouse until I spot some $250,000 comedy writer.

"I tell him the story. I say it's great. He looks at me like I've got two heads. To show how smart he is, he points out how it can be fixed. Now I've got $250,000 worth of comedy brains for nothing. I go back to the office and call Irv Brecher. I tell him how to fix his script, but I don't say where I got my ideas. And everybody tells everybody what a genius I am."

Not Brecher. He was friendly with Burns for the next forty years, but the sharing of profits obviously still rankled him.

As for Burns's description of the whole experience, as Paul Henning said, "When George starts to talk, it is virtually impossible to know whether he is engaging you in conversation, polishing a routine, or writing a letter."

Burns subsequently produced a series called *Mr. Ed* that, being about a talking horse, was just a little similar to *The People's Choice.* Comparing the two, the unremittingly bitter Brecher said, "In *The People's Choice,* the dog was thinking out loud. But his mouth didn't move. When McCadden did *Mr. Ed,* copping my original idea, they had the horse's mouth moving through trick photography—they wired the horse's lips. They semi-electrocuted the horse."

Not electrocuted, but bad enough. A nylon fish line was sewn through the horse's upper lips and then yanked from ten feet away by his trainer/persecutor, who was standing out of camera range. When the horse was supposed to be talking, the line was jerked. That irritated the lip and the horse would move his mouth.

Mr. Ed was yet another hit series. The McCadden office and its production facility at General Studios became a busy place, although George and Willie could always find time to dash over to the old office in the Hollywood Plaza Hotel. Those adjoining rooms were now used strictly for fun, and looking alike as the Burns brothers did, medium tall and wiry, with glasses hooked onto their big ears, they seemed like a couple of impish twins.

There was one new distinction. While George's idea of fun was still female, Willie was becoming more and more interested in booze.

It was amazing that Burns even had the time for play. In addition to performing on his own show, which was how the public knew him, Rod Amateau remembered that during production of *Love That Bob,* George would "sit in, walk out, take phone calls, have meetings, come back, go out to lunch."

McCadden Productions was thriving—and he supplied its energy. Once again, Burns was a success at what he was doing, a smash as a single everywhere but on the stage. He insisted that he did not especially enjoy being a businessman. There were no laughs, there was no foolishness. Business was business, it wasn't show business.

The slender, sandy-haired, rosy-cheeked, thirty-two-year-old Rod Amateau took advantage of one day's break at the Cummings show to stop in at the Burns and Allen writers' room.

As he said, "When you're sitting with those guys, you start pitching because it's fun."

It has often been observed that comedy writers are a strange lot, ranging from the eccentric to the downright extraterrestrial. For instance, one of the fellows on the Burns and Allen team, Norman Paul, always worked while stretched out on a couch. He claimed he was under doctor's orders because he had a heart condition.

"If they didn't accept his material," Amateau said, "Norman would roll over and turn toward the wall."

The new chief writer, Harvey Helm, whispered when he spoke, presumably so that everyone would have to keep quiet. And around the table, nobody ever laughed, whatever the idea and however funny the joke.

"It was a badge of weakness to laugh," Amateau remembered. "If you laughed, you were a schmuck. If everyone thought something was funny, they would smile, nod, and pound the table with their fists.

"But they wouldn't laugh."

As he stepped into "The Room," as all comedy writers' rooms were called, he found everything normal. "All the writers are yelling and screaming—except Harvey, who whispers."

While Burns came and went, the men followed the usual process, tossing ideas back and forth until somebody came up with something viable. Somebody finally did. A California state trooper, a motorcycle policeman, would give Gracie a traffic ticket. Then the other characters in the series, Blanche and Harry Morton (Bea Benadaret and Fred Clark, who had replaced Hal March) and the announcer Harry Von Zell (who had replaced Bill Goodwin), would come to her rescue. They all knew, Amateau said, "that Gracie was an angel, a confused angel."

Amateau was the rare person who saw the real Gracie Allen in the performing one. "There was no separating them. She is the most lovely angel that I've ever known— but *very vague*."

While the writers explored the comic possibilities of the exchange between the state trooper and Gracie as he asked for her driver's license and car registration, the secretary, Tommy Clapp, typed up whatever was considered good enough to save.

As the sequence was developing, Willie Burns said, "Wait a minute, guys. Is this cop being mean to Gracie?"

Amateau respected what Willie had to say, even if George didn't always seem to. "He was a man whose talent could have made him successful in his own right."

As Willie spoke, George stepped into the writers' room. "How's the show going, fellas?"

"It kind of sounds," Willie said, "as if the motorcycle cop is being mean to Gracie."

George snapped, "Mean to Gracie? Mean to Gracie? Who's playing that cop?"

Amateau said James Flavin, who was a busy television actor.

"Fuck him!" George said, "We'll never use him again."

Burns was serious about that. He looked around the room to make sure everybody understood what he had just said. But instead of being cowed, all of the writers were laughing. Then, realizing that he had been reacting to only a story, a sheepish George began to laugh along with them.

Young Amateau found the moment "so illuminating, how protective he was of her."

That was a professional as well as a personal protectiveness. Burns never forgot any lessons, certainly not about the Burns and Allen act. The act was at the core of his being, and a basic rule of the act was that the audience does not want to see Gracie threatened or hurt. He was not about to change the rule now. It was probably the only area in which he did not have a sense of humor.

Fred De Cordova left the show in 1954, for a more lucrative assignment with a series called *December Bride.*

"I've done a lot of big shows with a lot of big stars," he later said, "but I don't think I was ever as happy in television as I was in the George and Gracie era."

Before Rod Amateau was brought over from *Love That Bob* to succeed De Cordova, Googie again brought up the subject of retiring. She pleaded that she was exhausted. "She didn't have that same drive," De Cordova said, "that George did."

Paul Henning believed, "She was only doing the show to please him."

Henning's wife Ruth said, "She wasn't well but she was the only one who knew it."

"You couldn't tell from watching her," Paul added, "because she was so bubbly."

Natty again talked her into doing just one more season, and it seemed plain to Paul Henning that "George didn't think he had a career without Gracie."

Had he known the real state of Googie's health, it seems fair to say that he would never have talked her into working another season. Nobody who knew him doubted that, even though nobody who knew him doubted that he was afraid that she was the one who made the act work.

As they were lying on her bed one night watching television, Googie suddenly turned and said, "You know, Natty. The nicest thing you've ever done for me is that you never said anything about my bad arm."

Her migraine headaches, which couldn't get any worse, were getting worse. Sometimes it seemed as if she were actually willing to die for him.

13

If anyone had stopped to think about it, the role that Burns played on *The George Burns and Gracie Allen Show* was a rather odd one. He was simultaneously within and outside the show's reality. He was a character in the series but he was also the audience's surrogate, its interpreter and guide. In the French theatre, that is called a *compère,* but this was not esoteric. Rather, it was an extension of his role in their vaudeville act.

Rod Amateau thought of this as an observer's role. "It was a commentator's style. He commented on the show as if he were floating above it."

For instance, he would overhear Gracie in the other room and talk about it to the home audience. Then he would walk back into the living room and be part of the story. He interpreted Gracie for the audience, so that they might grasp what he perceived as being funny about her.

Then an idea came up. One Sunday morning, as he and Amateau sat beside his swimming pool, going over the next week's script, the director said, "Too bad you can't have one of those television sets on the show like they have in the department stores—where they watch for shoplifters."

Burns looked up and asked, "Why not?"

So they began to work out a magic television set that would be in George's den. Within weeks, he would be explaining this device to the viewers: He could now do more than overhear Gracie; he could watch her, too, wherever she was and whatever she was doing.

The psychological implications are self-evident—control, jealousy, and possessiveness, not to mention paranoia and simple snooping. But the era of psychological interpretation still lay ahead, and so this seemed like nothing more than a funny idea and, at worst, a benign paternalism.

One episode suggested, however, that Burns had anticipated a grimmer analysis. The episode was based, Amateau recalled, "on Gracie overspending on dresses, which she did in real life. And she's worried that George is going to land on her, so her friend Blanche [Bea Benadaret] comes up with a great idea:

" 'Why don't you tell him that you've been going to see a psychologist to cure you from overspending? And you've been paying his fee and that's where the money went. George'll buy that in a minute.'

"But," Amateau continued, "George is watching and strings her along. 'She thinks she's going to fool me,' he tells the home audience. 'It didn't work in vaudeville and it won't work now.' "

At the end of the episode, a psychologist unexpectedly turns up at the house. About the magic television set, he tells George, "I've been watching the show and I don't like what you're doing." It was as if Burns was one step ahead of criticism that had not yet been leveled. His mind was often one step ahead.

As an actress, Gracie was generally easygoing, although on one occasion she did get upset. Amateau had called for a "number two close-up," meaning the use of a two-inch lens, but the cameraman mistakenly screwed in a three-inch lens. As a result, the close-up was unusually tight. "At the collarbone," Amateau remembered.

When they screened the episode the following day for audience reaction, Gracie responded sharply as the full face close-up flashed on the screen. The director, sitting in front of her, heard that sudden, deep intake of breath. When Sandra Burns, sitting next to him, nudged him sharply with her elbow, he was positive that something was wrong. After the screening, Gracie simply said to him, "Rod Amateau, I'm going to have to have a talk with you. You come to breakfast tomorrow morning."

The relationship between Amateau and Gracie, always cordial, had become more than that when he began a romance with her daughter, now separated from Jim Wilhoite. Although Sandra had two small children, she had enrolled at UCLA.

When Rod called her that night, Sandy said, "Mom's mad. She trusts you so much."

"But Sandy," Rod said, "I would lay down my life for her."

"Just tell her you'll never do it again."

By the time he arrived at the house the next morning, he'd learned what had upset Gracie. She was afraid that the close-up had revealed her colorless eye, the one she had hurt in the childhood accident with hot kerosene oil. Amateau had already reshot the close-up and spliced the new shot into the show. He knew that while "Gracie wasn't sensitive about many things, she was touchy about her eye."

At the front door, he was greeted by the houseman, a Dane named Ovi, whose wife Adi was the cook.

"What's the climate, Ovi?" he asked.

"Threatening rain," the houseman replied.

Rod started to laugh, but Gracie was already coming down the stairs.

"Rod Amateau, is that you?" she said.

"Hello, Gracie."

"Rod Amateau, I want to talk to you."

As he remembered, she was wearing "a little pink house-coat, pink fuzzy slippers, and a headband. She had high color and her little eyes were dancing."

She started again. "Rod Amateau, I have to—"

He interrupted.

"Before you say anything—in that little housecoat, with those slippers and that headband and those cheeks, I could eat you up. You're so beautiful, and I mean it, Gracie."

He did mean it, too. ("I wasn't trying to butter her up.")

"But let's get on with it," he said to her. "What is it you wanted to say?"

She smiled as she looked up at him from her height of five-feet-in-fuzzy-slippers. "Never mind what I wanted to say," she said. "Go on with what you were saying."

Ultimately, she did get around to the subject of her eye and the close-up. By then, they were all seated at the breakfast table—George, Gracie, and Rod. When they finished eating, Gracie turned to the matter at hand while George opened *The Hollywood Reporter* and glanced through it. He seemed to be engrossed in the show business newspaper.

"What was it that went wrong, Rod?" she asked.

He did not say it was a simple cameraman's mistake, for fear of jeopardizing the man's job. Instead, he presented an analogy.

"Do you remember that great German cameraman who used to work for us?"

She nodded.

"You know, he photographed Marlene Dietrich when she made *The Garden of Allah*. And twenty years later he photographed her in *Rancho Notorious.* "

"She's a beautiful girl," Gracie said.

"Yes," Amateau continued, "but Dietrich said to him, 'I

can't understand what happened between those two pictures. I looked so nice in *Garden of Allah*. What happened to you?'

"The cameraman said to her, 'Marlene, darling, my camera's twenty years older.' "

Having listened raptly to this story, Gracie responded, "Well, he should be responsible for that. He should get a new camera."

This prompted George to look up from the newspaper. Glancing over to Amateau, he rolled his eyes toward the ceiling. Then he went back to the paper.

"Gracie," Rod said, "it isn't a question of the camera. You know, Walter Huston sings 'September Song,' about the days growing short to a precious few."

"Oh, that's a very classy act," Gracie said. "I do notice that the days grow short when you reach September and October and November. Sometimes I get up a little late, and by the time I have breakfast and make a couple of calls and go shopping, it's almost dark. But it all evens up in the springtime."

Amateau turned to George, if not for help then at least for sympathy, but Burns just stared straight into the middle of his newspaper as if there was something irresistibly interesting there.

Then Ronnie came bounding down the stairs and Gracie asked where he was going. To the beach, he said.

"Have some breakfast first. Sit down and talk with us. Rod and I are talking about September, October, and November."

"Right, Mom. That sounds great. But I've got to be going."

"And," Amateau said, "he ran like his hat was on fire."

It was because of such conversations as these that Amateau thought Gracie was an angel, only a little vague. In fact, he was convinced that George had taken the act from the way she really was, despite popular opinion to the contrary.

• • •

One very big party the Burnses hosted was given not at home but at Mike Romanoff's restaurant, which they took over for the night. Paul Henning's wife Ruth "just sat along the wall goggle-eyed, watching all the movie stars. Every star I ever knew of was there and the one who impressed me the most was Lauren Bacall—she was so classy."

Bacall did not impress herself. She believed that she was accepted among the Hollywood elite only because her husband was Humphrey Bogart. ("I wasn't a legend, I was just married to one.") And, she said, as a couple they were not part of the intimate dinner set. "We were just invited to the big parties."

She knew about Edith Goetz and the "A" list. "I was not in that inner circle," she said drily.

As she sat down at the restaurant bar, George was regaling the party with songs and anecdotes. Then Gracie came and sat on the bar stool next to her.

"Gracie was never 'on,' " Bacall remembered. "She wasn't what I would call an 'active personality.' And she wasn't stylish. That didn't seem to interest her."

Of course, "stylish" meant something quite different to Gracie Allen than to Lauren Bacall, who had been a successful model before going to Hollywood.

"She was just a sweet woman," Bacall said. "A very simple, charming kind of warm woman."

Gracie turned to Bacall, and as she watched her husband performing, she started to talk about how hard it was for her to get up in front of an audience the way Natty did. Then she sat back and enjoyed him as he entertained the crowd.

"She just *laugh*ed. How many times would you imagine she'd heard that stuff? But she never got tired of hearing it. She just adored him. She laughed as if she was hearing everything for the first time. She was his best audience. She wanted everybody to appreciate her George.

"She was just crazy about him."

Bacall was another one who appreciated the Benny-Burns friendship. "The minute George opened his mouth, Jack fell down on the floor laughing." Interestingly enough, she felt that "Jack wasn't the perfect fellow. He probably had more frailties than George had."

If he could be difficult to live with, which seemed to be her allusion, he also seemed aware of it. When a woman friend of his referred to his wife's tough reputation, saying, "I'm not like Mary," Jack replied, "If you were married to me you would be just like her."

He certainly was a more complicated personality than Nat, but even when he was baffling he was wonderful. Earlier in the evening, Rod Amateau had been standing at the same bar when Jack strolled over.

"How've you been, Rod?"

"Fine, fine, fine," the usually affable director said, but he was not feeling particularly voluble that evening. There was a lull in the conversation.

Jack looked at him a moment. As Rod remembered it, "There just was nothing to talk about. I was feeling uncommunicative and he was not exactly a brilliant conversationalist."

Then Benny asked the bartender for a glass of cold water. When it was brought to him, he drank half of the glass and looked at it. "Very good," he said.

"The water?" Amateau asked.

"You know," Jack said, "it's practically impossible to get a good glass of water nowadays."

"Regular water?"

"Well, that's the thing," Benny said. "You know, sometimes there's too much ice in it. And then it's too cold. And sometimes there isn't enough ice in it. And then it isn't cold enough."

"Right," Amateau said.

Benny wasn't finished.

"But a good glass of water. Like this glass," and he took a sip, "well, it's just right. Do you know what I mean?"

Amateau had to shake his head in befuddlement. He was convinced that Benny was not trying to be funny. "It's like Gracie talking about Dietrich's cinematographer getting a new camera, or about the days getting longer in September, October, and November. It isn't a comedy routine. That's the way their minds work."

Burns made Amateau repeatedly tell him about this encounter with Benny, just to laugh over it.

Meantime, as Benay Venuta observed, Mary Livingstone sat at a table with Edie Goetz and Danny Kaye's wife, Sylvia Fine, watching as Bacall talked to Gracie. "Edie Goetz would jump all over Bacall," Venuta remembered. " 'Oh, did you see her? She had three drinks!'

"They were the social leaders, Sylvia Fine and Mary Livingstone and especially Edie Goetz, who was the bitch of all time."

Venuta's ex-husband, the movie producer Armand Deutsch, had come to the party with Jack and Mary, as well as with Barbara Stanwyck and Robert Taylor. In the backseat of their limousine, the women were talking about a grand party to which they were going. Mary leaned forward and tapped Deutsch on the shoulder as he sat on the jump seat. "Ardie," she said, "I'm going to get you invited."

It wasn't every party that was grand enough for Mary Livingstone. She had boasted to Deutsch, "If I had a tooth pulled as an excuse for every time I wanted to back out of a dinner party, I wouldn't have a tooth in my head."

And so this party, to which she was going to get him invited, was sure to be something important.

"I refuse to go," he said.

"What do you mean?" Mary asked.

"I don't go to parties where I get a secondhand invitation."

Jack was in the front seat, sitting next to the driver. He

turned around and, almost bouncing with glee, he cried, "Don't go! Don't go! Don't go!"

That was Jack Benny in a rare moment of rebellion.

The Carnation Milk Company, which sponsored *The George Burns and Gracie Allen Show,* was presenting its two stars in magazine advertisements as "Carnation's Contented Couple." And because the product was supposed to be dietetic, Gracie made commercials standing on a scale holding up a can of the evaporated milk.

Carnation's advertising agency representative, Charles Lowe, said, "She looked young and vigorous and happy." But she was not that vigorous. Early in the spring of 1958, she suffered a severe, crunching, and prolonged series of chest pains.

The doctor visits began, the rounds of specialists and the repeated tests. She was finally diagnosed as having suffered a mild heart attack. "In those days," Burns's nephew, Lou Weiss, said, "There were no angiograms, there were no heart bypass operations. The advice the cardiologists gave my aunt was to stop working."

The issue was no longer that Gracie wanted a different life. Migraine headaches might have been tolerable, but the situation was now life-threatening. George was finally convinced that Gracie had to retire.

She was given a prescription for nitroglycerine tablets and was told to stay in bed as much as possible. George hired a live-in nurse. Finally, he had the office announce that *The George Burns and Gracie Allen Show* would go off the air at the end of the season.

It certainly seems as if he had been avoiding and delaying this decision for years, fearful of losing the act that was his life. In some part of him, he had surely pretended that Gracie was not as unhappy or as uncomfortable as she had been saying. It is likely that he was afraid he would now be proved without talent, which is the most common fear of creative people. George Burns had more reason than most to dread the truth of that. "If it hadn't been for Gracie," he told a newspaper interviewer, "I'd still be a small-time comedian."

The rest of that thought had unspoken resonance: without Gracie, that's what he would be again.

If he had jeopardized Googie's health because of these fears, it seems fair to say that he had not done it consciously. On June 4, 1958, Carnation's Contented Couple filmed the 299th and final episode of *The George Burns and Gracie Allen Show.* It was the last time they ever worked together.

14

After Gracie quit performing, George Burns joked that he wasn't going to retire from show business because "I was retired when I worked with Gracie." He realized that most people thought the funny partner was the star and the straight man did nothing but repeat lines and ask questions. Burns openly agreed with that. "Gracie's talent was on the stage," he said. "My talent was off the stage."

Well now it looked as if he wasn't a straight man anymore, just as he was no longer part of a team. He was half of an act, the wrong half. To become whole, he would have to become a one-man act, a single, which was something he had never even tried. Even a dog or a seal had been preferable to being entirely alone on stage. And he would also have to become funny, not at the Round Table at Hillcrest, but in front of an audience.

Like someone hit by a car who immediately tries to get up and walk away, the first thing he did was act as if nothing had happened. He tried to do the television series without Gracie. It became *The George Burns Show,* broadcast in the same spot (nine o'clock on Tuesdays), and on the same station (NBC). He kept Ronnie in the series and

Rod Amateau was again the director. The premise of the first episode was a funnied-up version of the truth, like all Burns material. Its premise was: "What will George do now that Gracie's retired?"

If the show represented the answer, it wasn't good enough. Even he admitted that everyone kept waiting for Gracie to walk through the door. But she was at home experiencing sporadic heart flutters. There were two nurses now, and she was in bed most of the time.

Variety noted that the show was "not enough for a strong tee-off for Burns as a single." Jack Benny had been the guest star on that first episode, and a newspaper interviewer asked him, "Can George do it alone?" Jack replied, "Of course he can. That's why I'll be on his show next week."

The George Burns Show was canceled after a single season, leaving Burns "convinced," Amateau said, "that his comedy persona, his style of humor—a smart aleck know-it-all—was not appealing to the public."

At sixty-two, he was close to retirement age. He had more money than he could ever spend, and McCadden Productions was an ongoing, lucrative enterprise. Yet instead of feeling fulfilled after a successful career, instead of being ready to go out and enjoy his new leisure, he felt like a failure.

"Why don't you retire, Uncle?" Lou Weiss asked. Lou was his favorite nephew, and George was proud that his sister Sarah's son had, independently of him, risen from the mailroom to become the chairman of the board of the William Morris Agency.

"What would I do?" Burns asked.

"You could relax," Weiss said. "You could travel."

"That's only good," his uncle glumly replied, "if you've got something to take a vacation from."

As George said it, "Here I was at the bottom again,"

which was a strange thing for a famous and wealthy television star to say.

Square one was exactly where he was, but not the bottom; he could hardly have realized that in a very different and exciting sense, he was just getting started.

The television series having failed, his only remaining option was to become a comedian. Perhaps it was not unprecedented for a straight man to survive a team break-up—Dean Martin had just done it—but Burns certainly did not impress Lou Weiss with his confidence. "I don't think my uncle ever perceived himself as a major monologist away from Gracie."

To succeed, he would have to unlearn thirty years of doing a double act, thirty years of feeding straight lines, thirty years of an essentially vaudeville style of comedy. And there was another kind of act he would have to develop. A person's "act" was a metaphor for his life, and "getting your act together" was a colloquialism for pulling up one's socks and coping. Burns was going to have to get that act together as well.

His first booking as a solo comedian was set for mid-summer of 1959 at the Sahara Hotel in Las Vegas. He arranged for a shakedown engagement in June at Harrah's in Lake Tahoe, Nevada. This was not even a hotel, but a gambling casino and show room. The owner, as Ronnie recalled, "kept a motel and a swimming pool next door for his personal guests and the performers."

George went to work on the monologue with his chief writer, Harvey Helm, and his brother Willie. Once it was written, he started to learn it. "He would always practice," Ronnie remembered, "even when he was driving. You'd see him doing it. He always rehearsed. When we drove to Palm Springs I would sometimes answer him like a dodo, because I thought he was talking to me when he was practicing his routine."

A star comes with an opening act. "I didn't take any chances," Burns remembered. "I took Bobby Darin with me, and the De Castro Sisters," who were a singing trio. In addition, he brought a dance team.

He had discovered Darin singing "Mack the Knife" on the Ed Sullivan Show, and telephoned Willie immediately. "Grab him. I don't care what you do. Grab him."

Burns doted on Darin. A new friend, a William Morris agent named Barry Mirkin, said, "Singing was very important to George. He loved singers. If you mentioned actors, he wouldn't know what you were talking about. He wasn't interested in the new generation of comedians. But he was always ready to listen to singers and talk about them."

He was right about Bobby Darin. This was a young man with a bright talent, but he had a dark future, for ahead lay great success and early death.

The opening-night audience at Harrah's was a convention of prison wardens, not a promising group. Of course Gracie, Ronnie, and Sandy were there, along with Jack and Mary. After the band played the Burns and Allen theme music ("The Love Nest"), Nat walked out to the microphone. He looked elegant in his splendidly tailored tuxedo. On his left ring finger he wore the unique "cat's eye" ring that Gracie had given him for good luck.

"Ladies and gentlemen," he said, "this is the first time I ever played a nightclub and I hate people who come out and say they're nervous . . . but I am."

An hour later, he was back in the dressing room, sponging off his makeup and perspiration while looking into the mirror as Jack and Mary told him how wonderful he'd been. Later, when Gracie was alone with him, she was constructively critical. As Burns recalled in *Gracie: A Love Story,* she apologized if she was hurting his feelings but said that he had seemed over-rehearsed. His old songs were charming, she said, but the monologue sounded memorized. Of course it was memorized, but it wasn't supposed to *sound* memorized.

He knew she was right, but it did not elate him. She followed it up with suggestions that he relax and simply do what he did at his sociables: tell his stories, smoke his cigar, and sing the old songs. "That girl knew what she was talking about," Burns remembered. Now, all he had to do was rehearse looking relaxed.

At the Sahara Hotel in Las Vegas the following month, he "was nervous. I was drinking a lot." But that memory was revised into comedy material. "I set up two glasses backstage, one with sand for my soft shoe and the other with Scotch. Reaching for a drink, I gulped down the sand."

The problem was his sense of humor. As Milton Berle put it, "His sense of humor was so wry and dry—so different, so special—you never knew whether he was being funny and when he wasn't . . . Show people would get it, but it wasn't commercial. It was all non sequitur and tongue-in-cheek."

Burns knew that he could not use such humor in his act. "That was his private sense of humor," Berle said. "He would never do that in public."

The first dictum of a professional entertainer is that the audience is always right. As Burns put it, "If you've got material that you think is funny but the audience doesn't, you don't use it again." His thesis, as he told his old television director Rod Amateau, was that "an audience is as brilliant as the sum of its parts. You can fool an audience of one or two a lot easier than you can fool a hundred people. A hundred people are a hundred times as smart.

"And if an act is *too* smart for the audience, that means it isn't funny."

There was another problem with his act, a psychological problem. Gracie was always sitting at a table and watching; he always introduced her from the stage. It kept him from being a solo act, and a solo was something he seemed to both want and be afraid of. With Gracie in the audience, they were still "Burns and Allen," even if she wasn't performing.

When he introduced her to the audience, "Gracie got more applause for showing up than I got for doing my whole act." Was there a trace of bitterness in this bit of modesty?

He attracted no more than satisfactory business in Las Vegas.

In the fall of 1959, he began preparing a television special, *George Burns in the Big Time,* which NBC scheduled for November. The theme of the show was vaudeville and the guest stars were Jack, Eddie Cantor, and George Jessel. There was a striking difference between Burns and Benny, who had transcended vaudeville, and Cantor and Jessel, who were still of it. George and Jack were dry and mellow, while Cantor and Jessel were as subtle as the black dye on their hair.

The four veterans reminisced while recreating some of the old routines. Burns sang "Syncopation Rules the Nation" and "Tiger Girl." It was an hour with almost as much nostalgia as it aimed for, and at the end, it reached a geniune high point—and yet, a high point with a nagging question.

George looked into the camera and said, "You know, this wasn't easy for me tonight. For many years, Gracie was always right there beside me. Seems strange to be out here alone."

Gracie spoke up, as if heard by the audience but not by him. She had become the one with the magic television set: she was now able to watch him the way he used to watch her.

"He's not alone," her disembodied voice said. "He's never alone. With those six beautiful girls on the show, I'm home watching him."

He continued, "It even feels strange to be making an

entrance alone and not hear Gracie say, 'George, are my lips on straight?' "

"Now," Gracie said, still talking in a voiceover, "George has the last laugh on the critics." She was getting dangerously close to truth. "They always said he was no comedian. But now that he's working alone, he's got a chance to prove it."

"And I never could retire," he continued. "I wouldn't know what to do with myself."

"Oh," Gracie pouted, "I wish I'd seen him when he was with the Peewee Quartet. Imagine an eight-year-old boy with a head of blond curls smoking a cigar!"

George continued on the subject of retirement. "At my age? I couldn't start fishing and playing golf. I'm too old to retire."

"Too old?" she repeated. "Why, he's got years and years of retirement left in him."

The laughs were hers as always. "I could never retire now," he said. "Here I am getting all of these laughs and I'm not even saying anything funny. Must be my—my—my delivery" (as he exaggerated his stammer).

"This would be a good time to get off," Gracie advised. "You'd always say, don't stay on too long. Always leave them wanting a little more."

She reversed the procedure. "Say good night, George."

It was the sweetest part of the show.

"Good night."

From a distance it seems plain that George could still not let go of her, and still depended on her to get the laughs. At this rate, he would never become a solo act, but there were signs that he had better, because Gracie was starting to faint in public.

The times were not cheerful. Friends were beginning to die off. In 1959 it was Benny Fields, and that left Blossom Seeley in money trouble. She tried to find work, but there wasn't much of a demand for a seventyish singer whose style was undiluted vaudeville. George started to send her monthly checks.

He tried to create another team for himself. "He was looking for another Gracie," his former production chief, Herb Browar, said. "Some young girl to take Gracie's part." He found an actress named Connie Stevens and they did one season of a series called *Wendy and Me*. It flopped.

He worked with other partners who could make him whole again in a nightclub act and part of a team once more. It was a little like happily married people who remarry soon after their spouse's death. That does not give their marital love the lie. They simply are people who enjoy marriage.

He landed somewhere between being a single act and a double. He would start with a short monologue, then he would sing a few songs. His actress-partner would have a few songs of her own. Then they would do some of the old Burns and Allen material. He tried this with Madeline Kahn, Bernadette Peters, and Ann-Margret. But, Lou Weiss said, "none of them was ever Gracie. Gracie was Gracie."

The most enjoyable of these experiences was with the bright and unique actress Carol Channing. She had married Charles Lowe, who once had represented Burns's television sponsor, Carnation Milk, and now managed her. Charlie Lowe had become a personal friend.

Channing was by then a Broadway star, but musicals were unpredictable ventures and more money could be made elsewhere. Lowe conceived a concert-style show for Carol, of the kind that Judy Garland and Danny Kaye had made popular. These were like vaudeville shows except that they played long engagements, toured across the country, and charged theatre prices.

Channing was not as great an attraction as Judy Garland or Danny Kaye, and her husband decided that Burns would make an ideal co-star. He was not a box-office attraction by himself either, and that was a fact he had to face.

Burns took care of staging *The George Burns–Carol Channing Show,* and their first booking was at the 1962 World's Fair in Seattle. The tour lasted for fourteen weeks, and toward the end of each show, Carol and George would appear onstage together to play some old Burns and Allen material. "It was so durable and so fundamentally logical in its humor," she recalled, "that people thought he'd written it for me. Yet he wrote it for a unique train of thought. Only a certain type of human being would think that way.

"As long as your feet aren't on the ground," she said, "it works."

Performing with and being directed by George Burns taught Carol what Gracie already knew. "He gave me the best moves and the best things to say. He had more sex appeal than anyone I ever worked with because he took *charge* of me, and I was feminine—a total female—in his hands. He turned me any which way he wanted to and I went there."

Not much later, when Carol opened her own engagement at the Tropicana Hotel in Las Vegas, George and Gracie brought along a glittering contingent of Hollywood friends. Carol remembered being warned backstage, "When you name the people who are sitting there, and introduce Gracie and George and Jack Benny, for God's sake don't forget Mary Livingstone."

Of course, as soon as the curtain plummeted down, Channing realized that she had forgotten to acknowledge Mary.

"That was a 'guillotine' curtain," she recalled, "it had a heavy rod on the bottom. But the people hadn't gone out yet, they were still applauding. I had to pick up that heavy rod, I pushed it up with my shoulders, got my head out like a turtle, and said, 'Sorry, I forgot to tell you—Mary Livingstone is sitting right over there.' "

She pointed to Mary, the audience applauded, and she ducked back under the curtain.

Afterward, when people came back to visit and congratulate, Gracie whispered, "I was so frightened that you were going to forget Mary. It would have wrecked the whole night."

And so now Channing was doing her own act while George was still trying to find a working partner. Nor would she remain in nightclub work for long. She was basically a stage actress and just ahead was a Broadway show—*Hello, Dolly!*—that was going to provide her with a fair success.

George, meantime, was looking backward, trying and failing to relive the past by giving Gracie's lines to somebody else. Smart as he was, he did not yet realize the futility of trying.

"Only Gracie could read those lines," was Rod Amateau's conviction. "You've got to believe those lines or the audience senses fraud. . . . It's got to be absolutely honest. If you don't mean it, if you try to be a naif and you're not, the audience will look right into your fucking heart and know it."

While it was probably rewarding for George Burns to perform in front of live audiences again, he had to recognize that there was a difference between a vaudeville show and a nightclub appearance. Audiences in the clubs expected risqué material, which vaudevillians considered the last resort of a second-rater. Nightclubs also served liquor, which brought out the loudmouths and the wiseguys. There were hecklers in vaudeville, but not like the ones he encountered now. For the first time, Burns had to deal with them. His approach was benign rather than cutting. A puff on his cigar gave him time, and his natural stammer became pronounced, a sign that his mind was racing ahead of his mouth. By then, he came up with a phrase to silence the noise-maker without being abusive.

"I try to be nice to them. After all," he said, "they did come and pay to see me."

In the early 1960s, he played an engagement in Vancouver. It called for two performances, one at ten o'clock and a late show at midnight. At that time, a local Sunday blue law went into effect, prohibiting the sale of alcoholic beverages. To prepare for the calamity, the audience all too literally loaded up on drinks at a quarter to twelve.

"By the time I came out," Burns said, "everybody was stoned."

As he began his monologue, voices cried out to him. To his relief, they were friendly.

"Hey George, how's Gracie doing?"

"What's she doing now that she's retired?"

"Tell us about the kids, George."

As he remembered, "I couldn't get into my act. I couldn't say, 'Shut up,' because these were people who liked me, and they liked my family."

He smiled and puffed on his cigar while the outcry persisted. When it became relatively quiet, he began:

"Let me tell you something. You people out there seem to be having a great time. You really don't want me to sing a couple of songs. Supposing I come out into the audience and join you. And forget my songs."

The response was rousing. "They roared and applauded, so I came out across the footlights and got drunk with all the people."

Even so, it was a strain to play to such audiences and, too, there wasn't enough of this kind of work to keep a performer busy. There were long gaps between lucrative engagements at clubs, state fairs, and conventions. In short, personal appearances were not an option unless he was willing to travel constantly and play in smaller clubs.

This left him unoccupied as a performer; at the same time, he was selling his production company. Attorney General Robert F. Kennedy had overseen an antitrust action that left the entertainment giant MCA to choose between personal management and production. Having chosen the latter, MCA was expanding by buying out smaller producers like Burns's own McCadden company. This sale provided George and Gracie with a considerable fortune. Unfortunately, making him wealthier was the only thing it accomplished, and he didn't need that. They were already secure and money never meant very much to him. He seemed to take a literal approach to working, defining it as "functioning," and money was merely a measure of how much his work was valued.

George tried to keep busy with make-work. He structured his days, going to the office each morning and the club in the afternoon. He hadn't gotten out of production entirely. He took space at Warner Brothers, where he produced the successful series *No Time for Sergeants* with Andy Griffith.

At dusk, he would come home to a martini. After dinner, he and Gracie, whose angina was worsening, spent the evening watching television. Fridays he still went to the fights with Jack—or said he did. Since Benny now had a regular girlfriend, the television singer Gisele MacKenzie, he was seldom at the Friday fights himself.

In the middle of a Thursday night in August 1964, Googie suffered a heart attack. Natty called for the ambulance and later told Sandy that he sat alongside her mother on the sirened ride to the hospital. Just after dawn on August 27, Gracie Allen was dead. She was fifty-eight years old.

It still was dark when Natty telephoned the news to Jack in Lake Tahoe, where he was performing. Benny woke Mary up and roused his daughter, Joan. He hired a limousine and by dawn they were on their way back to Los Angeles. Jack's agent, Irving Fein, canceled the balance of the engagement.

"We must have gotten to George's house at five in the morning," Joan remembers. "And we just camped there. My father moved in for the duration."

The next morning, an eerie spectacle of grief began, a "*shiva*/wake," as one of the participants put it. It was, Joan Benny said, "like a show business happening." Friends of

George and Gracie, from all parts of the entertainment world, arrived at 720 North Maple to gather in the living room, in the kitchen, near the pool, and out on the front lawn. Food and liquor were delivered continuously and Joan Benny made the cheesecake herself.

George's next-door neighbors, Larry and Leah Superstein, watched from the other side of the hedge that divided their homes. "It was kind of a hysterical atmosphere," Leah said. "Those people were saddened and funny at the same time."

The large contingent of comedians who came to honor and mourn Gracie put on a show without intermissions, while Nat remained sequestered upstairs. He kept to his bedroom with Ronnie and Sandy, and his sister Goldie. Gracie's last remaining sister, Bessie, was in a nursing home.

Downstairs, the pandemonium persisted. The house was filled to overflow, and the party lasted through the night, into Saturday and Sunday. Gracie wasn't being buried until Monday, and only on Sunday evening did George finally emerge from his seclusion.

He slipped down the stairs and into the library, and it was from there that he emerged, a curious sight without his toupee. Few had ever seen him bald-headed and some didn't even recognize him.

He strode into the throng, heading straight for Carol Channing and Charles Lowe. They had just arrived from New York on Carol's day off from *Hello, Dolly!*

Embracing these two seemed to signify the end of his initial period of shock and begin his time of mourning. With that, he turned toward the crowd. The room had fallen silent. Everyone looked toward him, as if to await his setting of the tone. And so he began a funeral oration that was unique in nature. It was a comic litany, an inspired rendition of his repertoire of vaudeville stories.

The crowd gathered around. "There must have been a

hundred people there in a circle," Joan Benny remembered, "and every one of them knew that it was George's catharsis."

He told stories about Gracie and her sisters, he talked about things that had happened to them when they were on the road. He reminisced about the old acts, those he was in and those he felt such fondness for—"The Cherry Sisters," "Swain's Cats and Rats," and of course "Madame Burkhart and the Cockatoos." He sang the old patter songs:

Where did you get that girl, oh you lucky devil?
Where did you get that girl, tell me on the level.

"He had everyone in stitches," Joan recalled. "That day became one of the funniest five hours I have ever experienced."

The next morning, George arrived at Forest Lawn Memorial Park leaning heavily on Jack Benny's arm and wearing sunglasses to protect his reddened eyes. The crowd was enormous, and speakers were placed outside the Church of the Recessional on the grounds of Forest Lawn Memorial Park, so that the service could be heard by the overflow audience. Afterward, the mass of friends again gathered at 720 North Maple, but this time the scene was more composed. Harry Ritz brought Jan Murray, and the younger comedian was "taken with George's calmness and his humor in that situation. He was wonderful in the way he handled the people and yet you could see that he was completely stricken."

He was approached by Herb Browar, his longtime chief of production.

"You know," Browar said, "of all the female stars I've worked with, Gracie was the only one who was a real lady."

"Yes," Burns said quietly, "she was."

He paused for a moment, and then added, "You know

that I wasn't a true-blue husband. But I loved Gracie. And we were always together in the evening. I always came home, I made sure to be there. We would go to bed together, and every night we would lie in bed, holding hands and watching television."

15

The day after the funeral, George went to the office at his regular time, sat in with the writers of *No Time for Sergeants,* and made his usual suggestions. "It was a good thing we had the show to distract him," Ronnie said, "because he was heading into a period of profound depression."

After thirty-eight years of marriage, the bond with Gracie was so strong, and so enduring, that he could not let go of it. Every week without fail, he visited the crypt where she was interred at Forest Lawn. He always brought flowers, and placed them at her tomb. Then he sat on a bench opposite, and stared, and wept.

As he wept, he choked out words, and when he grew calmer, he started to speak aloud. He talked to Gracie about the things that were happening in his life, telling her what he thought she might like to know.

This was a strange mixture of emotion and discipline as the heart-racked visits to Forest Lawn became part of his regular routine. Indeed, routine—like storytelling—was another way of neatening up and dealing with the mess that life could make. Routine tamed the unpleasant and minimized the unpredictable. It was like getting every part of an act right. Once learned, and when dependable after discipline, practice, and repetition, it could be played for years.

An act was life under control. Routine was self-discipline, and that was going to be George Burns's survival kit.

After one of his regular lunches at the Hillcrest Country Club, he sat morosely in the Men's Grill while Hugo, the waiter, cleared the dishes. The circle at the Round Table was changing as the original members died off. A new crop of comedians was filling their chairs, if not their shoes. Danny Thomas was the first Christian to sit there, following a liberalization of club membership rules. Sammy Davis, Jr., had already been admitted. His conversion to Judaism had been solemnly recognized as valid for credential purposes.

Milton Berle, one of the few left from the original group, sat across the table and watched as Burns first drew on a cigar and then stared at it.

"George," Berle asked, "are you sure you don't want to try a Monte Cristo?"

It was their running joke, but Burns's sole response was a wan smile. Milton knew that George was faithful to his cheap El Productos. Finally, Burns shook his head and said, "I can't believe it. They opened Gracie's will and she left it all to Catholic charities, every cent."

Berle was not the only one Burns said this to, but if it was true, it was not so serious. The bulk of the Burns estate had been in either his name or jointly held, and if Gracie had bequeathed anything to Catholic charities, it would have been an inconsequential sum from her personal savings account.

Burns's gloom would have seemed, rather, part of the "profound depression" that Ronnie was beginning to observe in his father.

"After Gracie died," Paul Henning said, "I believe George thought his career was over. And [Ruth and I] thought so too. We didn't know what in the world he would do."

Perhaps sixty-eight is an advanced age for a midlife crisis, but considering how long Burns was going to live, he was right on schedule. For the first few weeks after Gracie's death, he complained about not sleeping. When Larry Superstein, who lived next door at 722, asked how he was managing, he replied, "You know, Larry, the downstairs is okay, but the upstairs gives me trouble. I really miss her."

Her pink slippers were still at her bedside. One night he decided to try sleeping in her bed and found that he slept better there. From then on, that was where he slept, and her slippers remained where they were.

As this depression was hitting home with a vengeance, there were occasional remissions when George surfaced in giddy waters. Invariably, such relief came with Jack. The two of them were walking through a long marble hotel lobby when Burns caught his friend with an unexpected bit of whimsy and sent him reeling with laughter. Once that got started, it was hard to control. George, always merciless when Jack was on the ropes, kept punching while his pal turned helpless.

Benny was holding his head between his hands, trying vainly to stem the laughter, but it would not be stopped, and George made sure of that. Jack plopped down on a bench, shaking from laughing so hard. This prompted the second step of the ritual as Burns began talking to passersby.

"Do you know why this man is laughing?"

Jack was beside himself, the laughter now arriving on cresting waves. As he sat helplessly on the bench, his legs began to give way. They stretched straight out, and he started to slide right off the bench.

Burns shook his head in disbelief as Benny slid from the marble bench onto the floor. There he lay in a heap. Quakes of laughter were now sending shudders through his body and he pounded the marble floor with his fist in an effort to control himself.

"Jack. For God's sake, get up."

"Cut it out, Nat," Benny moaned. It was a catchphrase of his on the radio, but this time he meant it. The man was nearly in tears.

"Jack," Burns said, "you're embarrassing me."

That only made things worse for Benny, which of course made things better for Burns. He might have been healing.

Jack was headed for Las Vegas, where he was scheduled to open an engagement at the Sahara Hotel. He had been one of the first major stars to go the nightclub route. Others were following, such as Danny Kaye, Marlene Dietrich, and Noël Coward. Milton Berle was opening at the Latin Casino in Philadelphia, and George himself was booked into the Riviera Hotel in Las Vegas the following month.

He often sent telegrams to fellow performers on their opening nights, but he had ambivalent feelings about Berle. He could be put off by the comedian's brashness and then turn appreciative of his warmth, for there was a certain genuineness about Berle, and so when he was opening in the Philadelphia nightclub, Burns called to wish him well. He added that he had another reason for calling.

"Listen, Milton, I don't want you to think that I would do anything like this behind your back."

"What do you mean? What behind my back?"

"Well, I'm calling to ask your permission first. Since you're out of town and I'm all alone, you know, since Gracie passed away, I'd like to escort Ruth [his wife] to a benefit at the Beverly Hilton Hotel."

Berle was touched.

"Sure," Berle said. He knew that his wife was a fan of George's—"Crazy about him," Berle said later, "and his fast humor. Especially when he liked to surprise the ladies with something risqué."

"But let me just tell you," Berle said, largely to cheer up a man who was some ten years older and nearing seventy,

"I know your reputation. Don't fuck around. It's my wife."

He remembered that at the other end of the line, Burns seemed genuinely shocked. "You must be kidding. Do you think I would try anything with your Ruth? And anyhow, it's a funny thing you should ask me that. Because I happened to be reading an article—*just this moment*—about what you're talking about, a guy playing around with somebody else's wife.

"This I've got to read to you. Hold the line a minute, Milton. It's in the other room, I'll be right back."

"And," Berle remembered, "the son of a bitch never came back. I waited five minutes on the line."

When the same kind of prank was played on Burns, he was not amused. He once brought an accompanist along to a big party where he anticipated that he would be singing. The party was at Danny Kaye's home, and after the pianist walked through the door, Kaye shut it in Burns's face. George rang the doorbell again and when Kaye appeared, he said, "Hi, it's me."

Again, Kaye shut the door in his face. So Burns got back in his car, went home, and skipped the party. He was a good sport and could take a joke, but he did not appreciate anyone taking a joke of his. That was stealing material, which in vaudeville was a venal sin. Stealing a sense of humor was all the worse.

Better fun was in store for Jack Benny at the Sahara Hotel. George had arranged for a stunning chorus girl to be waiting in his friend's dressing room after the show. His plot was for her to be seated with her back to the dressing table, completely naked and facing the door. On each of her breasts would be drawn the face of a pig, her nipples the noses.

As Jack came in, she was supposed to cry, "Oinky! Oinky!"

This was something that Burns was not about to miss seeing. As Jack's performance ended and the applause began, George raced backstage and ducked inside the dressing room. The chorus girl was naked, all decorated and waiting. Like a detective in a movie, he stood with his back to the wall, next to the door.

When it opened, the chorus girl did as George had instructed. She lifted her breasts, cupping one in each hand, and squeezed so that the piggy faces moved, while she cried, "Oinky! Oinky!"

The first person through the door was Mary Livingstone. Jack was behind her, and his eyes followed where hers went, first to the piggy drawings, then to the chorus girl's startled expression, and finally to the culprit behind the opened door.

Mary shot Nat a single hot glare. Then she stormed out of the dressing room. Relations between them, already cool, went into the freezer.

Although Jack was under contract to the Sahara Hotel, he frequently had lunch at the Riviera, where his friend, Harvey Silbert, was vice-president for entertainment. Whenever Jack went over to have lunch with Silbert, Mary came along.

"Jack was a lovely, lovely man," Silbert said, "soft and gentle. But Mary was a tough lady. He was afraid of her and she totally dominated him. He didn't enjoy confrontations. It was easier to let it pass. He did his thing."

Mary's ulterior motive for coming along might have been to keep track of Jack, because she certainly did not come for lunch. "As soon as we ordered," Silbert remembered, "she would get up and head for the blackjack tables."

The first time she did it, he walked through the casino to check on how she was doing, and saw that she had no chips in front of her. When she said that she had lost her hundred-dollar limit, he told the pit boss to give her a hundred dollars in chips "and charge it to my account."

It wasn't just generosity, he said. "She was an attraction." Mary Livingstone was hardly a television star on *The Jack Benny Show,* but, Silbert felt, "people would recognize her and gather around and they would want to gamble at the same table."

The next time Jack came over for lunch, again Mary excused herself and went to the casino. Once more, Silbert passed through, saw that she had no chips, and arranged for her to be given a hundred dollars' worth.

"It happened several more times," he remembered. Finally, one of the pit bosses took the executive aside and said, "Mr. Silbert, I think you're being stupid giving her those chips."

"Why do you say that?"

"She hasn't been losing her money. She just puts her chips in her purse whenever she sees you coming."

Neither of the Burns children became practicing Catholics and Sandy was already divorced, so it was hardly surprising that when Ronnie got married, in early 1966, it was not in a Catholic church. The reception was held at the elegant Bel-Air Hotel, where his uncle Willie got so drunk that it might not have been wise for him to drive home. When he got there, before going to bed he took an overdose of sleeping pills. By the time Ronnie and his bride Peggy arrived in Honolulu to begin their honeymoon, a telephone message awaited them, urging him to call home. Uncle Willie was dead at sixty-two.

Louise Burns made it clear that she felt George was to blame for her husband's death. In those first months afterward, it took little prompting for her to recite a litany of Willie's mistreatment at Burns's hands. She thought that his contributions as a writer and a manager had never been appreciated; she knew that he had been frequently humiliated; she was certain that Willie had the intelligence and the talent to make a successful career of his own, and she was not alone in that conviction. "Had Willie not been

George's brother," Paul Henning said, "he would have had a different career, because he had humor and ability. But when someone right next to you shines as brightly as George, it's pretty hard to squeeze through."

Some people believed that Willie had committed suicide, but most seemed to agree that, as Herb Browar said, "it was one of those freak things." He and Willie had worked together at McCadden for many years, and Browar believed Willie "enjoyed life too much for that."

Louise apparently saw it as a psychological suicide. She continued a relationship with George, but there was a bitterness about it. One evening, when she'd brought her three daughters for dinner, a guest at the table innocently asked Burns how his brother had died. Ordinarily, when he found himself in an uncomfortable situation that he could not joke his way out of, he would turn away from the subject. That was not possible with Louise at the table, and so he described Ronnie's wedding reception and Willie's drinking, and then the overdose of barbiturates.

"He was very testy about it," the guest remembered.

He had always been disgusted with his brother's drinking, and could well have been angry about that being the cause of death. Perhaps he was remorseful for his treatment of Willie. Whatever his feelings were, he steadfastly refused to discuss them.

So it was that in 1966, of the twelve Birnbaum children, only Nathan and Goldie remained.

After Gracie died, he could hardly continue using "The Love Nest" as his theme song. It set too nostalgic and sad a tone. Burns and Allen had indeed had a love nest, though perhaps not the love nest that is portrayed in movie and song; perhaps not the love nest that the general public imagined was the same as their television show; perhaps a more realistic love nest. But it was a kind of love nest—and it no longer existed.

He found a new theme song that would confirm him as a solo act while still maintaining a connection with Gracie. The song was "Ain't Misbehavin'," which was sentimental but not maudlin. It seemed to say that as the country's best known widower, George Burns was behaving like one. Not misbehaving was a senseless suggestion of fidelity after death, and somewhat hypocritical in view of his life before her death, but that is why there is no business like show business.

In what is sometimes called the youth culture of America, a man of seventy is considered old, if not yet elderly. The entertainment business, trading as it does in fantasies of beauty and happiness, has little interest in performers who are old. The general public generally confirms that wisdom, and so few aging entertainers try to keep going. Burns, however, was not trying to keep going—he was trying to get started.

At the Riviera Hotel in Las Vegas, in May 1967, he made his entrance with a puff of cigar smoke, blown from the wings. Then he followed the smoke onstage.

His opening line was: "I get a standing ovation just standing." Thus he put his audience at ease about his age. The jokes were on himself, and that was how he hoped to evade the curse of being a smart aleck and a wise guy.

His opening act was a singing group called "The Kids Next Door." The seventeen-member chorus was the professional offshoot of a popular group of amateur singers, "The Young Americans."

A member of "The Kids Next Door," a young woman named Lisa Miller, was backstage, practicing a dance step, when Burns overheard her tapping and opened his dressing-room door. He was amused that a young person should be interested in such ancient vaudeville dancing and asked the girl where she had learned it. By the time she finished answering, he'd invited her to dinner.

Lisa Miller was a tall (five feet eight), good-looking, blond

Californian who had a background in piano and singing, and a preoccupation with show business lore. A dropout from Long Beach City College, she had played small parts in local productions of musical comedies before getting the job with this chorus. Burns pursued her. The vast difference between their ages—she was nineteen, he was seventy-one—discouraged neither of them. They went out to dinner almost every remaining night of the three-week engagement.

When it ended, Lisa continued touring with "The Kids Next Door" while George went home to do nothing. His nightclub bookings were sporadic, for he was not a strong attraction. Neither, for that matter, was Jack. At one of his recent openings, Johnny Carson had come with Fred De Cordova. The television director was now executive producer of the *Tonight Show*.

Carson, who was a great Jack Benny fan, glanced around the show room. The place was not filled to capacity, even on Benny's opening night. "It shows you," he said to De Cordova, "what a lousy business we're in."

When Burns was not appearing in Las Vegas, there was little to occupy his time, other than an occasional appearance at a charity dinner. His visits to the office were mere ritual and without purpose. This was the stretch of "profound depression" his son mentioned. There was no separating of grief and the gloom over being out of work. Gracie and work had always been related.

Lisa Miller was one of several women he had started dating. The actress Evelyn Keyes had been the first, and another was a Los Angeles woman named Lita Baron. She was his date at Chasen's one evening in 1970, and they walked into the restaurant with a large party. Jack and Mary were there, Joan Benny and her date, and Freddie De Cordova, the eternal bachelor who had finally gotten married to a beautiful actress named Janet Thomas. (When he'd first met her, he told Gracie that he believed at last he had met a woman to fall in love with. Gracie said, "Why don't you get married? If it doesn't work, you can just marry somebody else.")

Chasen's was one of the restaurants most favored by the Hollywood crowd, and as Joan Benny remembered, they were led to an "A-plus" table. After they had settled in and drinks were served all around, George sat back in his chair and asked across the table, "Jack, what do you think was the funniest line you ever heard?"

Benny thought for a moment. Then he replied, "Well, I know this sounds strange, but I think the funniest line I ever heard was said by Larry Adler."

Larry Adler was a superb harmonica player who had a good sense of humor and often would get laughs with his remarks between selections. Nevertheless, he was primarily a musician. Benny had become friendly with him on a trip to Korea to entertain the servicemen. Adler had been part of his troupe.

"Do you mean Larry Adler the harmonica player?" Burns asked.

Joan knew that Nat was never going to be able to resist this. "Their joking went on constantly. And the closer you were to it, and the better you understood this symbiotic relationship, the funnier it was."

"Jack," George said, "you are one of the leading comedians in America. You've heard Jessel, Cantor, Fay, Frank Tinney, Berle, Lou Holtz, Groucho. Those guys were the fastest in the business, and you say the best line you ever heard came from a harmonica player? This must be something."

The table was starting to giggle. Joan could see that her father was in trouble.

"I have got to know, what was the line?"

Benny was already looking sheepish.

"Well, let me explain," he said. "We had gone to a party and there was a big iron gate out front—one of those high things with bars. And as I came through the gate, I was walking behind Larry, and he turned around to me and said, 'Jack, don't slam the door.' "

The table looked at him in silence.

"Well," Benny said, "it was terrifically funny."

There wasn't a sound.

"That was the line?" Burns asked.

Now they were starting to laugh out loud.

"It was a very funny line," Jack said.

" 'Don't slam the door,' " George repeated. "That was the line?"

Joan was watching her father ("He wishes he had never opened his mouth").

"He must have said something else to go along with it," Burns said.

"No," Jack snapped. "That was it."

"That was the funniest line you ever heard? 'Don't slam the door'?"

The people at his table were laughing very loud now, and the director Mervyn LeRoy got up from his chair at a nearby table and walked over.

"What's all the laughing about?" he asked. "What did I miss?"

"What you missed, Mervyn," George said, "was the funniest line that Jack Benny ever heard. Remember, Jack has been on the stage since he was eighteen. He's heard everybody."

They were all laughing again while Jack looked glum.

"But he thinks that the funniest of all, funnier than Groucho or George Jessel, was this harmonica player. What's his name, Jack?"

Still grumpily but starting to exaggerate it, Jack said, "Larry Adler."

"Larry Adler's line, the funniest line Jack ever heard in all of his years in show business, was, 'Don't slam the door.' "

At this point, Joan remembered, "the whole restaurant was staring at us, because we were making such a racket with our laughing. Everyone at the other tables was wondering what in the world was going on. We were all in hysterics. And that was when George stood up."

Addressing the entire restaurant, he said, "Okay, anybody who wants to hear this, come on over and I'll tell you what Jack Benny thinks is the funniest line he ever heard."

Few people could resist an invitation to be part of such an evening with George Burns and Jack Benny. A crowd gathered around the table as George told the story yet again while everyone at his table was in stitches, none more so than Jack.

16

When Lisa Miller came home after finishing her tour with "The Kids Next Door," she began to see Burns regularly. The relationship was romantic, but there was no talk of marriage. The reason she brought him home to meet her family was simply for him to meet them.

Lisa's parents were divorced, and so "GB," as she called George, was spared the experience of being introduced to a father young enough to be his son. But then again, all of his life he either was or seemed to be unflappable. Social convention may frown upon a seventy-two-year-old man romancing a twenty-year-old woman, but an unconventional man does not have to wear his hair in a ponytail. He doesn't have to look like a freak. He may not even be one.

Burns certainly didn't act awkward when he met Mrs. Miller ("I felt at home with her the moment I saw her"), and as Lisa remembered, her mother was impressed to meet him. George Burns may have been only a former star, but he was still a former star. As for his age, "nothing," she recalled, "was said about it."

People seemed to assume that a young woman of her age could not be physically attracted to an old man of his age, but this young woman was. Lisa said she never even considered their age difference.

They acted as if they had nothing to hide. When they went out, Burns said, "we didn't sit in some dark corner." On the other hand, he wasn't oblivious to social convention. "I get a feeling," he said to her one night in Chasen's, "that some of the people in this room might think you're a little too young for me."

He wasn't shy about introducing her to his friends, and there apparently was no awkwardness in the generation mix. When Jesse Block and Eva Sully from the old vaudeville gang visited from New York, they all went out. As an act, the Blocks had expired with vaudeville, and Jesse had since become a successful stockbroker. Even so, George continued to pick up the checks. He was always generous and "never used credit cards," Lisa said. "He would walk around with two or three thousand dollars in cash."

GB told her he just didn't believe in credit cards.

"Eva wanted to be Gracie," she remembered. "Whenever we saw them, she would always talk about how she had been a dancer. She acted as if she was still in show business."

Lisa was sounding downright wifely, and that was because she was comfortable with George, so comfortable that before she was twenty-one, she moved in with him. He gave her Sandra's bedroom—his daughter was now thirty-five and had four children. Lisa hung her dresses in the closet, and put her sweaters and underwear in the bureau, but it was just for the sake of appearance. George had engaged a new couple to run his household, a Belgian pair named Arlette and Daniel D'Hoore, and he didn't want them to know that he was sleeping with a girl who was fifty years younger than he. After all, Gracie's slippers were still under the bed.

Every night, he and Lisa staged a little charade. They

retired to their separate bedrooms. When the house was quiet, she would tiptoe down the hall to his room and climb into his or Gracie's bed. In the chapter "And There Was Lisa" in his book *Living It Up* (1975), Burns chose to respect the usual morals and wrote, "Now hold it, I know what you're thinking! I admit I was thinking the same thing, but it didn't happen that way."

It did. As Lisa said, "We made love every night for three years." So Burns's vitality was not just mental or for effect.

She also saw people her own age, including dates—who picked her up at the house—and she registered at UCLA, majoring in theatre and music. Each morning, George's neighbors would watch bemused as the young woman emerged from Burns's house and met up with their own daughter. Then both girls would set out for school, book-bags slung over their shoulders.

One afternoon, George took Lisa to his bank and asked to see his safety deposit box. When he opened it, the long steel container was glittering with Gracie's jewelry.

"Pick out what you want, kid," he said.

There was even the bracelet and ring from the notorious George Burns smuggling scandal. Lisa, however, chose nothing. He himself selected a six-carat diamond ring, held it out, and asked her to marry him.

She declined. She had already told him that she was interested in a fellow she was dating. Like Burns's friends and his neighbors, that young man also assumed that Lisa's room at 720 North Maple Drive was in fact her room. She even introduced the young man to George.

He insisted that she take something, finally choosing the pieces for her. She estimated their value at $60,000.

Perhaps even more valuable to Lisa was Burns's invitation to work with him at the Frontier Hotel in Las Vegas. The notion was that as a break from his monologue, they would do one of the old Burns and Allen routines and then sing a duet (Sophie Tucker's "Some of These Days"). They would also close his act with a soft shoe dance, shuffling through sand that George sprinkled on the stage.

After that engagement, they performed together on two Jackie Gleason television shows. But as Lisa started her next year of school, she could see that George's career was virtually dormant. He went to the office, but he was only signing papers and talking on the telephone. Although in public he was cheerful and always funny, at home he would seethe. Why, he asked Lisa, wasn't his agent, Phil Weltman at the William Morris office, getting him booked?

Idleness made him feel his age. At seventy-three one was expected, at worst, to feel useless and self-pitying; at best, to act retired and leisurely. But to Burns, retired meant being in bed, it meant being inactive, and that was as good as dead.

The only concessions to age that he was willing to make were physical ones. He stopped playing golf and concentrated on bridge, playing every afternoon in the card room that adjoined the Hillcrest Men's Grill. He took the game seriously and was not amused or patient with incompetent players. He once grew so abusive about a partner's misplay that the fellow put down his cards, stood up, and told Burns that he would never speak to him again.

George followed him down the hall. "Wait a minute," he cried. "You don't know me well enough never to speak to me again." There simply was nobody quicker, or, on most days, more endearing.

Playing bridge would become the only hobby he'd ever have, his only non–show business interest. But because it was sedentary, he increased his exercising. For years he had started every day by swimming laps in his pool. Then he would briskly walk around its perimeter for fifteen minutes. To this routine he now added the Canadian Air Force Exercises, a popular regimen of sit-ups, deep knee bends, shoulder twists, and arm extensions.

"It keeps my spine flexible," he told the younger comedian Jan Murray, and his light eating habits did the rest for his health. As Murray noticed in the Hillcrest Grill, "George was following a good, light diet before anyone knew what a good, light diet was."

Murray also observed Burns's depression. "This guy who used to work fifty-two weeks a year on radio, and then television, was now going for years without working." But Burns insisted that he was busy at the office.

"Your office?"

"I go every morning. I'm there by nine."

"What do you do there?"

"I've got a secretary, I've got a writer. He'll write an article for a newspaper, or special material for a benefit or a roast. He'll put down notes for a memoir I might write. Hey, if we think of something cute, it's never lost. Funny is funny. Who knows, something will come up that they call me about and maybe something that we write tomorrow will fit that.

"I'm regimented, Jan. You've always got to go out and do something."

Murray was impressed with the older man's way of dealing with a bad situation. "He gives himself a place to go and something to do. He just wouldn't fade away, and watching him taught me something: what actually happens to you at any one time isn't that important. If you live long enough—unless you die young—everything will happen to you. Good, bad, happy, sorry, triumph, defeat.

"What the hell does that all mean? What it means is that what happens to you isn't as important as your attitude—*how you handle what happens to you*. It's how you accept it, and what you're going to do about it. That's what's important, and that's what I learned from him.

"This," Murray added, "is not the kind of conversation you could have with George. Probably, he would not understand what the hell I was talking about."

•   •   •

The president of Buddha Records was a man named Neil Bogart, and in an era of disco music, he had a notion of making an album of George Burns *singing*. Although Burns insisted that he took his singing seriously, he was sure Bogart was kidding. In fact, on the day he first met the album producer, Larry Fallon, he handed over a comedy script and said, "Here's what we're doing."

Fallon replied, "I didn't come out here to do a comedy album with a little piano music. I want to do a serious album with you."

"What are you talking about?" Burns said. "I can't sing!"

He kept trying to make it into a comedy album right up until the day he walked into Western Recording Studios in Los Angeles and saw the orchestra waiting for him. Then he stopped in his tracks and said shakily, "I don't know whether I'm going to be able to do this. I was never a singer. I was a hoofer."

He didn't look like a singer in the studio. "He wouldn't sing without a cigar in his hand," Fallon remembered. "It was like a security blanket." But after the producer used that most threatening of phrases—"Trust me"—he added, "I will work with you. If you can't do it live, we will record the orchestra first. Then you'll have as much time as you need to sing your songs."

Most of the material was contemporary ("Mr. Bojangles," "Satisfaction," "Feeling Groovy") with an occasional dip into nostalgia ("The Red Rose Rag"). Lisa also sang on the album, and for the Beatles' "A Little Help from My Friends" she showed off a beautiful and clear young voice.

It is not vastly rewarding to hear George Burns sing rock 'n' roll songs, but the album does capture his essential qualities. One selection alone—a rehearsal version of "You Made Me Love You," which includes Burns trying to get into key—makes the whole experience worthwhile.

More important than putting him on record, however, the album sowed the seeds of rebirth for this near octogenarian. In not being a nostalgia item for the older public but rather in being "directed toward the young," as Fallon said, it challenged the proscriptions of popular culture. It presented George Burns as a man who refused to play the traditional part of an old man. He was demonstrating that a person could be vital (or not) at any age, and that this old man was not going to obediently retreat into a rest home state of mind because of advertising's, show business's, and presumably the public's distaste for the elderly.

The album was called *Ain't Misbehavin'*, and Buddha Records put a publicity campaign behind it, booking him into Avery Fisher Hall in Lincoln Center. Jack Benny provided the introduction. "Tonight, for the first time," he told the audience, "a man is going to play this hall who can't spell it." Then Burns sang the album's songs and told some of his stories. Fallon accompanied him, conducting a symphony-size orchestra.

Lisa, now married, came east for the concert, and afterward, she and George went out to dinner with Jack. Mary wasn't there. She skipped many events that she considered beneath her. Her attitude toward Burns seemed reason enough to bypass this one. She was not likely to travel three thousand miles to see him play a concert.

Jack and his current girlfriend were waiting as George and Lisa arrived at "21." Benny stood up, wrapped Nat in an embrace, and whispered, "Oinky! Oinky!" It was boys' night out.

Promoting the record album kept Burns busier than he had been in years. He went to England to be the guest on a couple of Tom Jones television shows, and came back for two bookings on *The Dean Martin Show*. He might well have noticed that Martin was another straight man who had lost his partner, Jerry Lewis. Dean Martin had gone on to become more popular than Martin and Lewis had ever been, and even his oblique humor was like Burns's. George could well have taken that as an encouraging example.

One difference between them was that Burns was a perfectionist. Larry Fallon, who now was his regular music director, recalled that for *The Dean Martin Show,* "we worked until every word and every move was exactly right. It was as if even the cigar had to be held at the right height. Because George did not believe in ad-libbing or winging it even though he was as quick as anyone.

"Some people who worked with that kind of a performer," Fallon went on, "might think he was too rigid, too structured—doing every word and gesture exactly as rehearsed. But to Burns, that was the key to professionalism."

Dean Martin, on the other hand, did not even show up for rehearsals. There actually was a stand-in for him. "He had a closed-circuit television hookup to his house," Fallon remembered with continuing surprise. "He would watch the rehearsals from home. That's why he was so loose. The less structure there was, the better he was able to handle it."

If Burns was taking these television appearances as a sign that he was on the comeback road, he learned otherwise when none of the networks showed interest in a couple of musical comedy specials that he produced for himself. They finally were sold to a few independent stations, and the record album did only moderate business.

Sitting in a hotel restaurant, Fallon watched as George told a waiter, "Bring me a bowl of hot water. As hot as you can get it."

When it was brought to the table, he poured ketchup into it.

"I never got out of that habit," he said, "because when I was poor, that was all we had to eat."

He would never have to worry about food, but he was

poor in another sense. "He was an eighty-year-old comedian," Fallon thought, "and who wanted an eighty-year-old
comedian?"

In July 1974, while taping the *Tonight Show* with Johnny
Carson, Burns stumbled over his words in the middle of an
anecdote. One of the other guests, the writer-director Carl
Reiner, turned to see what the problem was, alarmed that
"George was dropping lines, searching for words, stumbling
over his own thoughts."

He decided that Burns was not ill, "just getting old." But
in fact, George had been suffering fainting spells; even saw
two doctors, Rex Kennamer and Gary Sugarman, about
them. Then one evening he was sitting with his son Ronnie
in the Universal Amphitheatre, watching a Linda Ronstadt
concert, and he started having chest pains. "He began
complaining that he hurt," Ronnie remembered, "and the
next day, August 9, 1974, he went into the hospital for
triple heart bypass surgery.

"At that time, he was the oldest person ever to have that
operation."

While George was in the hospital, the director Herbert Ross
was getting ready to start pre-production work on *The
Sunshine Boys*, a movie version of Neil Simon's 1973 Broadway comedy. The playwright had already written the screen
adaptation, and one of the two leading roles was cast.

His characters are a couple of seventy-year-old vaudeville comics who retired ten years before the story starts.
They had spent a half century together as the team of
"Lewis and Clark," but during its last year they were angry
with each other, and had not spoken since breaking up the
act. *The Sunshine Boys* could be seen as *The Odd Couple*—
only thirty years later, and with a show business background.

The crankier partner, Willie Clark, "was always Walter
Matthau," according to Ross. Ever since Matthau had cre-

ated the role of Oscar Madison on Broadway in *The Odd Couple*, he was considered the consummate Neil Simon player. At fifty-three, he was young to be playing a septuagenarian, but he would be given sagging skin and a bald scalp. Herbert Ross conceded that "movies are tough on makeup," yet he still felt lucky to have Matthau, "a wonderful, dimensional actor."

The other partner, Al Lewis, remained to be cast, and it seemed as if every older comedian in Hollywood was after the part. The movie's producer, Ray Stark, had his heart set on Red Skelton; Ross tested him—"terrible"—as well as Milton Berle—"not a good enough actor."

Burns, pretty much of a has-been, was not even under consideration. If nothing else, he was flat on his back on a hospital bed, his incisions still raw from open-heart surgery.

Jack Benny was in the same screen test with Skelton. When he was told that he was talking and moving too fast for a seventy-year-old character, he protested, "But I'm eighty."

One day shortly after George had come home from the hospital, Ronnie answered the telephone. It was a quirk of Burns's not to answer the phone except when he was alone. The call was from Jack, and Burns took it upstairs, where he was resting in bed. Afterward, he told Ronnie that Jack wasn't feeling well.

"He's having stomach pains. I asked him what the doctors told him. He said they can't find anything. I told him to go for a complete checkup."

Joan Benny was also concerned about her father's mysterious pain. "Nobody could detect anything."

Jack had been working a lot. His manager, Irving Fein, was good at that. "He made a ton of money for my father in the 1970s," Joan said. "My mother had spent every penny my father ever made. And that's why she didn't like

Fein, because Irving kept that money where she couldn't touch it."

In October 1974, Benny went to Dallas to play a private engagement. He planned to perform part of it playing his violin, but as he was rehearsing, his left hand became so numb that his fingers would not flex. By the time he went to a local doctor, he was complaining of dizzy spells. He was diagnosed as having suffered a mild stroke but insisted on going through with the show. He just skipped the violin part.

When his plane landed in Los Angeles, an ambulance was waiting at the airport to take him almost directly to Cedars of Lebanon Hospital. He asked the driver to stop so that he might buy an ice cream cone. He always did that when Mary wasn't around to refuse permission, and he wasn't worried about his diabetes at the moment.

After five days of observation and tests, he was given a diagnosis of "pancreatitis," and he told reporters that he was feeling fine. "I didn't even have a stomachache," he said, "until I got the hospital bill."

But it wasn't funny. As Mary and Joan already knew, he had terminal pancreatic cancer. His personal physician, Dr. Rex Kennamer, chose to spare him the news.

Feeling strong enough, Jack decided to pay a call on Natty, one pal mortally ill and the other surviving open-heart surgery. Benny arrived all dolled up in a sweater and a baseball cap. His convalescent chum was sitting in the garden, wearing the old beret and talking to his nephew, Lou Weiss. George's nurse sat close by.

"In the presence of George Burns and Jack," Weiss remembered, "I would usually sit and listen. These are giant, giant monologists. They always have something to say—great humor and big points of view.

"I suddenly realized, I'm sitting with two guys who are very tired."

And so he started to talk himself.

"Listen, Jack," Weiss said, "before coming out here, I had dinner with Neil Simon. You're going to hear it from Irving [Fein] anyhow. I've got wonderful news: you've got the part in *The Sunshine Boys*."

Jack was understandably elated even though he had lots of other work; nobody could have been more elated, except his manager. Before landing Benny as a client, Irving Fein had been a press agent at Warner Brothers, and his roommate at the time (1940) was Ray Stark, who then worked at the same studio and now was the producer of *The Sunshine Boys*. If Fein had used this connection to help get the part for his client, he could hardly have been faulted for it, but director Herb Ross was not comfortable with the choice. He loved Jack Benny as much as everyone did, but the best he could say about the screen test was, "Jack was charming."

The problem with Benny was that he was too familiar. His mannerisms would remind audiences that they were watching Jack Benny rather than the character of Al Lewis.

Like Jack himself, Irving wasn't aware of the desperate state of his health, but what Fein did know was bad enough for him. Even if Jack got well and was able to make *The Sunshine Boys*, he could not possibly fulfill that month's booking at the Fontainebleau Hotel in Miami Beach. Fein was a man with serious problems.

Even though Burns was seventy-eight years old and barely two months out of open-heart surgery, Fein invited him to step in for Jack at the Fontainebleau. While it was hardly surprising that George accepted the one-night engagement, this was exactly the kind of business obsession that did not endear Irving Fein to those close to Burns, particularly Sandy Burns and Lou Weiss.

Some weeks later, Jack realized that whatever was ailing him was not going to disappear in the near future. He himself called Herbert Ross to say that he would be unable to report for work on *The Sunshine Boys*.

He had another reason for making the call. "If I can't do this," he asked the director, "please consider George. He would be wonderful in the part."

Ross thought so too.

It was not a good year, 1974. The reason that Lou Weiss was in California was because his aunt Goldie had died. He had flown there to take his uncle to the funeral in San Diego.

Goldie was George's big sister, the next oldest. They had always been special to each other and she had been close to Gracie as well. She was also the only sibling who lived on the West Coast. She was important to Burns for all these reasons, and her death left him as the last remaining member of his immediate family.

When her casket was lowered into the ground, the rabbi passed a shovel around for the witnesses to toss the first earth into the grave. This was Jewish tradition, but George had a powerful antipathy toward death. Before the shovel came near him, he turned to his nephew and said, "Louie, I don't like this," and they left.

"The day that Jack dropped out," Herbert Ross said, "Irving Fein was on the phone pushing George."

On December 22, Joan Benny got a telephone call from her mother. "You'd better come right over," she said. "Your dad's in a coma."

He was still in a coma on Christmas Day, but by then his friends had started to stop by at the house. "It was one continuous party," Joan remembered, and Natty was the first one there. Then Danny Kaye arrived, and Billy Wilder, Jack Lemmon, and Freddie De Cordova. More came, and drank, and told Jack Benny stories until he died upstairs on December 26. He was eighty years old.

"My dad," Sandy Burns remembered, "was with Jack in the house in Beverly Hills just a few minutes before he died. I always used to say, I wished to God Jack would die after my dad died because I knew my dad would be just lost without him. And he was."

When Mary Livingstone came downstairs to say that Jack was dead, Natty asked if he might go upstairs and be alone with his friend for a moment.

"I don't think so," Mary said. "The doctor said nobody should go upstairs."

"I know him longer than the doctor," George said as he walked past her, "and I'm going up."

"When I went into the room," he recalled, "he was lying there with his hands clasped in that familiar manner and his head cocked to one side. He looked as if he were taking one of his long pauses."

Mary Livingstone once said, "I wasn't very much in love with Jack when I married him. My love for him came after."

Nat would bitterly comment, "She never did say after *what.*"

His own outlook was bleak. He had run out of vaudeville makeovers. "My best friend was gone, careerwise I wasn't in great demand, and I wasn't getting any younger."

It was actually an understatement for him to call this "one of the low points in my life."

That was precisely when his best friend, on his deathbed and knowing that he himself could not continue, had given George the opportunity for a new life. The last act of Jack Benny's life was to save George Burns's. He bequeathed the one thing Burns had wanted his whole life, and needed more than ever: the ability to go it alone.

Jack's mortal illness made George's movie break possible; his telephone call to Herb Ross set it up, and his manager could be counted on to sort out the details.

Fein was not George Burns's manager, not yet anyway. Burns's agent was Phil Weltman at the William Morris Agency, the man Burns had been blaming for not getting him any work. But Fein was facing a life-and-death challenge of his own, the loss of his major client in a business for which the primary goal was not getting the client the work, but getting the client.

He strolled into the office at General Service Studios, and, as Burns remembered it, said, "George, how would you feel about playing the part of Al Lewis in *The Sunshine Boys*?"

It would make him feel uncomfortable, said George. Still griefstruck and still mourning, he added: "Irving, I don't think I should do it. That was Jack's part and if I played it, I just wouldn't feel right." He did not know that Jack had telephoned Herbert Ross to suggest him for the part.

Fein, who declined to be interviewed for this book, said, "George, I think I can help you. I was Jack's manager for twenty-six years and nobody knew the man any better than I did. Take my word for it, nothing would make Jack happier than to have you do that part."

Then, with cavalier theatrics, he opened his briefcase, took out a script, and tossed it on Burns's desk.

"Think it over, and while you do, read this script."

On the way out, he said, "Call me in the morning."

17

Jack Benny's funeral on December 27, 1974, was one of the biggest in Hollywood history, and one of the most mournful. Some two thousand people made the pilgrimage to Hillside Memorial Cemetery in Culver City on a brilliant, sunny day. They arrived, a Los Angeles newspaper reported, "on bicycles and pushing baby carriages," and milled on a rolling hill as the beloved comedian was buried where Jolson and Cantor already were buried, in a black-veined Italian marble sarcophagus, inside a mausoleum.

There was room for only three hundred people in the glass-walled chapel where the twenty-minute service was conducted. Groucho Marx was seated in the front row, flanked by other members of the Round Table, including Milton Berle, George Jessel, and Danny Thomas. Governor Ronald Reagan was there with his wife Nancy, and so were Edgar Bergen and his daughter Candice, Andy Griffith, Johnny Carson, James Stewart, Henry Fonda, Walter Matthau, Raymond Massey, Merle Oberon, Cesar Romero, Billy Wilder, Mervyn LeRoy, Goldie Hawn, Dinah Shore, Robert Stack, Danny Kaye, and Jack Lemmon.

The pallbearers included Frank Sinatra, Gregory Peck,

Freddie De Cordova, and Berle. Jack's copper coffin was covered with a blanket of green and white flowers, and the chapel itself was banked with great sprays of red, white, and yellow flowers.

Whatever the animosity between Mary and George, she knew that he had to be the first eulogist. He told her, "I don't know whether I'll be able to do it," but he promised to try.

He was wearing a yarmulke and a *talles* (prayer shawl) as he approached the lectern.

"What can I tell you about Jack?" he began. "I've known him fifty-five years. I can't imagine my life without him."

Then he broke down. George Burns, a man who always kept his emotions to himself and who would, as his son Ronnie said, "put a vaudeville shine" on any unpleasant reality, just fell apart. Sobbing, he fled the podium and had to be helped to his seat.

Three months after his open-heart surgery, George was joking about it on the Johnny Carson *Tonight Show*. It is common for heart bypass patients to have a period of deep depression following the operation, but to hear it from Burns, the worst thing about it was being told that he shouldn't eat ketchup anymore—which he continued to do anyhow.

With Lisa's marriage, her relationship with him turned into a friendship and she asked whether it might cheer him up to have the house redecorated. The place had not been changed since Gracie had given it a postwar freshening in 1950, and Lisa thought the living room was beginning to look like "a seedy Palm Beach hotel lobby." The white area rugs had yellowed and the bottom of the sofa was sagging. "It actually creaked when somebody sat on it," she said.

"The overall style was *moderne*," she remembered, "and the dominant color was pale yellow. There were two stuffed chaises longues, one on either side of the fireplace, and a twelve-foot sofa, and everything was upholstered with foam rubber. The tabletops were leather and there were lots of nubby fabrics, like bark cloth."

George probably didn't know bark cloth from a washcloth. All he said was, "Make it look like it did when Gracie first fixed it up," and that was what Lisa did, covering the floors with Oriental rugs and replacing the old furniture with more traditional pieces.

In New York, Eva Sully told a friend that "Jesse's been crying ever since Jack died. Mary invited us out to the funeral but he wouldn't go." And it wasn't just to the funeral; for three weeks after Benny's death, Jesse Block wouldn't go anywhere. When he finally did show up for his regular lunch at the Friar's Club, he told his cronies, "I got a letter from Nat, and when I got the letter, I realized what's going on and I decided enough was enough."

This was George's response to what he described as a "very sad" letter from Jesse. The note was dictated to his secretary, Jack Langdon, on January 30, 1975, offering to share "a little secret" that he thought might help. Burns told Jesse how he cried every time he visited Gracie at the mausoleum. After a time, he decided "you can only cry so many weeks." Then, he said, you stop.

He stopped crying when he began to talk to her and "tell her everything." It was now eleven years that he had been visiting and chatting with her. "I still go," he said, "but now I tell her little humorous things. . . . Who knows, maybe she can hear me, and she always thought I was funny."

He concluded by telling Jesse there was no point in staying sad. "Life goes on," he said, "and there's nothing you can do about it. It's the only game in town." He signed his letter simply "Nat."

Mary Livingstone also suffered an intense depression, but hers was quite different from Nat's, or Jesse's. "She had been on a downhill path long before my father died,"

Joan said. "Afterward, her insecurities took over her life."

Her only real sign of vitality came when the first biography of Jack was published. It was written by Irving Fein, and "Mother was furious with him," Joan remembered. "He published that book before the body was cold. My mother was very upset.

"She said, '*I* should be the one to write the book.' "

With Benny's death, Mary went into virtual seclusion; she spent most of her days smoking cigarettes and watching television. Joan considered it "close to clinical depression." The family physician, Dr. Rex Kennamer, said, "Her reclusive tendency became more pronounced. She seemed to withdraw more and more into her bedroom."

The woman who'd even had her matchbooks imprinted "Mary Livingstone" now took to calling herself "Mrs. Jack Benny." This was a familiar phenomenon among women who took to wielding their important husbands' power or influence. When those husbands died and took the power with them, such women lost identity and purpose. Convinced as they were that nobody had ever been interested in them, in an eerie transmutation they abandoned their own existence for a marriage with death. Hence the taking of their husbands' names, so as to remain wed, dead or alive. Of course it never worked. Mary Livingstone was destined to live another eight gloomy years as Mrs. Jack Benny, but with Jack gone, so was her day in Hollywood society.

Burns was having a quiet lunch with Patricia Zeitman, the wife of one of the William Morris agents who took care of details for him. She asked George forthrightly, "First Gracie, now Jack—how do you handle so much loss in your life? How do you go on laughing and, well, living the way you do?"

For once he was serious. "Well, first of all," he said, "I have very bright friends. They don't go anyplace unless they are going to have a really good time. And so I know they're all having a *great* time—they wouldn't die unless there was a hell of a party they were going to.

"And in addition to that, you've got to keep making other friends."

Pat Zeitman had almost the same reaction as Jan Murray had had to George Burns's way of coping with life's vicissitudes. "He handled loss with acceptance," she said, "but with such love for the people in his life—even after they'd passed away. He had such appreciation for them. He might make a joke out of it, but what he was saying was that he appreciated the people he loved, and appreciated the fact that they were onto something that was pretty terrific."

George's reading for *The Sunshine Boys* in early 1975 was to be held at Herbert Ross's house at 806 North Rexford in Beverly Hills. It was only five minutes away from North Maple Drive and he climbed into his new Cadillac Seville for the drive. He always bought Cadillacs; he traded in for a new one every year. ("If Cadillac ever changed anything," Ronnie remembered, "Dad would have the guy come over and show him how it worked.") He was also a bad driver, not very long on concentration and getting short in height. In fact, recently a friend had been alarmed to see his car rolling down the driveway by itself.

He was at the wheel. He was just shrinking.

When he got to Ross's house, Neil Simon was waiting in the den with Ray Stark, the producer. George shook hands all around, sat down, and asked what scene they would like him to do. He did not have a script with him. To everyone's astonishment, he had memorized his entire part, which movies do not require as they are made in short takes.

The reason he did that was quite realistic: Despite all his efforts with tutors, he still had trouble reading.

Even more remarkable than his feat of memory was the performance in the den. It surprised everyone except Burns, who knew, as he'd told a friend, "I'm perfect for the part. They're looking for an old Jewish vaudevillian, and I'm an old Jewish vaudevillian."

That he was, although he hadn't seemed particularly Jewish during the years with Gracie. The quality began to emerge only after her death, and this was certainly an opportune time for it to show its kosher face. He was promptly hired. "Not only was he better than anyone we had tested," Ross said, "but he was better than Jack."

It was eerie for sure. As Sandy Burns said, "If Jack hadn't died, my dad would never have gotten into the movies. Who knows what would have happened to him?" The writer Irving Brecher felt much the same way. "That was a strange thing, a miraculous thing, how the death of his best friend gave him his biggest chance."

As an actor, Burns's anonymity gave him an advantage— and he had certainly become anonymous, having been out of the center ring for more than a decade. Even back in his heyday with Gracie, as a straight man invisibility was part of the role.

George's recent Las Vegas engagements, Herb Ross said, had had "no immediate impact. You're not getting national attention. It's just hard work." And so he was an unfamiliar face to the public, one of a legion of the formerly famous.

That and an instinct for character acting were going to make his performance in *The Sunshine Boys* a startling achievement—and more so when reviewed decades later. For even after George Burns had become a very familiar personality, he did not seem to be playing himself in the movie. The vaudevillian Al Lewis was another character entirely, a character of his creation.

Besides the team of Lewis and Clark, the other figure in this essentially three-character movie is a young agent. He is the nephew of Willie Clark (Matthau), the young man who arranges the reunion of the feuding team. Harvey Keitel was engaged for the role and rehearsals began.

Burns, without mentioning Keitel by name, described him as "a Method actor who needed a motivation for everything he did." Herb Ross felt differently. "Harvey," he said, "is a wonderful actor but he never understood the tone of the play. Neil has a particular style. George understood that style." Ultimately Richard Benjamin replaced Keitel.

Directors not only direct, they also do parenting. Matthau "adored George," Ross said, "and so he was on his best behavior—and Walter can sometimes be tricky."

He was "tricky" with a bit player. Early in the picture, Willie gets lost and goes to the wrong address for an audition. Instead of walking into an advertising agency, he goes to a garage. A then unknown actor, F. Murray Abraham, was playing a mechanic who worked there. For whatever reason, Matthau was annoyed with the young actor and told Ross, "I hate that guy. I won't play the scene with him."

The director put Abraham at work under a car. He stayed there as long as Matthau was in the scene. After Matthau made his exit, Abraham crawled out from under the car and spoke his lines. (Ten years later, F. Murray Abraham would win the Academy Award for *Amadeus*.)

There was also a "nasty moment," Ross remembered, "when Frank Rosenfelt [the new head of production at MGM] suddenly got panicky and decided that he didn't want George. He was nervous about the project and said he wanted Jack Lemmon."

Lemmon had played opposite Matthau before, most notably in the popular movie version of Simon's *The Odd Couple*. Ross considered him a marvelous actor who was wrong for this part, and both he and Simon walked off the picture, refusing to do it unless Burns was kept. Ray Stark stood up for them, and ultimately, Rosenfelt backed off.

The movie version of *The Sunshine Boys*, as Ross said, "was essentially the play with only one new scene, where the nephew comes to try and talk the Burns character into reviving the act." Ross persuaded Burns to play that new scene without his toupee, and it was the only time in his career that he went topless. The sacrifice in vanity was worth it, for disguise is one of a character actor's most valuable tools, and the scene established Al Lewis as having a face all his own. Unfortunately, this scene is also inconsistent with the rest of the story, for it presents the man as intermittently senile. Burns plays that sensitively and with compassion, but Simon never conformed the rest of the screenplay to the new scene and subsequently—inexplicably—Lewis has all his wits about him.

There was another new scene written, an epilogue at the Actors Home in Teaneck, New Jersey. The idea of that scene was for Lewis and Clark to finally patch up, living out their last days together in the Actors Home, as their prototypes, Smith and Dale, actually had. In fact, Joe Smith—the partner Burns understood he was portraying—was still living in the Teaneck Actors Home when the scene was filmed there. But although the epilogue was made, it was cut.

The most disappointing sequence in *The Sunshine Boys* should have been its highlight. This is when Lewis and Clark perform the act that made them famous. It is inspired by the classic Smith and Dale sketch "Dr. Kronkeit."

In Simon's variation, he attempted to combine every element of burlesque comedy, a genre as ritualized as commedia dell'arte. Like the figures of Harlequin, Columbine, and Pantaloon in commedia, burlesque comedy had its stock characters in the quack doctor, the punchy patient, and the bimbo nurse, traditionally played by a gorgeous stripper (in this movie, Lee Meredith).

Simon's sketch uses these ritual characters faithfully, and captures some of the qualities of traditional burlesque comedy.

NURSE
Is there anything else you can think of?
DOCTOR
I can think of it but I can't do it.

Matthau, as Willie Clark, does a good job playing the doctor in broad German dialect. Both he and Burns wear outlandish wigs for this sketch. George's is a full head of blue-black hair, which sits on his seventy-eight-year-old face like a ridiculous hat. Walter flaps around in a fright wig. This is all in the right spirit.

Simon also made much of the scene's assorted props, especially an "ah stick"—a tongue depressor.

But with the set "dressed," the lighting settled, the camera angles prepared, and Ross ready to start shooting, Burns whispered to Matthau, "Listen, this sketch is not going to work."

"Why won't it work? I think it's fine."

"It won't work," George said, "because the props are funny.

"You see," the doctor of vaudeville explained, "you can't play funny dialogue against funny props. People won't know whether to watch the props or listen to the dialogue. You'd better tell Neil."

Matthau was not about to do that. He told Burns, "He's one of the most successful playwrights in American history."

"The sketch won't work," Burns insisted. "Tell him."

"Why don't you tell him?"

"Walter, it'll sound better coming from you."

This was a typical Burns set-up, but not without reason. He called Simon over and said, "Neil, Walter has something to tell you."

Simon looked at Matthau.

"The sketch won't work."

"Why won't it work?"

"Because," the newly educated Matthau explained, "the dialogue is funny and the props are funny and you can't make funny dialogue with funny props."

"Walter, I don't buy that," Simon said. "The sketch stays the way it is."

Burns popped up, "I'm with you, Neil."

That was funny, but he was right. The sketch didn't work. The props are too funny, the wigs are hilarious, and they overshadow the writing.

The picture was shot in eight weeks, much of it on location in New York City. Matthau was paid about a million dollars, Burns less than a third of that. As far as the director was concerned, he was worth much, much more.

"Because of George's simplicity and directness and honesty," Ross said, "he set a tone for the picture . . . and you had to play within that tone. It didn't allow for lying by an actor. It stripped away a lot of that 'stuff' which I worried about with Walter. He was being too bombastic, there was too much 'acting.' "

If George was aware of this admiration, he didn't let it distort his perspective. At the first screening, he watched the movie and said, "I didn't know I was bald. This is going to ruin my sex life."

His neighbors on North Maple Drive were an educated couple. The Supersteins pursued cultured and intellectual interests. One such interest was participating in a study group at UCLA. It involved a series of ten Thursday evening philosophy lectures, which were followed by "salons"— coffee, dessert, and discussions—in one or another of the subscribers' homes.

On an evening when they were themselves hosting a discussion in their luxurious, art-filled home, the doorbell rang. Larry was startled to find George Burns standing there, at ten o'clock in the evening. Even more startling, George asked if he might come in.

Thursday nights had regular but different connotations for Burns and his neighbors. In both cases, it was the maid's night out, consequently theirs. But if going somewhere meant a philosophy lecture series for the Supersteins, to George, as Leah knew, it meant going out to dinner with his show business friends in a show business restaurant.

Her husband appreciated Burns's inviting himself in but knew "this wasn't the group for George." And so he said, "I'm sorry, we've got some people in."

As in all things, Burns was undeterrable. "I know." He smiled. "That's why I came over. I just came back from Chasen's for dinner and saw you had a bunch of people over. I thought I'd come in for a cup of coffee."

Superstein tried to dissuade him. "You know you're welcome anytime, George, but we've got a university professor here and our study group . . . Maybe you wouldn't enjoy it."

"Well, why don't I just say hello?" Burns said, already walking through the door.

As he entered the enormous living room, it fell silent. He was hardly a star, but this was Los Angeles where show business was the town industry. He was at least still remembered for the *Burns and Allen* television series.

He sat down on the sofa. All eyes fell on him.

"We were all waiting for him to say something," Leah remembered.

Finally, a "rather imposing woman," she recalled, "who was a duenna type," turned to him and said, "We were having this philosophical discussion about the relationship between the body and the universe."

"Oh?" he said, puffing on a cigar. She expanded on that relationship. Burns listened attentively. She digressed to the other cultural issues that demanded her time. Beyond even them, she said, there were the various causes and charities that she served as supporter and hostess.

"It sounds like you're very busy," Burns said.

"Well, you don't know what kind of a house I run."

"No, but maybe you can give my sister Goldie a job."

The room roared. George knew how to bring down any house and it was all the merrier for him if he could include his sister in the joke, speaking of her as though she were still alive.

He "totally took over," Leah remembered. "We all had the best time. He charmed everybody. He stayed until twelve o'clock and he was just adorable."

He actually was just starting to become adorable and he was looking it too. In his dressing room on the set of *The Sunshine Boys*, Herbert Ross had asked how he managed to keep his complexion so smooth and free of wrinkles.

"Revlon's Eterna 27," George said. "I've been using facial cream all my life but this is the best. I put it on every morning." This was true, as Lisa Miller confirmed. He certainly knew the secret of youth. Call it Eterna 27.

When *The Sunshine Boys* was released, George received the first personal rave reviews of his career. In February 1976 he was deservedly nominated for an Academy Award as the Best Supporting Actor of 1975.

This was amazing for a man who had never acted. "He was able to inhabit his role," Herbert Ross thought, "because he was an incarnation of that character—and he understood perfectly who and what those people were. And George is very simple. He has no big acting theories. He was able to play an aspect of himself which had not been tapped before.

"Also, he was used to being on the stage and he was a very skilled artist at that, so he always knew what he was doing. And after all, the act with Gracie was a form of acting."

His competition for the Best Supporting Actor award came not only from Brad Dourif, but from the picture he was in, *One Flew over the Cuckoo's Nest*. It appeared headed for a sweep of the Oscars, and there was no telling how many of the awards would be swept along with it.

Lisa, now separated from her husband, was Burn's date at the March awards, and when he walked down the aisle to claim his Oscar, he was cheered as the sentimental favorite he was. Eighty-year-old Academy Award winners were as rare as eighty-year-old comedians.

Every other prize seemed to go to *Cuckoo's Nest*. Michael Douglas, as its producer, accepted the Academy Award for Best Picture; Milos Foreman won for direction, Jack Nicholson for Best Actor, and Louise Fletcher for Best Actress.

George had a broad grin on his face as he accepted his Oscar from Linda Blair and Ben Johnson. Noting that he'd made his last movie in 1939, he said, "I've decided to keep making one picture every thirty-six years. Getting this award tonight proves one thing: if you stay in this business long enough, you get to be new again."

He wasn't new yet. The movie did not change his life or his work. Reporters talked to him like an old man and he knew what they expected. He gave them old man answers. Asked how he planned to celebrate, he replied, "I'm going home to have a bowl of soup."

There weren't many old man parts and the Academy Award wasn't leading to any more movie offers. There was no more of a market for an old actor than there was for an old comedian. "I'm thinking of taking on Gentile roles," he said, "and becoming the new Robert Redford," but it wasn't that funny.

He went back to playing Las Vegas, whenever he was booked.

18

When an actor writes a book of memoirs, it often means he's out of work. Nobody becomes an actor to write memoirs.

In the case of George Burns, the concept of memory assumes new dimension. He always refused to talk about the hard facts of his life, and yet his monologues were increasingly about his life—at least, his "life." When one version didn't get laughs, he tried another, until his life was his act literally as well as figuratively. So it was appropriate for him to write many different memoirs.

Like most celebrities, he didn't exactly write them. *I Love Her, That's Why!* (Simon and Schuster, 1955) attests to Gracie's greater fame. It was essentially about her, written by Cynthia Hobart Lindsay from Burns's recollections. In 1976, he published *Living It Up (Or, They Still Love Me in Altoona)*. This time, his own people did the writing. He related anecdotes to the office secretary, Jack Langdon, and when enough were recorded, the one-man writing staff, Elon ("Packy") Packard, put them into readable form. This was published by G. P. Putnam's Sons.

The book begins with a potpourri of homilies on the

subject of age—young at heart, as old as you feel, and so on. What follows is a random series of essays on Gracie, open-heart surgery, Carol Channing, Lisa Miller, Jack Benny, and *The Sunshine Boys*.

Whatever the book's shortcomings as literature, it conveys a voice that is unmistakably Burns's, and because of that, it is charming. *Living It Up* was not a great commercial success, but George wasn't busy at the time, it was good money, and it passed for work.

Even as it was being published, another book, Avery Corman's novel *Oh, God!*, was resurfacing at Warner Brothers after having been given up for dead. The studio had bought it years earlier, but nobody wanted to make the movie.

One of Hollywood's best writers, Larry Gelbart, had been hired for the screenplay. Mel Brooks had already accepted Gelbart's suggestion that he play God, and the writer had Woody Allen in mind for the young man chosen by God to be a messenger. "But Woody was working on *Love and Death,*" Gelbart remembered, "and anyhow, he had his own vision of what God was." Larry Gelbart did not think of this movie as being seriously about God, but it is surprising how many in Hollywood did—or perhaps it isn't surprising.

Gelbart's friend Carl Reiner was approached to direct it. The former comedy writer had made three movies, the last of which—*Where's Poppa?*—had been such a *succès d'estime* that he hadn't been asked to direct since. Even so, he rejected *Oh, God!* because the notion of Mel Brooks as God, he thought, "would have been 'The 2,000 Year Old Man' all over again." That was a reference to the popular series of comedy records that Reiner and Brooks had made in the 1950s.

After the Corman novel had picked up several years' worth of dust at Warner Brothers, Gelbart saw *The Sunshine Boys* and was inspired with the idea of Burns playing

God. When he suggested it to Reiner, the director said, "Now that is a picture!" and agreed to make it. The casting reminded him of George's role on *The Burns and Allen Show,* with its magic television set. "He played God then. He stood outside the scene and he'd say, 'She's going to walk out the door now. She's going to come over to me.' "

The only time Gelbart had ever written for Burns was when he'd been in the Army, writing for the Armed Forces Radio Service. It was a sketch for Burns and Allen, but since it was slightly racy he put "Written by Paul Henning" on the cover. "He [Henning] was George's senior writer," Gelbart explained, "and his name with Burns and Allen guaranteed approval."

Reiner never considered anyone but Burns for the title role, and when George came to read for *Oh, God!,* "well," the director remembered, "the first reading was absolutely *there*. He was exactly right for the part."

In 1976, despite winning the Academy Award, Burns was not considered a name and he certainly wasn't paid like one. Jerry Weintraub, the executive producer of *Oh, God!,* negotiated a fee that was no bigger than what Burns had received for *The Sunshine Boys*. Reiner was startled when Irving Fein agreed, because "it wasn't a price."

Gelbart said, "I don't think Irving knew who George Burns was yet." Then again, George hadn't become *George Burns* yet. Certainly, the low fee did not indicate much prestige for an actor who had just won the Academy Award. "So what?" Gelbart said, wise to the forgetful ways of Hollywood. "That was Monday."

To broaden the picture's appeal, the popular folk singer John Denver was hired as the co-star. The idea was that George would attract the old-timers while Denver brought in the kids. That made for one star with a single movie role to his credit and the other with no acting experience at all. But as Reiner pointed out, at that time, Burns was not a star. "He wasn't a star even when he worked with Gracie.

She was the star. And even after she died, his monologues were never anything special."

Oh, God! is basically a "what if?" movie: what if God paid a visit to earth? Jerry Landers (John Denver) is an average guy with a wife, two children, and a job as the assistant manager in a Burbank supermarket. One day, he receives a mysterious memorandum: "God grants you an interview." The appointment is at an office on the twenty-seventh floor of a seventeen-story building located at, if you please, North Hope Street.

At first, God speaks to Landers through an office intercom, then from the car radio. He finally shows up in the person of a big-eared, pint-sized old man in a white fishing cap, red plaid shirt, and poplin jacket, a male version of the proverbial little old lady in tennis sneakers.

More disarming than God's appearance is His accent. One does not expect the Lord Almighty to speak like a Jewish man from the Lower East Side of New York City. As Burns grew older, his accent was becoming more pronounced, and he would say "tawk" for talk, "wit" for with (and, in private, "hoo-a" for whore). Much of his speech was inflected with a Yiddish-style tone of querulousness. An occasional Jewish expression in the script, "Sue me," for instance, seemed to cater to this accent.

In the picture, America's loss of trust in God has piqued divine concern. "Religion is easy," God tells Jerry Landers. "I'm talking about faith. You're going to help me change that."

Because there are "too many non-believers," He wants it known that He still exists, and also that He is fretful about the way people are carrying on. As Avery Corman put it in his novel, mankind has everything it needs for happiness. "I set up the world to work," God says, "only I can't do it for you. It's up to you to do it yourself."

After the young man is convinced that this definitely is God, he tries to spread that word, only to be ridiculed as a crank. To test his claim, he is locked in a hotel room with a list of fifty questions only God could answer. These have been posed by a panel of religious professionals—a minister, a priest, a rabbi, a television evangelist. When Burns shows up as God at Landers's door, he is in the guise of a bellhop, carrying a private joke, a bottle of ketchup. His response to the theological questions, besides providing the answers, is to give his opinion of the religious panel. The movie, having been at pains to be non-denominational ("Jesus was my son, Buddha was my son, Mohammed, Moses, you"), tiptoes respectfully around the sensibilities of various churches and synagogues, before pouncing on the safe target of the television evangelist (Paul Sorvino). When the holy roller sues the young man for slander, the picture arrives at its climactic trial scene.

On the first day of rehearsal, Burns astonished Reiner as he had astonished Herbert Ross, having memorized his part, indeed, the entire script. When work started, "he was respectful of the role," Reiner recalled. "George was an old Jew and the word 'God' impressed him. He played the part with total respect. In fact, he questioned that God would be wearing this funny cap."

Reiner explained to him, "God came down in that guise. He could be anything. Let's assume that he didn't want to scare people." And, the director said, "George accepted that."

There were several changes that Reiner made in Gelbart's script. One was to make the Denver character an agnostic, perhaps in the cause of honesty, for the director himself was not a religious person. "The picture served two purposes," Reiner said. "It served the people who believe that God is the Almighty who knows everything; and it served the purpose of those of us who believe that life is being fouled by man's stupidity and irresponsibility about what we have here. We're poisoning the atmosphere and the water."

Another contribution of Reiner's was a miracle for God to do, a card trick with cards that appear and disappear magically. Gelbart considered it corny, but Reiner said, "The way George plays God, a card trick is what he'd do. He spread out a deck of cards that wasn't there and said, 'Pick a card.'

"When I told George about it," Reiner remembered, "he clapped his hands and said, 'Oh, that's perfect! Perfect!'

"It was the simplest trick in the world, but in his hands it was a trick that God would do, because it was simple, and God would be a simple man."

During filming, Burns conserved his energy, lying down in his dressing room between takes. Reiner took precautions too. One scene called for God to make it rain inside a car. "We knew we had to drench George with water for however many takes it was going to require. He had a few lines in the scene and it's easy to muff lines when there is so much 'business' going on.

"So I made sure that he was wearing protective waterproof material under his clothes. But all he needed was one take, and he was stronger than anyone would imagine he would be at that age."

Reiner was also solicitous about Burns's attention span. "As with all older actors," he said, "you are aware of them getting tired. He had two long speeches in the courtroom scene, and I said, 'Let's get two cameras on this one,' even though it isn't the kind of scene where you *want* two cameras. Because you want to light it well, but I felt that because of his age, I had to. So that we would get the close-up as well as the long shot, and if he slipped up, we would be able to cover it up.

"Well, we were finished by noon. We had nothing to do. He did both speeches from four different angles and did them perfectly; I mean, *usable perfect.*" Reiner had to conclude about Burns: "Nobody stays alive for that long, and keeps his senses, unless he's gifted with the best genes in the world."

The director occasionally visited with his eighty-year-old star during breaks in the shooting. A show business aficionado, Reiner would ask about the early days with Gracie, and the even earlier ones when Burns was growing up in New York. "I wanted to know about his family. I'd heard it all in his act, but I wanted to know what was fact and what was fiction."

Reiner came to realize that "everything there is to know about him, he said himself and he doesn't want to say much more. . . . He remains a mystery to me.

"I tried to talk to him," Reiner said, "but it was frustrating."

He could never get a straight answer.

"I ask you a question," Reiner complained to Burns, "and you always tell me a joke."

"Ask," Burns said.

"How old are you?"

"I was eighty in January. "

"Well, I'm fifty-five," Reiner said, "and it's getting me worried. Tell me honestly, when I'm eighty can I look forward to any kind of a sex life?"

"Sex life?" Burns marveled. "Let me tell you something, Carl. It's like trying to get a raw oyster into a coin slot."

Reiner knew it was hopeless.

Oh, God! did not provide as rich an acting opportunity as he'd had in *The Sunshine Boys*. As written, God was not a layered character. He didn't even have moods, and all of George's scenes were played with John Denver because none of the other characters could see God. Denver was giving an acceptable performance, but it was understandably tentative and passive. He did not have the experience to interact with Burns the way Walter Matthau had in the Neil Simon movie.

Even so, Reiner recognized that "George was a natural as an actor and listened to the other actor in a scene."

Who, if not a straight man, would know how to listen?

A movie courtroom scene is always climactic, but there was not nearly enough of a buildup in *Oh, God!* to anticipate the fireworks when Burns came to John Denver's defense. These fireworks could not have been set off without the script, and screenwriter Gelbart deserves credit for that. But it is Burns's radiant performance that makes the scene so compelling.

As Reiner pointed out, these are two very long courtroom speeches. Burns begins the first one gently and softly. "I know how hard it is in these times to have faith," he says understandingly to the judge, the courtroom, and the movie audience. "But maybe," he suggests, "if you could have the faith to start with, maybe the times would change. You could change them. Think about it. Try. And try not to hurt each other. There's been enough of that. It really gets in the way. . . ."

This is quite nicely written, forcing the issue of what is simple, what is simplistic. When the picture tries to deliver words of wisdom, it sounds platitudinous ("The heart is the temple where all truth resides"), and when it attempts to deal with theology, it is certainly simplistic ("What is the true origin of the universe?" "Did man fall from grace in the Garden of Eden?").

But in this courtroom scene, the picture starts to soar beyond the glossy surface of its celluloid heart. The screenwriting becomes simple in the best sense, and God's courtroom speeches would strike inspirational chords among audiences.

Pictures may be made by movie people in Hollywood, but they are experienced by everyday people who offer themselves up to the dramatic experience. They watch the moving pictures in theatres where they can make their emotions available, safe in the company of others, protected from embarrassment by the dark. What was contrived in a Hollywood office can be legitimized in a neighborhood movie house. In that gathering place, there is always the chance for awe and rapture. Audiences watching *Oh, God!* in 1977 sensed an affirmation from it, an affirmation for which they apparently yearned; a sign of decency and virtue in a time of little faith in the existence of goodness, let alone God.

George Burns, vaudevillian, was providing that. As if himself inspired rather than intimidated or even shamed by the presumption of playing God, he rose to the occasion. He evoked the majesty of a simple man, which is all that most people hoped for in a deity. He found a way to be, or at least to portray a being who was, both intelligent and decent.

His second courtroom speech built from the first with conviction and strength. "However hopeless, helpless, mixed up and scary it gets, it can work. . . . If you find it hard to believe in me, maybe it would help you to know that I believe in you. . . . Just talk, I'll listen."

Such a speech is fraught with risks of being hypocritical or maudlin. Burns slipped those risks. He brought his own decency and compassion to the performance, and it glowed almost palpably from the screen. And so at this time he himself was born anew. If he had proved himself an actor in *The Sunshine Boys*, he now transformed himself in a much bigger way than playing a character in a story. Within and beyond *Oh God!* a hitherto unseen George Burns emerged: wise and benevolent, yet impish and droll, "everybody's idea," as Reiner said, "of who you would want to sit and be advised by."

This person was God in the guise of a sagacious, grandfatherly old showman, and that was the new act. He could now work alone, as himself, and he would be able to play this act for the rest of his life. At the age of eighty-one he became at last, for the first time in his life, a major star. And that is what he got paid for doing *Oh, God!*

Larry Gelbart was dissatisfied with the movie, and he not only wrote the screenplay, he was nominated for an Academy Award for it. "I thought I would have a chance to make it better," he said. "They really shot a first draft. [But] the writer of a movie is just not around."

The picture might have been worse; it might have been sanctimonious. Burns himself dries the sweet out of it. It is sometimes coy, for instance, when it suggests that God might have made trees lower so that animals could eat the leaves, or that his avocado pits are too big. *Oh God!* was also blatantly calculated to appeal to the young, not only through the casting of John Denver but with such speeches as, "Young people cannot fall from my grace. They're my best things."

Perhaps the calculation brought the youth audience in, but Burns walked away with them. Young people became some of his greatest fans, and "they stayed with me," he said.

Oh, God! was a huge success. Produced at a cost of $2.2 million, it grossed either $30, $60, or $100 million, depending on whose figures are to be believed. "It was the biggest surprise of my life," Reiner said. "It was a sweet picture . . . it was also the only picture I was ever involved with that stayed in some theatres for almost a year."

That fascinated him. "For a lot of people," he said, "it was a religious experience."

After the picture was released, and while it was a national hit, George was in New York City, heading for the Friar's Club with Walter Matthau and Lou Weiss. They were going to lunch, but stuck in traffic at Park Avenue and 55th, they decided to get out and walk the remaining half block. The Friar's was just around the corner.

The taxi driver wouldn't let them pay the fare, and as they got out of the cab, they saw that the usual traffic snarl had been compounded by construction work. Much of East 55th Street was torn up, and as the three men walked along the temporary wooden sidewalks, they passed groups of hardhat workers on lunch breaks.

"Hey, George!" several cried.

"Hey, God!"

An autograph seeker stopped him and Burns obliged. The man said, "My little boy will ask me, 'Did you really see God in person?' "

Burns turned to Matthau and Weiss. "Can you imagine this happening to me? I was never this big in the days with Gracie."

The new act was one he could never have dreamed up. It was not listed in the vaudeville book of routines. He was not a comedian and he certainly was not a dancer or a singer. The act was George Burns himself. At an age when most people were retired, inactive, or driving on memory, he was just getting started. And that act was a smash.

19

"*Oh, God!* showed a side of GB that nobody had ever seen before," Lisa Miller says. "It was a side of him that he only showed in private. Nobody knew the human side of this sweet, gentle man, this perfect, gifted human being."

A newfound sense of him certainly was heartening audiences in movie theatres across the country, and, Carl Reiner thought "this incarnation defined him in his later years."

The movie's success, and Burn's tremendous popularity, had more mundane meaning for his manager. An elderly star was an unprecedented phenomenon, and Irving Fein wasted little time exploiting it. Between 1977 and 1979, he contracted for George to write two books, appear in four movies, and play the top show rooms from Las Vegas to Lake Tahoe and Atlantic City. He was now being paid between $25,000 and $50,000 a week for such engagements.

Besides these bookings, Burns made regular appearances on the late-night television talk shows and in idle moments played the occasional state fair.

This was a lot of work for a man in his eighties, and those close to Burns were concerned about it. Lou Weiss was one of them, but being chairman of the William Morris Agency complicated his situation. "I was very careful not to be involved—I didn't want to do anything to disturb the relationship with Irving. He keeps my uncle working when he shouldn't. Sometimes, my uncle played dates when he wasn't feeling well enough."

Burns's son Ronnie, on the other hand, thought that rather than killing his father, work was keeping him alive, and perhaps there was something to both views.

Burns was also available for a new kind of private engagement, which the comedian Jan Murray marveled over. "This idolatry," he said, "this appearing in person— the love, the affection—people were paying him $50,000 and $75,000 just to fly down to be at their parties. Just so they could say they know George Burns."

He also made appearances at benefits, although Fein discouraged it. Joan Benny asked her father's onetime manager if George might show up at a major Hollywood benefit with which she was involved. She got an excuse in return. "I knew damn well," she said, "it was because George wasn't getting paid. Irving Fein is an agent from the top of his head to the tip of his toe, and if George doesn't get paid that means Irving doesn't get paid."

There were some unpaid appearances from which Burns could not be dissuaded, such as the roasts at the Friar's Club in New York, or at Hillcrest in Los Angeles. But while so much work was taxing, he seemed to revel in the activity.

Every Passover, Jan Murray would host two seders, on the first and second nights of the Jewish holiday. The first ritual feast was for his family, and the second was for his comedian friends. They were not the Round Table crowd, but a younger generation of comics, including Buddy Hackett, Red Buttons, Shecky Green, and Jack Carter, as well as Milton Berle who, Murray said, "bridged us with the older generation of Groucho and Jessel and Benny and Burns."

Murray's wife Toni suggested that he might invite some of the older comedians (those who were still alive). Groucho Marx declined. "I appreciate being asked," he told Murray, "but I'm an old man and I can't wait that long to eat. I have my dinner now at five-thirty. Besides, I went to a seder last year and it's the same material."

But Burns accepted. "I haven't been to a seder since I was five years old," he said, "back on the East Side with my grandfather."

He never knew his grandfather, but it was probably true that he hadn't been to a seder for most of his life. That didn't surprise Jan Murray. "Jewish had nothing to do with guys like Cantor, Benny, Berle, and Burns. They were performing since they were kids. All they knew was show business and all they spoke was show business. It's amazing that any of them had any degree of humanness."

Besides, he added, the older comedians tried to rid themselves of Jewishness. "In that generation," he said, "it was important to appear Gentile. It was tough to be on radio or television if you had a Jewish 'thing' about you. They wouldn't say it. They would say you were too *New York*. But that was what they meant."

Others at that seder from the Burns generation were Lou Holtz and Edward G. Robinson.

"At my house," Murray said, "we do a serious seder. We don't fool around. If we were going to fool around, I might as well just invite everyone for dinner.

"But afterward"—he grinned—"of course, anything goes."

He and his wife took all of the furniture out of their sun room and set up an enormous horseshoe table to seat the thirty-five to forty guests they were expecting. "And George," he remembered, "was just magnificent that night, telling stories and singing all those obscure verses to famous songs."

As he caught the rhythm of this crowd of younger

comics, he paused to light a cigar, which every one of them knew to be part of his routine. During that pause, one of the non-entertainers, a "civilian," asked a question that Murray considered "very stupid."

The question was, "Mr. Burns, do you believe in the hereafter? I mean, do you think there's a heaven and a hell?"

Murray was appalled. "There were other things you could think of discussing with a man who was eighty-two years old."

But the benign Burns simply twinkled his eye and said, "I don't know what they've got waiting for me, but I'm bringing my music." The laugh from the crowd of professional comedians told him that he had a line he could use again. He certainly would. It was in this way that he created material and built it into monologues.

"It was a joke and it was true," Murray said. "If he could sing three songs and tell three jokes, he was happy." More to the point, he was learning how to disarm audiences with a light approach to his physical functioning and his mortality, which were the aspects of the elderly that made most people uncomfortable.

The younger comics seemed to vie for his approval. Murray himself kind of bragged about an evening when Burns was sitting at his table at a party and a stranger walked over. "Forgive me, Mr. Murray," the man said, "but I saw you a few nights ago in Las Vegas. And I just want you to know that I think you're about as good a stand-up as I've seen in years. And I just wanted to say this."

Murray was embarrassed. "It looked as if I'd hired this guy to come over and flatter me in front of George." Turning to Burns, he said, "I swear, I don't know this guy."

"Well, kid," George said, "you're *pretty* good," which of course thrilled the younger comedian. But George Burns never changed his mind about who was the greatest of all comedians. This was the man he admired and detested beyond all others. "I'll tell you who the best was," he said. "The best was Frank Fay."

Buddy Hackett recognized Burns as the resident sage of show business, which was why he took issue with Jan Murray's story. Then again, he always took issue with Murray, just for sheer love of the man. These two were pals the way Jack Benny and George were.

Hackett insisted that a Hollywood doctor, while giving Burns the regular examination before a movie, asked who George's favorite comedian was. This, Hackett reiterated, was a doctor.

"Buddy Hackett," was Burns's immediate response, at least according to Hackett, who said, "George told the doctor, 'Buddy Hackett is the best stand-up I ever saw. If I had thirty minutes left to live and had to spend them watching a comedian, it would be Buddy Hackett.' "

Buddy couldn't leave it at just that. " 'And if the kid was hot,' " he insisted George continued, " 'I'd stay alive an extra twenty minutes to listen.' "

That actually sounded as if it might be true. There weren't many comedians funnier than Buddy Hackett in his prime, and Burns liked to fool with him. At a Friar's Club roast being held in the Beverly Hilton Hotel, Hackett was seated on the dais, between Burns and the actor George Raft.

Burns turned to him and whispered, "Don't eat the dinner. I'll get the waiter to give us a couple of orders of ham and eggs. You've got to have the ham and eggs here at the Beverly Hilton. There's nothing like them anywhere."

Hackett turned to George Raft and asked the suave star of gangster movies, "Are you going to have the ham and eggs?"

"No," Raft said, "I'm going to eat a steak."

Burns motioned to the waiter and asked whether, as a personal favor, he and Mr. Hackett might have the Beverly Hilton's celebrated ham and eggs.

"Meanwhile," Hackett said, "George Raft got that steak and it was gorgeous, a New York strip, plus a baked potato and peas."

He turned to Raft and asked, "How's the steak, George?"

"Excellent," Raft said. "As good as ever."

Hackett and Burns waited. Finally, the waiter brought their orders of ham and eggs.

Hackett examined his plate. Then he began to eat.

"It was the most ordinary ham, boiled ham, nothing special. And eggs. Two regular fried eggs."

After eating a few forkfuls, he turned to Burns.

"This is regular ham and eggs. Why did I have to order the ham and eggs?"

Burns replied, "Because they don't make just one order."

Jan Murray thought that was so funny he insisted that he, not George Raft, had been there at the Beverly Hilton, sitting on the dais with Burns and Hackett. And then he would tell the story as if he'd been there when it happened.

But it was Hackett's story, a real experience that he found funny, and could make funny for others. Like George Burns, he drew his material from reality, and he could communicate his sense of humor. For such fellows, being funny was a serious matter, a way of getting through life.

In 1978, Burns made a television movie, *The Comedy Company*, and played a cameo role in a feature film, *Sgt Pepper's Lonely Hearts Club Band*. The next year, he made even easier money. At Warner Brothers, production had just been completed on a picture called *Movie/Movie*. Made from a Larry Gelbart script, it consisted of two separate one-hour satires of old movies—a valentine to the double features of the 1940s and 1950s.

The Warner executives were having second thoughts about audiences understanding what the picture was all about. Hollywood is famous for its distrust of originality, which is exceeded only by its distrust of the audience's intelligence. Gelbart was asked to write a brief prologue explaining the whole idea of *Movie/Movie*, and Burns was hired to read it.

"For two hours' work," Gelbart remembered, "he was paid $50,000."

When George arrived at the studio to do the reading, his manager was with him. As always, Burns was fully prepared and he started promptly.

"This is a movie house," he spoke. "We used to have these. Those were the days when the only four-letter word you saw in a movie was 'Exit.' "

But just when George was getting started, Fein became ostentatiously impatient. As Gelbart remembered, "Irving stood there looking at his watch."

"Irving," Gelbart whispered to the manager, "come on, this is a first take, $50,000, give us a break."

After all, the last time Gelbart had anything to do with Fein, it was *Oh, God!* and Burns was doing it, an entire movie, for a minimal fee. This was quite an improvement, especially when the fee was figured on a per-hour basis.

However, "by now," the writer said, "Irving had found his balls."

George was being deluged by fan mail, but one writer outdid herself. Her first letter simply enthused over his book, *Living It Up*. Her subsequent letters continued the enthusiasm. Then she wrote with personal admiration, and she continued to write. She wrote so many letters that finally George added a postscript to one of the thank-you notes that Jack Langdon sent out from the office. "If you're ever in L.A.," he put down—his handwriting a childish scrawl—"here's my telephone number. Let me buy you a drink."

The writer's name was Catherine Carr and she had been writing from Dallas. She was a divorced mother of two, she was wealthy, she was forty-five years younger than George, and she finally took him up on the invitation. Flying to Los Angeles for the evening, her one dinner date led to several, and after she came out a few times, she grew infatuated with him, or so it seemed to Lisa.

Cathy Carr began to fly in from Dallas every couple of weeks. The relationship between the forty-five-year-old woman and the eighty-three-year-old man appeared to be a chaste one. She always stayed at the Beverly Hills Hotel.

"She seemed to intrigue him," Lisa said. "He must have been flattered that a very young and very wealthy woman with blond hair down to her waist was mad about him."

Larry Gelbart said, "I don't know how sexy it was, but it was romantic." He'd watched them during the filming of the *Movie/Movie* prologue. "George would stroke her hair fondly, tenderly."

Cathy was very generous, perhaps too generous. As her gifts became more elaborate, he had to reciprocate in kind, and he told a friend, "That woman is going to break me."

Lisa, unable to resist, asked outright, "GB, are you sleeping with Cathy?"

She should have known better than to expect a straight answer.

"Kid," he replied, "I can hardly pee on my shoes."

One thing Lisa did know was that he was potent and active, but some of the older women in his circle were irate about a general pattern of aging male stars being smitten with presumably treacherous and deceitful young females. Groucho Marx had been involved with a young woman named Erin Fleming, who, so a friend of his said, "came into his life when he was beginning to slip. She was a disturbing force. She took advantage and tried to take over. She alienated many of his friends and tried to drive us away."

George's friend Fred Astaire was another old-timer who had the ladies muttering. He'd just married a young jockey.

Burns, however, did not appear to be part of this endangered subspecies of the male elderly. His mind seemed as sound as his body, although some began to rethink that when he went to Texas to meet Cathy's parents.

"I would have liked to be there for that," Carl Reiner said.

Cathy Carr was frank about wanting to get married. When a reporter asked her about "May-December unions," suggesting a bit snidely that "it may sound like Erin Fleming and Groucho Marx all over again," she rejected the mean comparison with composure. There were two differences, she explained, between Marx's girlfriend and herself. "I certainly don't want an acting career and I have more money than George does."

She was quite sensitive to their age difference ("I hate it") and was afraid of just the kind of suggestion that the interviewer was making: that she and George would be likened to "these sugar daddies and these young girls with minks. *How can they do it?*"

But she did it, insisting that she "wrestles with the fact that our relationship is not, quote, legally contracted in the eyes of God."

In short, Cathy Carr was not only from what she called "a very Christian background," but operated on a different level of sophistication than Burns. "I've never met anyone like him in my life before," she admitted.

As for Burns, he was taciturn and terse. "If I was younger, I'd marry her. I love her and she loves me, but I don't think I'll ever get married again."

His physical condition might have been excellent, his mind sharp, his energy astonishing, and his life spirit inspiring, but whatever Eterna 27 could do for his complexion, it could not change the fact that he was an octogenarian.

When he worked in Las Vegas, he would be booked only for a weekend, just three performances. That was every three months. He signed a major contract with Caesar's Palace on that basis, four engagements a year.

He played the occasional one-night stand, even a business event if the price was right. For instance, Fein extracted a huge fee from General Motors for an appearance at a sales convention in Disney World. George let the automobile company arrange the rest of the show because that way, they paid for it. He used to be concerned about his girl singer because there would be a couple of comedy exchanges. Those little routines harked back to Burns and Allen, but there weren't many who remembered Gracie Allen. These audiences came to see George Burns.

So he now worked completely alone. He would fly in, do his fifty-five-minute monologue, and go home. The old act, having been put to rest a quarter of a century earlier, was finally dead.

He began the new, post-*God* act by disarming his audience of any defensiveness about his age. Since he always received a standing ovation, he had plenty of time to light his cigar, look at it, take a puff, and then smile until the audience quieted down.

"If I can stand, you can," he'd croak. Or he'd use the line he had been using for ten years, "I get a standing ovation just standing." Or, "I can hear you saying to each other, 'How do you like that? And he walks too!' "

Sometimes he would use all three lines, but he would never improvise. He always prepared a monologue line for line for line. That was hardly for want of quickness. Not many were faster with a riposte than George Burns. It was simply that he had always believed in preparation and discipline, and that was off the stage as well as on it.

"You know," he would say to his audience, "people ask me about the young girls I go out with." He inserted his El Producto into a little plastic holder, struck a match, and inhaled. Blowing out the smoke, he looked at the cigar to make sure it was lighted.

It was all in the timing.

"I would go out with women my age," he'd say, and pause. "But there are no women my age."

It was important to make his audience comfortable with his age. "When I walk, I walk," he would say. "I take *steps*. And not little steps. Little steps, you'll never get there. At Hillcrest, which is my club, I never ask anyone how they feel. Everyone there is old. A member comes over to the table taking little steps, am I going to ask him how he feels? I *see* how he feels. I'll say, 'Nice to see you.' Then he'll sit down. Drop a little food on himself."

Never a joke-teller as such, he had burnished his reminiscences to a warm and easy glow, and he could be gracefully sage. "You can't help getting older," he'd say, "but you don't have to get old."

That was his stage manner, relaxed, quiet, casual, and yet curiously formal—"courtly," as he so often was described.

Carl Reiner noticed that "he kept something back. He presented much less than he was. He was the most economical monologist ever. He was always very quiet, and so, as he told you these stories between puffs on his cigar, you thought you were in the presence of a pundit."

His punditries would have sounded like homilies from anyone less charming. "Don't worry about little things," he told his audiences. "It's little things that upset you the most. If the food is no good, send for the ketchup.

"And never get discouraged."

That was from the heart.

"Whenever I was canceled, I just thought, 'Poor audience, missed a lot.'

"Imagine getting up every day hating what you have to do. That's what shortens your life. It's better to be a failure at something you enjoy than a success at something you hate."

Such philosophizing would last only so long. He knew

when to stop. When he sensed that moment, a twinkle came to his eye and he would take a quick puff on the El Producto cigar. This was the signal that his mind had gone ahead on the humor circuit, and it was time to lace the pensive mood with wit.

As Gelbart put it, "His humor is so fast, but he just does not press. He's a fountain."

Burns always stood as he performed, but he was beginning to complain about it. He traveled with Barry Mirkin, whom he'd met at Hillcrest, and one evening after a performance he said, "You know, Barry, it's getting to be tough standing for an hour."

"Why don't you try the act sitting down?" Mirkin suggested. "If Perry Como can sit on a stool, why can't you? You're older."

George replied that it wasn't the way he was taught. But one evening in Las Vegas, the two of them were watching Bill Cosby perform. It was the comedian's closing show at Caesar's Palace, on the night before Burns opened. As the show room's glittering curtain rose, Cosby was not standing, and he wasn't sitting on a bar stool. He was sprawled across a sofa.

"He did the whole act that way," Mirkin remembered.

"If Cosby can do it," he said to Burns, "so can you."

It took a while to defy the old conventions, but finally George acceded to his body's demands. He would look out across the darkened audience and say, "Now I'm going to do something I like to do more than anything else." And he would sit down. First it was on a bar stool, soon it became an easy chair.

His informality never went as far as Cosby's. Cosby wore a sweater while he performed. Such casual costuming was one trick that this old dog refused to learn. George Burns had been dapper as a young man and he remained that way. He was strictly a tuxedo man, with a red silk handkerchief in his breast pocket, a pair of patent leather shoes on his feet, and on the ring finger of his left hand, Gracie's good-luck "cat's eye" ring.

Canny vaudevillian that he was, he knew that an audience's eyes are attracted by a moving prop. The prop was the cigar in his left hand, so that hand was where he wore the cat's eye ring for good luck.

20

People would walk directly up to Burns and speak without embarrassment or awkwardness. They got the feeling that they could. They seemed to assume that he was approachable as well as forthcoming, and they were right: he had patience for anyone who was polite. As he strolled through the lobby of New York's Helmsley-Palace Hotel, he responded to good wishes and greetings with smiles, handshakes, and when requested, autographs.

However, when several youngsters rushed up to George in a group and shouted for autographs, he laughed and waved them aside. As he continued on through the lobby, he said to Irving Fein and a visiting writer, "You get back what you give out. I like people, I enjoy people. For instance, I felt bad just now, passing those kids and not signing autographs for them. I enjoy people and people enjoy talking to me."

A dramatic figure approached, a towering man who wore a glamorous ankle-length brown suede trench coat and a matching wide-brimmed hat. The fellow was tanned to a deep bronze, and even though it was indoors, he was wearing sunglasses.

As he came closer, he stopped and cried, "Hello, George!"

Burns peered up into the face which, now that the man was upon him, made him crane his neck. He did not recognize who it was until the man removed his sunglasses and flashed a friendly grin.

"Billy Graham!" the man cried. "How are you, George?"

They had been friendly since the evangelist was a guest on *The Burns and Allen Show* on television. Graham was always a good sport, as long as the kidding was not irreverent. George enjoyed him. In his own way, Billy Graham was also in show business.

Burns had been talking without pause, his mind so alert and impatient that he sometimes stammered. That was a matter of his mouth playing catch-up with his thoughts. Onstage, when his concentration was in absolute focus, he exaggerated the stammer so that he could fine-tune a monologue while delivering it.

He jumped from one topic to the next, stream-of-consciousness style, although always within the bounds of show business. Arriving at the hotel's cocktail lounge, he took a seat and ordered a Bloody Mary while moving on to the subject of comedy. "You know what's funny by instinct," he said, taking a slight turn off the subject. "The audience tells you what's funny.

"Audiences are very happy to see me."

There was a theory that comedians tended to perform in a hostile psychological atmosphere. "I don't have that kind of a problem," he said. "But you can't go by me. I'm sort of an accepted commodity."

Irving Fein squeezed in a comment. "George was always never working." The seventyish manager, tall and slender, wearing horn-rimmed glasses and dressed in expensively tailored tweeds, resembled the newscaster John Chancellor, and had a general appearance that might be described as show business Ivy League. "All of the actors," said Fein, "used to hang out in front of the Palace between shows.

George wanted to look like he was working so when he hung out there, he'd put makeup on his collar."

Burns kept talking. "The audience finds everything," he said. "The people that come in to see me are people who know me. The material I do is familiar to them. The routines I do today are about my age, they're about my size. I don't talk about what I'm doing. I talk about what I've done. I talk in the past.

"The *Oh, God!* picture with John Denver really helped. All the John Denver kids came to see it.

"I love to work; you can't make any money in bed. Wait a minute. No, it's not the money. I don't need the money. I enjoy it, I enjoy working."

Fein interjected. "Tell the story about—"

"It [show business] seems the same to me," Burns continued briskly. "It hasn't changed for me. The words are different—they say all kinds of things today. You couldn't say anything in vaudeville. The secret to Mae West was her delivery. 'Come up and see me sometime.' What the hell was dirty about that? She could make anything sound as if she had just slept with you. If Gracie said, 'Come up and see me sometime,' it would mean the guy came up, we gave him some eggs, and he went home.

"I don't think I would have enjoyed sleeping with Mae West. She would put on her makeup and you would have to applaud her. I was always a great lover.

"In fact I wasn't. I never kissed Gracie where she applauded me. Now my sister Goldie, she had a whorehouse in San Diego."

Burns made two movies in 1978. In *Just You and Me, Kid* he was typecast as an old vaudevillian who has become wealthy and is giving his money away to other aging vaudevillians—much to the consternation of his greedy daughter.

By chance he becomes the protector of a young girl,

played by Brooke Shields, who is in trouble with a drug dealer. The situation allows his character to deal with familiar George Burns subjects such as show business, young women, and age. In short, the picture seems calculated to appeal to Burns fans.

The script provided little in the way of plot detail or structure. Much of Burns's character comes directly from his material in monologues and memoirs. Director Leonard Stern's memories of production seem set in subtext. "I could sense," he said, "that the earlier George, the one I didn't know, could be autocratic and authoritarian," but it would seem as if the later George had similar characteristics. Stern says, "It was an energizing experience, working with somebody that age who is active and creative," which sounds as if George had plenty to say about the script—and from the look of the movie, there was plenty that he did say about it, perhaps because something had to be said.

Whether these were suggestions or responses to requests, there are obvious and substantial contributions of his own. They are not always beneficial to the movie. Because they were allowed, *Just You and Me, Kid* often sounds like a George Burns routine. He sings, dances, tells familiar anecdotes, and renders words of wisdom about age; his character even has Burns's own birthday. What is missing, in both the picture and his performance, is the professional discipline that George Burns demands of his own work.

Making the movie, he was spry for a gentleman of eighty-two. "He would hurry across the set," Stern remembered, "nimbly sidestepping wires and cables and all the paraphernalia, but then he had always been a dancer and he still had that agility."

The wrap party seems to have been better than the picture. George hosted it at his home, and Stern brought his wife Gloria, as well as her mother Bianca.

As ever, guests in Burns's home meant an audience for

his songs. There was always an accompanist invited, and a moment when he started singing the old songs. George never wearied of them.

I'd love to call you Honey
But honey runs away,
I'd much prefer a name like Clinging Vine.

And if I called you Buttercup,
The dandelions would eat you up—
So I'll buy a ring and change your name to mine.

Leonard Stern's mother-in-law was old enough, and enough of an aficionado, to know the song. When she began to sing along with Burns, it brought him to a halt.

"Lady," he said. "I work alone—but later you can come on up to my room."

"That depends," the feisty Bianca said.

"On what?" George smiled.

"On whether or not you insist on smoking that cigar."

Of course he was just kidding about his room. He had always been interested in younger women, starting with Gracie.

He made *Going In Style* later in the year, and it is the best picture he ever made. Like Burns himself, it is mischievous, sweet and not unwise, dedicated to his proposition that being old doesn't have to be a terrible thing. It is about three septuagenarian roommates who have given up on life in old age. They idle away their time, sitting on park benches and collecting Social Security checks. Burns (there is no point using characters' names) suggests that, for a little excitement, they rob a bank. His pal Art Carney is game, but Lee Strasberg cannot believe they are serious, especially when George says, "We're going to need guns."

Burns's understated reading of this line begins his best pure acting since *The Sunshine Boys*.

After deciding how to dress, and whether to shave for a bank robbery, the three codgers, armed with guns and wearing Groucho Marx masks (which surely amused Burns), pull off the heist without a snag. The robbery makes for a grand scene and George is priceless as the amiably snarling ringleader of this improbable gang.

They agree that it "feels great to be doing something," but Lee Strasberg doesn't feel that great. In fact, he dies as soon as they count up their loot ($36,000). That is just as well because Burns and Carney were giving better performances. Strasberg, guru of the Actors Studio, looks as though he is always thinking about how to play the next scene.

More than half the picture remains after the robbery, but there is plenty of plot left in Martin Brest's impish screenplay. The two remaining thieves give away most of their take and fly to Las Vegas for a lark, bringing along a $5,000 stake. George takes to the craps tables like a character out of the Damon Runyon stories which could well have inspired this movie. He seems to know everything about betting at craps—a game that is all but unfathomable to the uninitiated.

In the gambling scene, Burns also has the manner of a man who is generally in control. This is the man Gracie was crazy about, the Burns whom Carol Channing trusted her performance to, the Burns who took charge of his career, his business, and his life. The character who emerges in this scene is a rich and full combination of all George Burns's qualities—street smart, confident, wily, warm, simultaneously trusting and skeptical—and funny, of course.

After putting these facets of his personality into the character, he never breaks that character. Unlike his other recent movies, there is never a wisecrack or a song to suggest this is George Burns the nightclub comedian.

Nor does he ever shuffle his feet like an old man. Rather, he strides through this delightful movie, without question at the center of its stage.

That is not to slight the work of Art Carney, whose performance is ingeniously detailed, from the tipping of a hat in a crowded elevator when a lady enters, to a joyous dance improvised to the music of a Jamaican street band. Indeed, the Burns-Carney interplay has the timing of a dance team and it is simply delightful to watch these two old professionals at work together.

Their performances are certainly indebted to Brest, who directed as well as wrote this thoughtful, entertaining, and crisply professional movie. It is not surprising that Martin Brest subsequently had such great successes as *Beverly Hills Cop* and *Scent of a Woman*.

It was inevitable that Warner Brothers would want to make a sequel to *Oh, God!,* but neither its director nor its writer was interested. Carl Reiner remembered, "Larry Gelbart and I were called to the Warner Brothers offices. They said, 'We have to do a sequel. The picture did over a hundred million dollars.' "

As the director recalled, "Larry and I said, simultaneously, '*You* have to do a sequel. *We* don't. And God doesn't.' "

When the studio executives asked for his reasons, Reiner said, "For God to come down one time and give a message to people—maybe that's possible. But for God to come down twice, you're making him *a nudge*.

"To keep coming down? His own messenger? Where are the angels? For those people who believe in God, it's a disservice to Him.

"Besides, if He comes down more than once, it's a genie picture."

Of course, *Oh, God! Book Two* was made anyhow. Gilbert Cates produced and directed it, and five writers worked on the script, including Lisa Miller, who was now using her full name, Melissa Miller. They did not work on it long enough.

"George didn't mind doing the sequel," Reiner says. "He loves to work and he loved being God."

The role did seem to have a transforming effect, at least on his public personality. As Melissa Miller noted, he allowed his inner self to emerge. It was as if he had faith in himself at last. But there was also another transformation, and in its own way it was miraculous, for what was the *Oh, God!* miracle of rain inside a car compared to superstardom at the age of eighty?

The performance had also transformed *God*'s life. Audiences do suspend their disbelief, and millions seemed to momentarily identify God with this little old man. The Lord Almighty, usually pictured as bearded, thunderingly majestic, and quite furious if not downright frightening, had evolved into a grandfatherly vaudevillian with a sweet heart and a wry sense of humor.

As a title character, God got shorter shrift in the second movie. *Oh, God! Book Two* is the original without the glow, leaving the formula bare. God simply says, "They're still not getting my message," and the same story starts all over again.

Although Burns as God was supposed to be the movie's main attraction, the most important character is a little girl named Tracy who is the chosen messenger, this picture's John Denver. As the daughter of an advertising man, she suggests that a catchy slogan be used to spread the Word, and her slogan is, "Think God."

Like Denver in the first picture, she is disbelieved, but this time a panel of psychiatrists stands ready to commit her to an institution. It is not a lighthearted notion for a movie.

God comes to her rescue, and with the help of a few miracles, the psychiatrists are convinced that she was not hallucinating. In the bargain, her separated parents reconcile.

A young actress with one name, Louanne, played Tracy, and hers is the larger role in the picture. Burns's scenes are brief statements of his Godliness, with none of the inspired touches that gave the original movie its thrilling moments. *Oh, God! Book Two* plays and looks like a television movie, and Reiner said he hated it.

Because it starred the tremendously popular Burns in the role that made him tremendously popular, it performed satisfactorily at the box office. At least, it performed satisfactorily enough for Irving Fein to talk Warner Brothers into another sequel, *Oh, God! You Devil.*

The idea of the third movie in the series was for George to play two roles in it, the Devil as well as God, battling over the life of a young man who may or may not have sold his soul to become a rock star. The larger of Burns's roles was as the Devil, and that alone would have undone the picture. For the success of *Oh, God!* was based on his perceived goodness. Audiences did not want to see him as a figure of evil. *Oh God! You Devil* was hoisted, then, on its own Satanic petard. The moviemakers, apparently sensing that, merely made him *devilish*. This is a hoofless and tailless Satan, an evildoer whose evil doings run to making a waiter lose his trousers in the middle of a restaurant.

The movie is just another exploitation of the Faust legend, without a tone of voice, or even a touch of malice. The most amusing thing about it is that on earth the Devil assumes the guise of an agent. Yet there aren't even agent jokes. Perhaps that was because the picture's executive producer was Irving Fein himself.

Burns was eighty-seven when he made *Oh, God! You Devil*, but he hardly looks it in the movie. Costumes contribute to that youthfulness. As the Devil, he makes a snappy appearance in a blue blazer and rose-tinted glasses. It is smarter than God's fishing cap and poplin jacket, but it is not only the clothes that are youthful. Extreme close-ups show a smooth, glowing complexion, and his movements are vigorous. The only suggestion of dotage is an ill-advised attempt at tap dancing.

Larry Gelbart didn't think he could sit through this

movie, and didn't try. Burns told him that he had an idea for yet another sequel, but after *Oh, God! You Devil*, the studio wasn't interested.

His movies, and his regular appearances on the late-night talk shows, helped to stimulate sales for three more books, and each made it to one or another best-seller list: *The Third Time Around* (1980); *How to Live to Be 100—or More* (1983); and *Dr. Burns' Prescription for Happiness* (1984), all published by G. P. Putnam's Sons.

The latter two were pocket-sized collections of anecdotes, priced at $12 and $13 for impulse buying. Their titles are meaningless. Inside the jackets, the anecdotal material is familiar from previous books, in style and sometimes in substance.

However *The Third Time Around*, while limited in period and scope, came closer to being autobiographically truthful than any of the four books to which Burns had thus far put his name.

As before, Burns dictated the stories in these books to the actual writers, but unfortunately he abandoned his previous, admirable practice of giving them credit. For whatever the books are worth, they do capture the idiosyncratic George Burns tone of voice, and for that alone, their authors deserve mention. In the case of *The Third Time Around*, even more credit is due.

As for *How to Live to Be 100*, it was tempting fate to offer such a title at the age of eighty-seven. Were that not daring enough, Burns was already entering bookings in his 1996 datebook. First thing, Ronnie Burns remembered, "Dad said, 'I want to celebrate my hundredth birthday at the Palladium in London.' "

And so Irving Fein contracted for the engagement. "That doesn't mean I'll make it," George told a *Washington Post* interviewer in 1984. "But I think I will, because they're paying me enough."

The shred of doubt was something new in a man who had always been certain he would live forever and meant to accomplish it through sheer life force. That certainty suddenly seemed to waver, for though it was optimistic to arrange for bookings on a hundredth birthday that was still a dozen years away, it was also a fearful thing to do. It was a hope that the future could be made real with an engagement on the calendar; that once a date was made it would be kept, because Burns always adhered to his schedule.

George seemed to be thinking about death, when he began to say, "I can't die—I'm booked."

He was certainly booked for the interim. Just that year, he signed a five-year contract with Caesar's Palace to play its show rooms in Las Vegas, Lake Tahoe, and Atlantic City. He was also under contract to CBS for more annual television specials like the ones he'd been doing for ten years since 1976, such as *George Burns in Nashville*, *George Burns's Early, Early, Early Christmas Special*, and *George Burns and Other Sex Symbols*.

He was even on the cover of *Penthouse* magazine. The headline on the September issue read: "Oh, God, She's Nude!" Pictured was a beaming Burns with a cigar in one hand and his other arm around the new Miss America, Vanessa Williams. The scandalous pictures of her within were going to cost Miss America her tiara.

"Somebody asked me if I was suing the magazine," George told the *Post* interviewer. "I said, 'What for? She sings very good. She's going to be a big star.' "

He certainly called that one right. Within ten years, Vanessa Williams would be a major recording artist and receive rave reviews for starring on Broadway in *Kiss of the Spider Woman*.

He was giving the interview in the Sherry-Netherland Hotel in New York, where he was staying during a promotional trip for *Oh, God! You Devil*. Cathy Carr was openly with him and spoke freely with the man from the *Post*. She and George were obviously having more than a passing romance.

In fact, the relationship was now four years old and working well in its own way. The grandfather of six (Sandy's four children, Ronnie's two) was comfortable enough about it to tell his interviewer that this fiftyish girlfriend always accompanied him on the road. Moreover, there was nothing sleazy about it.

"I respect him," Cathy told the man. "I admire him, I love him. My children adore him. There isn't anything I wouldn't tell him."

"What's wrong with going around with a young girl?" he asked. "I love her and she loves me. It's better than sliced tomatoes. Maybe some of Cathy might rub off on me and maybe some of what I've got will rub off on Cathy.

"If it doesn't drop off first," he said.

"Listen," he added somewhat more elegantly, using several words of wisdom from *How to Live to Be 100*. "The idea is to keep a young mind and a healthy body."

His office put out a press release:

In 1983 a poll of a thousand comedians selected George as "King of Comedy." A poll in *People Magazine* found George preferred by women as their "favorite well-known older American." *Playgirl* found George Burns to be one of America's ten sexiest men. *US Magazine* readers named George Burns "Man of the Year." And *Harper's Bazaar* picked him as one of America's Seven Sexiest Bachelors.

21

On January 17, 1986, three days before George's nine-tieth birthday, CBS celebrated it with *A Very Special Special*. Since a birthday, after so many of them, was not that special, he treated the program like any party and sang his heart away. He let the audience take the old songs as silly, but he was enamored of them and the audience could appreciate that as well.

Down in the garden where the red roses grow,
Oh, my, I long to go
Pluck me a flower,
Cuddle me an hour,
Lovie, let me learn that red rose rag . . .

The special was taped at the Beverly Theatre in Los Angeles, its host the actor John Forsythe, then starring in the popular television series *Dynasty*. Among the guest stars were John Denver, Walter Matthau, Diahann Carroll, and Ann-Margret.

Ann-Margret had a special history with George. It stretched back twenty-seven years, to 1959, when she had gone from majoring in theatre at Northwestern University to being his opening act at the Riviera Hotel in Las Vegas. Burns had "sort of discovered her," according to Harvey Silbert, then the hotel's vice president for entertainment, and had hired her.

The executive questioned her inexperience but took Burns's word about "this wonderful nineteen-year-old girl who sings and dances," booking them for the big Christmas weekend. After the first show, there was no doubt about her talent.

Silbert went backstage to congratulate both of them and found the youngster weeping. Burns was trying to console her.

"What's wrong, kid?" George was asking.

"I'm very lonesome," she said. "I love doing the act but this is the first time I've been away from home like this. It's Christmas Eve and I miss my mother."

George said, "Well, for chrissake, go into my dressing room and call your mother. Talk to her as long as you like and while you're at it, invite her up here to see the show, if that'll make you more comfortable."

The two men left the sniffling youngster in the dressing room and stepped outside while she made the call. Finally, they forgot that she was there, and strolled off to the bar.

An hour later, she came up to them with a broad smile across her pretty face and said that she felt "a million times better."

"That's great," Burns said. "Did you invite your mother to come see the show?"

"I can't do that, Mr. Burns," Ann-Margret said. "She lives in Sweden."

That brought the cigar out of his mouth. "Sweden!" he cried. "You were on my phone to Sweden for an hour?"

The story became part of his material and their friendship endured, even though Ann-Margret never completed that engagement. Halfway through, she was offered a movie contract by 20th Century-Fox, and George released her so that she might accept it.

For the week that they did work together, she had read some of Gracie's lines with him. Now, on his ninetieth-birthday television special, he showed the real thing—film clips of Burns and Allen in their prime. Once again, the young and dapper George danced with the young and beautiful Gracie and the young and elegant Fred Astaire in *A Damsel in Distress.*

Then John Forsythe quoted the most famous of all Burns and Allen lines—the lines, he explained, that they had never uttered at all.

GEORGE

Say good night, Gracie.

GRACIE

Good night, Gracie.

That was not how George wanted the act to end. He wanted sincerity. He wanted to say, "We were only kidding." This wasn't the moment for Gracie to be dumb-funny, and so after George said, "Say good night, Gracie," she just replied, simply and straight, "Good night."

Then the television special moved to George's closing monologue. The foxy old vaudevillian was now complete; what he did was who he was, and he did not have to "lie a lot" anymore—at least, hardly anymore. Speaking of life after Gracie, he said, "By the time I found out I had no talent, I was too big a star to do anything else."

This was an endearing boastfulness. He was surprised by his own success, he really was.

The ninetieth birthday began a decade to amaze. Anyone who is active at *anything* while in his nineties is a surprise. Usually, such a figure is to be humored and honored, trundled out on special occasions like the Kennedy Center

Honors (Burns would get the award two years later, in 1988), then trundled off with relief to a waiting oblivion.

A performer at that age who actually performs was unheard of, yet George Burns was still strolling onstage under his own steam, preceded by a puff of smoke, with cigar in hand and twinkle in eye. He was alert, he was charming, and most important for him, he could still do the job.

But could he do so many jobs and did he need so many jobs? There was some question whether he was strong enough for all the work that Irving Fein continued to get for him. Some even wondered for whose benefit all the work was. Fein was now producing everything George did, the television specials as well as the movies.

Work had always been good for George's spirits, and as for his health, obviously *something* had been good for it. Regarding the act itself, only someone his age could have done this material. For his act was not only about the subject of age, it was also a result of age. It was what a person's act *should* be after a lifetime of practice. It was comfortable, it was experienced, and it was secure unto itself. For the benefit of all cynics and pessimists, here was the hitherto inconceivable—an acceptable, attractive, and vital elderliness.

In 1988, writing in the *San Francisco Chronicle*, Gerald Nachman reviewed the ninety-two-year-old George Burns at Caesar's Tahoe:

> You're ready to laugh . . . what you're not ready for is to be touched. In George Burns you have the essence of entertaining, everything rolled into seamless, artless charm, pure humor wedded to pure style. As we watch him, warmed and awed by this foxy grandpa in a natty tuxedo, we want him never to leave—not just the stage, us.

At Caesar's Palace in Atlantic City, Lucie Arnaz was his opening act. She was already smitten with him, if for no other reason than his insistence that they get equal billing on the giant marquee outside the hotel.

When he was asked why he did not demand star billing for himself, he replied, "They know who I am."

Before the first show, the tall, beautiful, and smart Lucie noticed that "at half hour," thirty minutes before curtain time, "George was dressed and ready to go. That was when his pianist arrived."

There was always a piano in a George Burns dressing room.

"Other people have their own warm-up exercises," she said. "Dancers warm up their bodies. Singers warm up their voices."

She found that George's warm-up was unique. He stood at the piano and went through the nostalgia songbook with his accompanist, Morty Jacobs. Leaving the door open, as if to invite a backstage audience, they ran through songs that had nothing to do with his act. The pianist would ask, "Do you remember this one, George?"

He would play a snatch of melody.

"Oh, yes!" Burns would cry, and he would sing the lyrics.

"They would play 'Name That Tune' before every show," Lucie said.

Reversing the process and taking his turn, George would say, "I'll bet you don't remember this one." Then he would start singing.

"The guy would know it, and play it," Lucie remembered. "So they would go back and forth and it would kind of get him back in time. It was a fabulous thing.

"And people in the hall would stand there and get into it."

Of all the kinds of warming up that she had seen among performers, this was the most unusual. "George," she said, "would warm up *his mind*. He has kind of a mode he gets into—and his memory kicks in."

Almost every night after her performance, she went into

the audience to watch him perform, "because it was fabulous to watch. He did most of the act standing up. He did a little dance. He told jokes. He sang songs. It was absolutely charming.

"Every show was almost exactly the same but he could never be thrown. If somebody said something to him from the audience, he would go with it."

Burns surely knew who Lucie Arnaz was. Her parents had been part of the Hollywood community. They had lived on the same street as Jack Benny. They had even rented studio space from Burns in the early days of television.

"Of course he knew who I was," Lucie said, "but he didn't make a big deal out of it. He was very kind, very polite. He was sweet and a complete gentleman, but it was never 'I knew your folks,' or 'I knew you when you were a kid.'

"It was always performer-to-performer. I was the person sharing the bill with him and that was how he treated me; which was the way I really wanted to be treated."

Playing the perfect grandfather was now central to the George Burns career and he seemed relaxed in the role, certainly proficient at it. The 1988 movie *18 Again!* was tailored to it, a Cinderella variation on *Oh, God!* As if in acknowledgment of that, the expression "Oh, God!" is used twice in the picture with a broad wink at the audience.

18 Again! is a harmless and sometimes sweet little movie designed to appeal to adolescent fantasies. Its protagonist is an eighteen-year-old college freshman who feels that he is the class twit, being nervous with girls, bad at sports, and hazed by his fraternity brothers. After he and his rich grandfather are nearly killed in a car accident, their souls exchange bodies. With Burns at the controls, the boy becomes confident with girls, great at sports, and revenges himself on the fraternal tormentors.

Unfortunately, this story keeps George offscreen for much of the time. That often happens when an actor is playing a character who is in a coma. Only Burns's voice is heard. He speaks the old man's thoughts while the audience watches the boy he is inhabiting.

There is a fair amount of charm in Charlie Schlatter's youthful, cigar-smoking impersonation of Burns, and sometimes the mimicked gestures, shrugs, pauses, and stiff grins successfully evoke the grand master.

There is also a strange moment in the picture when the grandson is introduced to his girlfriend's parents and the George Burns within materializes before our eyes, as he imagines what it would be like if they actually saw him. The parents' reactions (bewilderment, anger, disgust) to the ninetyish suitor of their eighteen-year-old daughter are quite fascinating in view of Burns's real-life romances with young women.

The script of *18 Again!*, written by Josh Goldstein and Jonathan Prince, does not provide much of the wisdom that distinguished *Oh, God!* in its best moments. Burns sometimes sounds as if he is delivering a monologue, which dispels the make-believe, yet overall, *18 Again!* is one of Burns's better pictures. A bonus is his singing, start to finish, of the enchanting and gently nostalgic title song.

Only six years before this picture was made, Burns had been valiantly resisting all signs of dotage. "When I walk, I walk," he said. "I take *steps*. And not little steps. Little steps, you'll never get there."

Sad to say, in *18 Again!* he was starting to take little steps. Perhaps at that age he was entitled to, but it had been good hoping that this would never happen to George Burns.

•   •   •

The longer the life, the richer the nostalgia account. He was booked into the Concord, the famous resort hotel in the Catskill Mountains. This engagement was for a single performance on a holiday weekend. He shuffled out with his usual cigar to the usual standing ovation.

He could still remember his lines, could still hold attention. But something unusual happened as he took his bows at the end of the precise, fifty-five-minute turn. An executive of the hotel walked onstage and said he believed an old friend of George's was in the audience.

Burns smiled, took a puff on his cigar, and peered into the darkened room.

The executive said, "You once were in a team with a man named Billy Lorraine."

For once, George Burns was startled, and his eyes opened wide behind his glasses while the old partner, the old friend, the old man made his way down the aisle toward the stage.

For almost one whole year, Billy Lorraine had been George's partner. The act of "Burns and Lorraine, Broadway Thieves" had been the last time George had been second-rate or small-time. It was the last time he had failed.

They had not seen each other since the winter of 1923, backstage in a Union City, New Jersey, vaudeville theatre. It was the night that Gracie came to meet Billy, hoping to find a new partner.

In such whimsical ways are lives re-routed and then destined.

Over the years, in books and monologues, George Burns had told lots of stories about the old days with Billy Lorraine, but he hadn't seen his old partner in more than sixty-five years!

If he was moved by the reunion at the Concord Hotel, he didn't lose his composure over it. Turning to his piano player, he asked for "Seems Like Old Times." There were no singing impressions by the "Broadway Thieves" this time. This time they sang for themselves.

A friend of Burns remembered, "It was one of the most emotional nights of all time." Two years later, Billy Lorraine was dead.

22

In 1987, Lou Weiss told Burns that he expected to step down as chairman of the William Morris Agency.

"What would you do?" George asked.

"What do you mean, Uncle?" said the sixty-five-year-old nephew. "I'm going to retire."

"Retire to do what?"

"To enjoy life," Weiss said. "To spend more time with my wife Alice. To travel."

"Great," George said.

The best of the Burns books is the seventh, *Gracie: A Love Story*, written with David Fisher and published by G. P. Putnam's Sons in 1988. Although much of its material appeared in previous memoirs, this is the best organized and the most gracefully written. That was appropriate, considering the subject.

It opens with the lovely remark, "For forty years my act consisted of one joke. And then she died." With that, Fisher and Burns turn to the beginnings of Gracie's life. That is where most of the new material is concentrated, offering details of her childhood, her home and family, and of her genesis as a performer.

When the story arrives at George, the anecdotes begin to sound familiar and for the most part are revisions of prior revisions. He has not yet applied the final polish, and reality still had mistakes worth deleting.

Such indelicate subjects as sterility and infidelity, for instance, are bypassed in *Gracie*. Burns would probably argue that they would be inappropriate to a valentine, and it seems all right to accept that. For such reasons, this memoir is like a tinted photograph in a rotogravure. It is prettified. But even such photographs are photographs.

The bestseller led to yet another memoir, *All My Best Friends* (G. P. Putnam's Sons, 1989), again written with David Fisher. As the title suggests, this book is about the stars Burns had known—and since so many of them were dead, he was free to express himself about those he disliked. Even so, he had been diplomatic for a lifetime, and it was difficult to break so longstanding a habit. He did take the opportunity to say his piece about a Mary Livingstone who "felt it was her duty as his wife to prove to people that Jack wasn't really cheap by spending as much of his money as fast as she could. But Jack never stopped loving her. There's an old expression, politics makes strange bedfellows. Well, sometimes, so does marriage."

Joan Benny read that with relief, and then telephoned Burns. "Thank you for doing that, Natty," she said. "You opened the door for me." The passage freed her, she felt, to express her own long-suppressed feelings. "I don't think either Gracie *or* George liked my mother," she said. "I didn't like my mother, either."

As a book, *All My Best Friends* was a sound enough idea, but much of it rehashed George's often-told tales, in still different variations. A collection of anecdotes without structure or chronology, it was a commercial success, though not as great as *Gracie*.

To help publicize *All My Best Friends*, George went on the Larry King television show on November 10, 1989.

His appearance had changed sharply, as if a funny thing had happened to him on the way to the studio and he had become an old man. His eyes appeared huge, magnified as they were by the strong lenses of his glasses. His toupee looked dry, like straw on glass, with all the hairs stuck together in a solid piece about a half inch off his head. And for the first time, this snappy dresser whose nickname actually was "Natty" looked as if he hadn't dressed himself, and hadn't been able to.

King was less interested in the new book's anecdotes about the old stars than he was in Burns's own history.

"Would you ever remarry?"

"No way," George said.

"Has anyone ever come close?"

"I went around with a little girl, Cathy Carr, in Dallas. She wanted to get married but I was fifty years older than she was. So I told her to get married."

King supplied the punch line. "But not to you?"

In fact, Burns seems simply to have gotten used to living alone. Coupling at this point hardly made sense. "Listen," he told a friend some months earlier, "I'm ninety-two years old. She wants to get married. What am I, crazy?"

Crazy he never was.

King was a student of show business, and recalled some of the novel techniques that were introduced on the Burns and Allen television series.

"You went outside the sketch," he said. "You talked to the audience. They all do it now, but you did it first."

George seemed to be missing the point. "You see," he irrelevantly responded, "my talent was off the stage. I was able to think of the things and Gracie was able to do them."

"And then," King persisted, "you would tell us what was happening. You'd walk out of the living room and look at the camera."

George got it now. "I also had a television set upstairs in the library. When Gracie was planning to do things to me, I would watch her upstairs on the television. Our sponsor said, 'You can't do that. It's out of reality.' I said I certainly would."

King dutifully turned to the book Burns was promoting and inquired about Jolson and Durante. Al Jolson, George said, wasn't the most modest man in the world, "he wasn't even the most talented entertainer, but he was the greatest of all," and as for Jimmy Durante, "Everybody loved him because he was a religious man."

It was a curious remark and King asked, "How do you mean, religious?"

"He was a nice man," Burns said, "a good man, and there was no scandal about him." What Burns was really saying was that Durante's whole act was being nice and there was nothing else to his act *except* being nice.

Lou Weiss had said, "I thought Jimmy Durante was the most loved man in show business, but Durante's circle of people who loved him was relatively narrow. Burns—I would walk with him on Fifth Avenue and truck drivers would call out to him."

It was hard for George to be evasive when King asked directly whether he'd liked Groucho Marx. "I liked Harpo," he replied.

The reason for liking Harpo was love. George once asked Harpo and his wife Susan how many children they expected to adopt. They had just brought the fourth one home.

Harpo said, "We want to adopt as many kids as there are windows in the house, so that whenever we leave, there's a kid waving from every window."

He was certainly warmer than Groucho—whose nickname was deserved, and became an understatement as time went on. Burns eyed Larry King carefully and paused, as if reconsidering what he had just said. "I liked Groucho," he finally conceded. "I just never danced with him."

Then he was asked about Jack Benny, and that turned him serious. "Jack didn't give the impression but he was a very strong personality on stage, a powerhouse." There was a long pause. "He was my best friend."

Perhaps not realizing the depth of that friendship, King asked about Jack's death. "Was he very ill?"

Burns stayed quiet.

"Was his a sudden death?"

George looked up.

"It was sudden for me."

Some of Larry King's success was based on asking human-size questions, for instance, "Do you ever get nervous?"

"Never. To get nervous, you have to have talent. Gracie got nervous. Jack got nervous."

"Why do you put yourself down?" A good question.

"I've got talent. You ask me questions, I'm able to answer them. When I worked with Gracie, well—" He was thinking on the spot and evidently decided to skip his usual remark about having talent offstage. Instead, he said, "You've got to time your jokes, so I've got talent. I just didn't have that kind of talent. But *now* I've got talent."

"In fact," King said, "you've gotten bigger as you got older."

"The best time in my career is right now."

Another reason for King's success was a certain innocence. He was able to venture into sensitive areas without assaulting.

"You're older than our century, do you realize that, George?

"You're older than our century!"

"Let me tell you something," Burns responded. "When I go out on the stage now, I don't do anything that isn't my age. I allow myself to get old. It's very important."

What he meant was that a performer should never lie to himself. An audience is never fooled. An actor's material should be appropriate to his age.

"Blossom Seeley was a great entertainer but when she was booked on the Ed Sullivan Show she was eighty-two years old. And she sang 'Toddling the Toddle-O.' You can't toddle the toddle-O at eighty-two. You can only toddle until you're twenty-one.

"I tell the truth. I tell my age. I talk like a ninety-three-year-old man would talk."

By that time, at the end of the hour with Larry King, his toupee fit fine and he looked as if he could dress himself perfectly well.

At Hillcrest Country Club, George was in the card room for his daily bridge game. A member of the club watched and waited until the game was finished, then said, "George, I'd like you to do me a favor. I've got my father here for Father's Day and he would love to meet you."

Burns smiled. "Well, bring him in," he said.

"Bring him in?" The man laughed. "My father is a hundred and four years old."

"Really?" Burns said. He pushed back his chair and started to stand up. "Let me go to him."

He rose and walked slowly out of the card room, allowing the member to guide him by the elbow. They approached a table in the Men's Grill, but as they did so, the old man who was seated there pushed back his own chair in order to stand.

"No, no," Burns said. "Don't get up."

"Why not?" the fellow said. "I can get up."

And he did.

Burns, enjoying the rare pleasure of speaking to an elder, asked, "Are you really one hundred and four years old?"

"Yes, I am," the man said.

"Why do you want to meet me?" he asked. "Do you want to fuck my sister Goldie?"

In 1989, he made a forty-five-minute videotape called *The Wit and Wisdom of George Burns*, to be sold on television. While there are some elements of the home movie about it ("I'm going to take you through a typical day of mine"), like most home movies these are moving pictures of real life.

In the house on North Maple Drive, he lies on his bed and demonstrates his daily exercise routine. One would imagine that any movements would be strenuous for a ninety-three year old, even touching the toes as he does, sitting on the edge of the bed, but he seems quite spry.

He walks around the swimming pool and says he has been doing it for decades, although he is now down to ten laps.

He introduces Arlette and Daniel D'Hoore (the couple who takes care of him), as well as his cats, and then goes to his office, where he visits with his manager, Irving Fein; his secretary, Jack Langdon; and the staff writer, Hal Goldman. From there, Daniel drives him to Hillcrest for lunch, after which he plays bridge with his friend Barry Mirkin and the comedian Red Buttons.

Then he goes home for his regular afternoon nap. "I do the same thing every day," he admits. "I keep the same hours, eat the same food, smoke the same cigars, drink the same martinis." But unlike the everyday routine, on the day of this video his accompanist arrives for a session of songs.

My girl is a high-toned lady,
Won't say "yes," might say "maybe."
Struts like a peacock night and day,
Beautiful, and she was born that way.

In the old days, Burns sang the song in blackface, but these are not the times to mention that. Singing it now, he looks radiant, and in the flush of health.

The *Wit and Wisdom* videotape ends with a performance before a college audience. It is a performance in which he talks offhandedly about his age, sings a few songs, and takes a momentary shuffle in the direction of a soft shoe dance.

Before our eyes, his selves have merged. There is no longer any distinction between the George Burns talking to the camera at home, visiting at the office, playing bridge at the club—or entertaining onstage. George Burns can be and has become himself all of the time. He can also be and has become the performer all of the time.

He is seen taking his bows for the college audience ("You were afraid I wouldn't be around this long"), and in a narration for the videotape, he sums up his views on aging. It is wisdom as material:

> Age is a state of mind, an attitude. I see people that the minute they get to be sixty, they start practicing to be old. They start taking little steps. They drop food on themselves. They take little naps when you're talking to them. By the time they get to be seventy, they've made it. They're now a hit. They're now old. Not me . . . I like young people. I don't think it's good when older people just hang around each other comparing gravy stains . . . unless it's expensive gravy. And I'm not interested in yesterday . . . I'm ninety-three and I love my age.

Cathy Carr had refused to disappear. George was learning that no matter how old one grows, certain aspects of romantic relationships are never outgrown. It all may seem adolescent but breaking up, as they say, is hard to do.

Cathy Carr was not very tall, but when she came back she was even taller than before because George was almost visibly shrinking. Moreover, she could raise her voice, which he never allowed himself to do, and so, from her greater height and with her greater volume, she declared that she was back; moreover, she was back with demands.

For instance and first of all, she was not going to travel with him, then stay at the Beverly Hills Hotel when she came to Los Angeles. That arrangement, she said to the ninety-three-year-old man, was only his way of keeping up with other girlfriends. Since he would not marry her, she announced, she was moving in.

His lifelong approach to objectionable behavior now had acquired a name, "passive-aggressive." But whether it was a good tactic or a bad personality type, it was useful in the relationship-ending department. He put up no resistance to Cathy. He simply told her to move into the back bedroom.

Undiscouraged, she had a truckload of clothing shipped from Dallas, and moved into 720 North Maple Drive.

The first night, she took a long hot shower in anticipation of the premiere conjugal bed. It was a very long shower, Burns remembered: a two-hour shower.

By the time Cathy was finished, the shower steam had curled the wallpaper on her bedroom ceiling and that ignited a tantrum. She raged at Arlette and Daniel, insisting that the back bedroom was uninhabitable and intolerable. It was musty and damp, and even the wallpaper was peeling on the ceiling.

The next evening, however, she was calm. George had, without discussing it, invited Melissa Berry and her two children to dinner. Burns told her that he had no intention of changing any of his habits or activities because Cathy was there.

Cathy Carr was not a socially inexperienced woman. She adeptly handled the dinner situation, politely hosting the ex-girlfriend and her children. "She was the perfect hostess," Melissa remembered. "She sat with the same little smile glued to her face all night."

But afterward, George remembered, there was another tantrum, that one about entertaining an ex-girlfriend. The next morning she moved out and so, thanks to passive-aggressive techniques, that was the very end.

His 1993 television special was called *George Burns Celebrates Eighty Years in Show Business,* and this was a remarkable event. In a way, it was a miracle on view, although once again, it didn't seem that way at the start.

It began with a rowdy gang of comedians firing fusillades of sex and old age jokes at Burns in the manner of a roast. Their styles of attack were sufficiently antiquated so that they seemed as quaint as vaudevillians. The show appeared destined to be a standard show business tribute.

Burns listened attentively, with a game but blank smile on his waxen face. The tone at the start of the show was something less than elegant. Like many variety programs of the period, it was modeled on the roasts held by the Friar's Club.

Too, like those roasts this show was set in a hotel ballroom, except that instead of being on a dais, the comics and assorted guest stars were seated at tables. They included Bob Hope, Carol Channing, Milton Berle, Danny Thomas, Don Rickles, Phyllis Diller, Red Buttons, Buddy Hackett, Johnny Carson, and the Reverend Billy Graham.

The program took on its first glow when Bernadette Peters sang the seldom heard lyric to the old Burns and Allen theme song by Louis A. Hirsch and Otto Harbach:

Just a love nest, cozy with charm
Just a love nest, down on a farm.

Then Ann-Margret appeared, singing:

Lovey Joe, that ever lovin' man
Way down home in Birmin'ham

George joined her, with cigar in hand,

He can do some lovin' and some lovin' more
And when he starts some lovin'
Then you'll ask for more . . .

He seemed to rejuvenate on camera, his flesh tightening, his color rising, his eyes brightening. That was now happening at every public appearance. He greeted Billy Graham with a generous smile. The minister seemed to be the first adult male on the program.

"The Bible," he began, "says the merry heart doeth good like a medicine. . . . There is something else here tonight, it's a feeling of love for this man who has given us eighty years of himself. Of his unique talents, his warm humor, his positive attitude, and his tremendous zest for life."

Although George replied, "I love old age," he no longer seemed old as he sang the song from his movie, "I Wish I Was 18 Again." Recovering from the wistful moment, he picked up the mood with one of the patter songs that had become his trademark:

Oh, I forgot the number of my house the last time I
    went out
I forgot the number of my house so for hours I roamed
    about
So I've unscrewed the number from the door
And I've got it here tonight
All I've got to find is the door that it belongs to
Then I'm all right.

He surely did not know it was the last time he would be able to run his own show, to stand and deliver from start to closing. Yet before the show he had feared that he wouldn't be able to remember his monologue. And he'd said to Irving Brecher, one of his former writers, "I don't think I can remember my act."

Brecher put an arm around his shoulder and replied, "The audience will remind you."

Perhaps that was sweet, but it did not change facts. Henceforth, George would have to move from center stage to a seat of honor.

Even so, his inventive manager, Irving Fein, had already conceived a way to keep him performing without the necessity of learning a monologue. Fein booked him into Disney World, where he sat before an audience in a chair at the center of the stage and answered questions. George did this for an hour and a half, quipping in a lively and responsive way, and the performance was videotaped. It was subsequently broadcast as a special on the Disney Channel.

Without a doubt, Burns would have preferred to be at center stage doing a monologue. Even so, this was handled with poise and charm. Never did anyone age with greater finesse.

23

As the hundredth year began, a squiggle showed up in what had been George Burns's lifelong streak of grit, perseverance, and spirit. Having lived so completely, having done the thing he loved to do for so long, so well, and so successfully, he began to falter.

One day in September 1994, he stepped out of the shower in his bathroom and sat down on the stool to towel himself off. Nobody seemed to know how it was that he happened to be alone. As Ronnie Burns reconstructed it, "Dad stood up and either fell or blacked out. He hit his head on one of the bathroom fixtures."

He gashed his scalp and suffered a mild concussion. Daniel heard the fall, rushed upstairs, and telephoned for an ambulance. He also called Sandy and Ronnie, and all of them converged at the hospital.

"It was really bad," Sandy remembered, "with Daddy in intensive care and all three of us just watching helplessly.

"But he wouldn't stop joking around. He had Ronnie and Daniel and me laughing hysterically. Other people in there, they stared at us like they were saying, 'They're laughing and their father might be dying.'

"But he was just funny."

He was, but the situation wasn't, and "from there," Ronnie said, "the spinal fluid that cushions the brain began to accumulate. So that caused pressure, which had to be drained."

The draining required the drilling of a small hole in Burns's skull, a gruesome-sounding but straightforward surgical procedure. However, no operation is simple when the patient is almost a hundred years old. On the operating table, September 14, 1994, Burns suffered a heart attack and a mild stroke.

Lou Weiss broke off his vacation in France and flew directly to Los Angeles. He found his uncle at home, working with a speech therapist and, Weiss said, "looking like a sparrow." The debonair agency executive watched as the therapist asked Burns questions calling for simple answers and logical thought processes.

"What is a large auditorium with rows of desks?"

"School," the old man whispered.

"And what is a large auditorium with a big screen at the front?"

"Movie house."

"Now, Mr. Burns, if you are sitting in a large auditorium and you are in a pew, where are you?"

He spoke up more forcefully.

"I'm in a Presbyterian church."

The therapist clapped her hands over the five words and cried, "Wonderful!"

George was holding up a finger. He had more to say. "When I was eight years old," he began, "I sang in the Pee-wee Quartet and we worked at this Presbyterian church. And I got an Ingersoll watch. I went home and I said, 'Ma, I've been a Jew for eight years and I never got anything. I was a Presbyterian for one day and I got a watch.'

"My mother said, 'Help me hang the wash.' "

The therapist positively glowed.

"That is just remarkable."

Burns held up his finger again. There was a kicker to the anecdote.

"Three days later, the watch stopped. I became a Jew again."

Even an audience of one served as an elixir for him; but was this therapeutic, or just a shot of adrenaline?

Sandra Burns was fearful that if her father tried to play his centennial engagements, he would be embarrassed. Ronnie was less worried. "If the band plays Dad's music, he'll just stand up, walk out, and do the fifty-five minutes."

That would have been thrilling but it wasn't likely, and of course Ronnie knew it. Facts had to be faced and some of the dates had to be canceled. This was heartbreaking, for cancelations were not George Burns's line. He had gone idle for too long when he was young to volunteer for it when he was old.

His cancelations were like the vital organs of a failing body that were starting to shut down. The first to go was the London Palladium. His feisty explanation for that was, "The Brits wouldn't give me a three-year deal."

Other bookings remained, for instance, a two-hour television special that CBS planned to tape in October 1995 and broadcast around the date of the hundredth birthday. There was also the longstanding engagement at Caesar's Palace in Las Vegas, scheduled on the centenary itself, January 20, 1996. It had been sold out since being announced in 1994, but even Ronnie Burns was beginning to doubt it. "You've got to take that with a grain of salt too," he said. "Whatever nature and God do, that's what'll happen. Hopefully he *reaches* his hundredth birthday.

"He's looking forward to that, and however it's celebrated, it'll be great. Only he knows whether he's going to make it."

But there was something more important than reaching the centennial. Unlike the finish line in a foot race, a hundredth birthday was not the end of a measured run. It was merely a milestone in an unfinished life. After it was reached, it would be *passed* and continuity was the important thing. Perhaps the festivities would be over; the celebrants would certainly go home; but for the runner, the journey was continuing. A life's circuit was not a matter of distance but of endurance. That did not end at a marking point, the tenth year or the hundredth. It ended when endurance ended.

However, George's endurance was becoming an issue. Where, now, was the getting older but not old—the wit and wisdom of George Burns?

He had always planned ahead. Plans signified a confidence in a future, another date meaning another *date*. But another engagement was out of the question. His friend Charles Lowe said, "I never thought this would happen." Burns looked as if he knew it. For the first time in his life, this man of hope and optimism seemed depressed.

Lou Weiss had only semi-retired, too young at sixty-five to be doing nothing. Graying gracefully and youthfully slender, perhaps he shared some of the Burns genes, mental ones as well as biological. Perhaps, too, he had learned the good lesson. George gave him a very special present, the gold and platinum cat's eye ring that Gracie had given him for good luck. "I love you, Louie," Burns said, "and Gracie did too. She would want you to have this."

Weiss was moved by the gift. "My uncle was always very proud of whatever success I had." He took the gesture as more than affectionate; he read it as a sign that his uncle did not intend to ever perform again.

Charitable institutions were prominent among the interested parties who were cheering George on as he approached the hundred-year mark. He had become a familiar after-dinner speaker at Los Angeles fund-raising affairs. He enjoyed doing the brief monologues, and prepared them as diligently as full-length routines. If, in the process, he helped a worthwhile institution, so much the better. But he preferred helping people rather than institutions.

Lou Weiss was an active supporter of the Museum of Radio and Television Broadcasting in Manhattan. He once asked Burns whether he might like to contribute to the institution. The museum had been founded by George's old friend at CBS, William S. Paley, and its purpose of preserving broadcasts was certainly pertinent to his own career. Even so, George asked Weiss, "Does this mean a lot to you personally?"

"Not personally-personally," his nephew replied. "I'm just active in the museum's affairs and I think it does important work."

"But not *personally,*" George said. "Because you know, Lou, I'm asked by everyone to contribute everywhere. So if it isn't personally, I'd just as soon not do it."

Like anyone who has something that other people want, whether it is money, celebrity, or beauty, George Burns resented being courted as if for that alone. Secure as he was with himself, even he was susceptible to the fear that he wasn't loved for himself. Bernie Kamber, a friend of his at the New York Friar's Club, said, "Everybody wanted to use George. Jesse [Block] and I once went up to see the Hebrew Home for the Aged in New York. They wanted to build a house and call it 'The Burns and Allen House' because, they said, 'Burns was the perfect example of how a man should age.'"

Burns turned them down. "If I do one," he told Kamber, "I've got to do four hundred of them." But Bernie believed that George's real reason was "he felt he was being used." Nor did it mean anything to him for a building to bear his name. He believed, as he said to his nephew, "Louie, all actors will be forgotten."

That was why, when he did give money, he gave it to

help individuals, particularly actors. He contributed a million dollars to the Actors Home in Los Angeles, and another million to victims of the 1989 San Francisco earthquake. "My fantasy," he told Weiss, "is to leave all my money to poor people."

The big philanthropic tap was opened when he gave a million dollars to Cedars-Sinai Hospital in Los Angeles. With that, he did agree to a nearby street being christened "Gracie Allen Street." That was followed by a gift to an institution in Israel, the Ben Gurion University of the Negev. This was so magnanimous that George was offered, and accepted, his name on a building, the George Burns Medical Education Center.

Thus began his serious philanthropy. He gave another three million dollars to Cedars-Sinai in Los Angeles, and the hospital administration began drawing up plans for the "Burns and Allen Research Institute." Immediately, a "George Burns Road" was dedicated at an intersection with Gracie Allen Street.

Fund-raising is a sophisticated business and institutions publicize major contributions, hoping the publicity will encourage other major contributions. Two simultaneous galas were scheduled by Cedars-Sinai to celebrate and publicize the Burns gift, one at a Los Angeles dance hall called, coincidentally, the Palladium, and the other in the nearby Pantages Theatre. The show at the theatre was to be a two-hour tribute to George, climaxing with his monologue.

The event was planned to serve as the show for CBS. Irving Fein had been producing all of George's television specials, and in recent years they had been linked to anniversaries of one kind or another. As the keynote of a show, his hundredth birthday was a natural.

After the taping, the city of Los Angeles had already agreed to close off the streets connecting the theatre with the dance hall so that, as a Cedars-Sinai spokesman said, "the audience can walk between them. A huge buffet dinner will be given after the taping.

"Hopefully, George will be there."

Meantime, Fein said, "We're working on another book." This memoir was going to be put together by the office writer, Hal Goldman. "We're going to make one last million with George," Fein said.

On good days, Burns seemed wise to it all. As he was being wheeled into the office and past Fein's desk, he turned to his driver-valet, Daniel D'Hoore, and said, "Isn't that what's-his-name?" Fein had only been with him for twenty years.

Irving was not a popular man, but few agents or managers are. Most people who knew him were willing to give him credit for the money he made for Jack Benny and George—his only clients in four decades. Fein had certainly made a lot for them, and for himself too, although George had been well fixed before he signed on with Irving.

Some, like Melissa Miller (now Berry), thought that Irving was not malicious, but just singleminded and obsessive about getting the job done. She thought he could not distinguish between the client's income and the client. "He just doesn't seem to get it," she said.

Others had stronger views. The television producer Fred De Cordova once said to Irving, "You killed Jack [Benny] by working him too hard. And you're certainly doing the same thing with George. What happens to you, Irving, if he goes?"

Fein's unfazed reply had been, "I've got my eye on Jimmy Durante."

Buddy Hackett's remark seemed to sum it up for everyone. "A lot of people think that Jack Benny died," the comedian said, "but Jack didn't die. He's just hiding from Irving."

Irving Fein also had his defenders. Ronnie Burns said, "A

lot of people don't like the man who can say no, but [Irving] was great at protecting my father."

Only in private did George Burns ever express any displeasure with the people who were fussing over the centennial and its events. He would tell Daniel and Arlette that outside of the plans, nobody called and nobody visited, except for Ronnie, Sandy, Lou Weiss, Carol Channing and Charlie Lowe, and Melissa Berry. The regulars who went out with him on Thursdays only went out with him, he suspected, because they liked to be seen in a restaurant with George Burns.

When Melissa came, she often brought her children along. Like their mother, the boys—Nathaniel, who was named for Nathan Birnbaum, and three-year-old-Ben—called their godfather "Papa."

"Papa is a moon, isn't he, Mom?" Ben asked in the car as they were driving home.

"What, sweetie puss?"

"Papa is a moon," the boy repeated.

"You mean he's a star," his mother said.

"I mean," Ben explained, "he's up there in the sky."

George had been so strong, so active, and so alert for so long that everyone seemed to believe he would always be up there in the sky. If the bathroom accident wasn't itself responsible for the change, it marked the time of the change. In the summer of 1995 Ronnie Burns was saying, "Everything [medical] that happened in that fall is now fine, but—"

He didn't have to finish the thought. Burns's mental state was in decline, and not because of the accident. "Right now," Ronnie said, "all it is is age."

Even so, George struggled to keep his days structured, making a brave but shaky gesture toward the regimen he had maintained for more than a half century. Mornings he still went to the office, even if Daniel had to lift him in and out between the car and the wheelchair. There was no function for the office, nothing happening there and certainly nothing for him to do. As soon as noon came in sight, he went to Hillcrest for lunch.

On such an average day, he sat with Daniel in the Men's Grill. At eleven-thirty, it was too early for the lunch crowd and the big room was virtually empty. A shrimp cocktail was before him, set in a large silver bowl filled with ice. He held one shrimp between his fingers, shakily poised for a dip in the saucer of ketchup.

Jan Murray and a visiting writer stopped by to chat.

"It's Jan Murray," announced the good-looking, athletic comedian. Now about seventy years old, he still looked youthful. He was shouting to make certain George heard him.

"I know it's you," Burns said, as if accustomed to people questioning his mental state as well as his hearing. The croaking voice was as familiar as an old radio.

"How come you're having shrimp, George? I thought you always had boiling hot soup."

Burns's smile was wan. "Come back tomorrow," he said, looking up at Murray. "I'll order the soup. I don't want to disappoint you."

Daniel rolled him into the card room for a few hands of bridge. He could hardly hold his cards, and one of the other players had to shuffle the deck and deal for him.

"He's making mistakes," another of them said. "He's not playing the game, but the other players never criticize him. We make believe it didn't happen."

By three o'clock he was home and sleeping, until two hours later, when he arose for his daily martini. For the last year, the housekeeper Arlette had been making it with only a whisper of gin to give the vermouth a scent at the top.

Supposedly at six o'clock, but earlier all the time, the nurse brought his dinner upstairs to the bedroom.

One spring day in 1995, Arlette had prepared an unusually elaborate meal of grapefruit, shrimp and rice, with peas and black beans on the side. She handed the tray to the nurse, who carried it upstairs, setting it on the desk in his bedroom. There, with a robe over his pajamas, the bald-headed little old man sat and ate in silence.

Some people watch television when they eat alone. Nat Burns seldom used the television set upstairs. There was a time when he watched the California Angels baseball team, but he had lost interest in them as in everything.

He used to go to bed with the radio tuned to the talk programs. He enjoyed the Larry King and Michael Jackson shows and fell asleep with them on. He didn't do that anymore either.

He had never been a reader. Despite the tutors he'd hired, he never learned to be comfortable with reading. The only materials anyone had ever seen him read were scripts and "the trades"—*The Hollywood Reporter* and *Daily Variety*.

Downstairs, Melisssa had come to see him and was visiting with Daniel and Arlette in the kitchen. They told her that it had not been a good day for Mr. Burns. She trudged upstairs dreading that he might not recognize her.

"Hiya kid," he said flatly, and stared through his lenses.

He looked over her white shorts and sneakers.

"Out playing tennis? Siddown."

She kissed him while he continued to eat, seeming "a little spaced." He asked about her teaching, and about her children. He put down his fork, looked up, and asked, "When are you leaving town?"

He was confusing her with his daughter Sandy, who lived in San Diego.

"Whenever you want me to, Papa."

"But I don't want you to. Stay as long as you want."

"I'm not Sandy."

"Did you just talk to Sandy?"

"Yes. She's coming in to see you. I just live across town."

"I forgot," he said.

He picked up a cookie and nibbled at it, and sipped from a cup of tea while the nurse cleaned him up. Taking the tray, she spoke as if he were not there, telling Melissa how amazed she was that he'd eaten so much. As she padded out, the room turned silent. After a moment, Melissa announced, "Okay, Papa, you go to bed. I'm going to go home."

"When are you going to drop by again?"

He seemed to have renewed energy. His voice grew stronger and the old gravel was rolling around in his throat.

"GB, I'll come every day if you want."

"You come as often as you can come."

Now he seemed to want company.

"Why don't we watch some baseball? The Angels are on."

He shook his head and said, "Carol [Channing] is coming over for a drink on Saturday."

"That's pretty funny, Papa. I haven't seen you drinking lately and she never drank."

He narrowed his eyes and winked.

"You know what I mean, kid. Come on, let's rehearse the monologue."

24

Sammy Lewis was ninety-eight years old, one year younger than George Burns. He lay flat on his back in a closet-sized room at Berkley Convalescent West, a rest home on Santa Monica Boulevard in Los Angeles. His bedclothes were soiled with medication, spittle, food, and blood. Motionless, a vacant expression in his half-opened eyes, he gaped at the ceiling of the airless room. Tacked to the wall over his head were two discolored publicity photographs. They showed a youthful couple, smiling brightly, poised to entertain. They were a song and dance team.

Lewis had never done as well as Burns—not when he was young, not when he was in show business, not when he was older, and certainly not in 1995, even considering George's present condition.

For ten years George's friend Harvey Silbert had been paying the bills at Berkley. It seemed as if Sammy's only visitors were the former Las Vegas hotel executive and his friend Jan Murray.

George Burns also took care of needy vaudevillians. When Benny Fields died, he helped support Blossom

Seeley, and of course there were all the show people in the Actors Home in Los Angeles; beyond his original million-dollar donation, he had just bought a half million dollars' worth of land for the Home.

When vaudeville died, many mourned, but few cared for the surviving vaudevillians. It is easier to feel for the dead than the dying. The last of the dying vaudevillians were very old now and tended to be more like Sammy Lewis than George Burns. Done in by time and taste, these gay and rambunctious entertainers had fallen like waves of good soldiers. Only the last of them, the grizzled veterans, remained.

Burns had refused to be part of the rout. "Vaudeville didn't put me out of business," he said. "See, vaudeville went out of business but I didn't. The [other acts] allowed themselves to go out of business . . . I said the hell with that.

"I loved what I was doing."

But there was only so long that anyone could say the hell with it. One Thursday evening, he was out for dinner with a group of friends, as he always was on Thursday evenings. But instead of going to his regular place, Trader Vic ("The Trader's"), at the intersection of Wilshire Boulevard and Santa Monica Boulevard, for a change he agreed on a Beverly Hills restaurant called Da Vinci's.

As the group of men arrived, Dean Martin was perched on a stool at the bar. Harvey Silbert, who was in the party, stopped to greet the former star, and when the Burns group was seated, he suggested that George say hello. Years earlier, Dean Martin had twice booked Burns on his television show. At that time, George needed the work.

Burns looked over, smiled, and waved his cigar.

Dean Martin was some twenty years younger, but having once been handsome and athletic, he was now gaunt to the point of appearing wasted. He looked catatonic behind eyeglass lenses as thick as George's. He showed no sign of recognition and seemed to be in a trance, some kind of mental twilight zone.

In the 1960s, Silbert had hired Dean Martin to perform at the Riviera. The roguish singer was such an attraction that his contract included a 5 percent stake in the hotel.

At the time, Martin was a smash playing the rascal. Like Burns, he had not merely survived but transcended the loss of a partner who had been considered the main attraction of the team.

But Dean Martin hadn't worked in a decade. Most in George's younger generation of fans would not remember either him or his off-the-beat sense of humor. Probably, many young people had never even heard of this once raffish, once cocksure bon vivant.

He wasn't supposed to be drinking but, "in this condition," Silbert said, "it hardly made a difference." And so every night, a dazed and emaciated Dean Martin was propped up on the same bar stool in Da Vinci's Restaurant. A wraith in a tuxedo, he might have been knocked over with a whisper. Silbert could only say, "Terrible." As Burns said, "Nobody remembers an actor."

In the rest home, Sammy Lewis—né Dambrowski—was actually in better shape than Dean Martin, since he was occasionally lucid. The glossy photographs on the wall over his head were labeled: "Sammy Lewis and Patty Moore." Patty, his wife, was long dead.

"Sure we played the Palace," he rattled in what remained of his voice. " 'Lewis and Moore, Songs and Dances.' We sang 'Shine On, Harvest Moon.' "

They could not have sung "Shine On, Harvest Moon." That song belonged to Nora Bayes and Jack Norworth. It didn't matter now.

At Hillcrest, Daniel D'Hoore was rolling George's wheelchair through the lobby and into the Men's Grill. Daniel was built like a physical trainer. His muscles bulged through a tight white T-shirt, which made the little man in his charge look frightfully frail. A waxen and infantile George seemed swaddled within the folds of his gigantic blue sweatsuit. His eyes were embryonic and glistening. He looked like "E.T."

"He was becoming like a child with Down's syndrome," Melissa said. "As if he knows something that you don't."

In August 1995, when a final commitment had to be made for the Cedars-Sinai gala and the CBS television special, the fact of Burns's condition had to be faced and both events were canceled. Irving Fein was outspoken about how much the loss of the television special was costing him.

That left Natty Burns with only one engagement in his datebook: the hundredth birthday engagement at Caesar's Palace in Las Vegas.

Fein, always resourceful, suggested that Burns make that entrance by riding onstage in a chariot drawn by showgirls.

"Well," Lou Weiss said to his uncle in the bedroom, "come January twentieth, Alice and I are going to be at Caesar's Palace to see you break a hundred."

Burns looked up. "I'm only doing fifteen minutes. I can't stand an hour anymore." He paused, and then added, "They'll have [film] clips."

"And," Weiss said, speaking very loud to make sure his uncle could hear, "the following year on January twentieth, Alice and I will be back there for your hundred and first birthday."

"That's if they're still in business," George quipped.

There were still flashes of humor, but with faculties failing, so was his vitality. Perhaps everyone gets a supply of energy for exactly a lifetime, and not one day more. The lesson his life taught was that it isn't enough to exist, you have to do something. But "there's nothing I feel like doing anymore," he said gloomily. "All I'm doing is sleeping."

He seemed frightened by that, as if sleep were pulling him down, no longer serving for respite and revival but itself a sign of inertia and decay. "The bed will kill you," he'd always warned. "Get out of your bed. Get out of your house. The biggest hedge against old age," he had been saying for years, "is not to fall in love with your bed."

Now he was awake only a few hours each day. He spent them trying to learn his monologue for Las Vegas, and that was a strain. "GB is angry about his mind failing him," Melissa said. "He is angry about being confused. I see desperation in his eyes."

He seemed bewildered by the uncontrollable drifting of his mind, by his inability to recognize people or to understand what they were saying. For the first time in his life he was not interested in anything.

He used to say that he never thought about dying because "it's been done," but death could no longer be joked away. Perhaps he'd already had the last laugh. After a lifetime of denying and revising the unpleasant—and getting away with it—he was now being forced to confront the meanest event of all.

Herbert Ross had noticed that Burns had "never dealt with Jack's death. He had a very strange view of that, of death."

There was this same rejection of death in Burns's visits to Gracie at the mausoleum, keeping her alive by talking to her. And there was hatred of death in his refusal to shovel earth over his sister Goldie's casket.

Once, when asked what he would like for his own epitaph, he said, "I'd like to be standing there reading it."

Gambling is the least sentimental game, and the management of Caesar's Palace was not in the wishful thinking business. Wary of betting on George's delivering a monologue at his centenary, it had to be assured by October 1995 that he would make his January date.

The answer was obvious.

• • •

For a decade, Burns's friends had debated whether work was keeping him alive or killing him. He had known the answer all along: Activity was not a reason to live or a cause of death. Activity was life itself.

"I guess," Melissa said, "Papa is going to celebrate his hundredth birthday in the upstairs bedroom."

With the cancelation an accomplished fact, all he wanted to do was sleep. He had to be dragged out of bed, and when he was, he tried to crawl back into it. It had been charming when he'd say, "I can't die, I'm booked," but he could not say it anymore.

There was scarcely anything left of his little body when Cathy Carr arrived in Los Angeles for a surprise visit. George hadn't seen her in nearly five years, not since the day she had moved out of the house in a temper over the curling wallpaper on her bedroom ceiling.

Daniel answered the telephone when she called.

Cathy said that she had flown to Los Angeles because she had received a message from God. Always a church-going woman, she had become even more religious.

"God told me to come," she told Daniel. "Because George is getting ready to go see Gracie."

Index

Picture Credits